ON THE RUN IN NAZI BERLIN

ON THE RUN IN NAZI BERLIN

=== a memoir ===

BERT LEWYN

WITH BEV SALTZMAN LEWYN

CHICAGO
REVIEW
PRESS

Published by Chicago Review Press Incorporated
814 North Franklin Street
Chicago, Illinois 60610
ISBN 978-1-64160-110-8

On the Run in Nazi Berlin was first published in 2001 by XLibris Co.
This edition has been substantially revised.

Library of Congress Cataloging-in-Publication Data
Names: Lewyn, Bert, 1923- author. | Lewyn, Bev Saltzman, author.
Title: On the run in Nazi Berlin : a memoir / Bert Lewyn and Bev Saltzman
    Lewyn.
Other titles: Holocaust memoirs
Description: New, revised edition | Chicago, Illinois : Chicago Review Press,
    2019.
Identifiers: LCCN 2018049845 (print) | LCCN 2018050797 (ebook) | ISBN
    9781641601115 (adobe pdf) | ISBN 9781641601122 (kindle) | ISBN
    9781641601139 (epub) | ISBN 9781641601108 (paperback)
Subjects: LCSH: Lewyn, Bert, 1923- | Jews—Germany—Berlin—Biography. |
    Holocaust, Jewish (1939-1945)—Germany—Berlin—Personal narratives. |
    Berlin (Germany)—Biography. | BISAC: HISTORY / Holocaust.
Classification: LCC DS134.42.L49 (ebook) | LCC DS134.42.L49 L49 2019 (print)
    | DDC 940.53/18092 [B]—dc23
LC record available at https://lccn.loc.gov/2018049845

Cover design: Preston Pisellini
Cover photographs: AP Images
Interior design: Nord Compo
Photo credits: All photographs courtesy of Bert Lewyn's collection unless
indicated otherwise.

Printed in the United States of America
5 4 3 2 1

This book is dedicated to my parents,
Leopold and Johanna Lewin,
as well as all other members of
my family who perished in the Holocaust.

CONTENTS

FOREWORD

Since World War II, many books have been written about the Holocaust. This book is about my own experiences before, during, and, to a lesser extent, after that period.

I decided to record these events primarily because I want my children to know what happened to me before I arrived in America. When they were young, they asked me to tell them about my life in Germany, but the demands of establishing a new business and my feeling that they would be unable to comprehend the horror of the Holocaust prevented me from doing so. I told them that I would answer all their questions when they were older.

Now I feel differently. I want them to know as much as I can transmit, as much as I can remember about myself and about my mother and father, their parents and families. Time is rushing by, and if I don't attend to the task of writing now, I may not be able to do so later.

Then there are my grandchildren, who should know of the trials of those who came before them. It is my hope that my sons and daughters will pass my story on to their children and they to their children, so that knowledge of the Holocaust will become a legacy binding the generations together, never to be forgotten.

In 1933, Hitler took power and became Supreme Ruler and Dictator of Germany. Berlin had a Jewish population of around 165,000. When World War II ended in 1945, about fourteen hundred Jewish Berliners had stayed alive by hiding out in the city, and about three thousand more had survived the concentration camps. Fewer than five thousand of Berlin's Jews were left to inform the world of what they had experienced. I am one of them.

It is with a profound sense of obligation that I relate to you my memories of life on the run in Nazi Berlin.

PART I

THREE MIRACLES

1

ENDINGS AND BEGINNINGS

WHEN I FINALLY OPENED MY EYES, the first thing I saw was a ceiling.

That by itself was not enough to upset me. But the fact that I could not remember ever having seen this particular ceiling before, much less the rest of the room, set off internal alarms. I attempted to swing my legs over the side of the bed and sit up but soon learned that even this small effort was beyond me. Worse, in my weakened condition I couldn't remember where I was. I didn't know if I had been recaptured by the Gestapo or if I had found the sanctuary I had so desperately sought.

I heard a woman's voice. "Come see, he's awake!"

I turned my head in the direction from which the voice emanated. Before me stood my friend, Jenny Lebrecht. Within seconds, her sons, Horst and Heinz, joined her. All of them stared at me as if surprised that I had woken at all.

"We're very glad to see you, Dagobert," Horst said. "Do you know what happened?"

"Not really," I muttered. "I remember escaping from the Gestapo prison, walking here, and knocking on your door, but I don't remember anything past that."

"Well, my boy," Jenny said, "I think you could stand some nourishment. Then we'll talk."

Jenny disappeared, returning with a tray loaded with bread, cheese, and milk. I struggled to a sitting position and wolfed down the food while they gathered around me.

"You haven't had much to eat recently, have you?" Leo Lebrecht asked.

"Well, no one has invited me to any banquets lately," I responded, grinning weakly.

Jenny smiled at me. Her expression was so sweet and welcoming that it was a relief just to be in her presence. She was petite, although somewhat heavyset, wearing her black hair in a bun on top of her head. Jenny was a rare individual in those days, all the more precious to me because she seemed genuinely interested in my well-being. After making sure I was comfortable and had enough food, she sat down next to me and started to speak.

"Now then," she began, "I will tell you what I know and then you can fill in the blanks. Two days ago, shortly before I was to go to work, I heard a knock at the door. It was unnerving, as it always is these days. The boys and Leo hid and I went to the door and looked through the peephole. Lo and behold, it was our sweet Dagobert, leaning against the wall.

"No sooner had I opened the door than you collapsed. I called the boys to help me and they carried you to the couch. You must have done a lot of walking, because when we took off your shoes, your soles were worn through. Then when we removed your socks much of the skin from the bottom of your feet came off with them. It was very unappealing. You have been unconscious and we have all been terribly worried about you. But now you are awake and so we are happy."

"So tell us, Dago," Leo interjected, "tell us what has happened. How have you come to us?"

I looked at him, almost too exhausted to speak. "I just missed you too much, Herr Lebrecht. I had to come back to say hello." Finishing the last of the food, I said, "Give me a few minutes to catch my breath. Then I will tell all. In the meantime, why don't you fill me in on what has been happening here?"

The Lebrechts sat around the couch, eyeing each other, as if unsure how much to tell me in my present state. Finally, Leo took the lead.

"Well, as you probably know, Berlin is about to be invaded by a few Russians. With the Russians coming, the end seems to be in sight. I know that we had to turn you away before, but conditions have changed. I think that you can stay here without putting us in danger. Still, having Russians in Berlin is no guarantee of safety for the Jews, and we're all very afraid of what will happen when the Red Army arrives."

Heinz nodded. "We've heard rumors that the Russians are stealing anything not bolted down and that there have been numerous instances of rape."

Jenny got up. "I can't stand this talk. Let's not talk like this. We just have to pray and hope for the best. Dagobert, you are not yet well. You are going to lie on that couch until you feel better."

All this was great news for me. Even though the Lebrechts had refused me sanctuary in the past, with the end of the war so near it seemed probable that I would be allowed to hide here for the duration.

And now, we bided our time, waiting for the end to come. The fighting in the streets grew louder every day. The echoes of artillery and rifle fire and other types of explosions became much more frequent. It should have been clear to every living being in Berlin that this war was going to end and it was going to end soon. The Russians were unstoppable.

The next day, Jenny walked upstairs to her job in the Nazi district headquarters building. It was one of the ironies of the war that not only was Jenny employed by the Nazis without ever having been discovered to be Jewish, but she was also allowed an apartment directly under headquarters.

When she went into the office area, no one was there. Although it was early, the building should have been humming by now with people going about their assigned tasks. Instead, it was deserted. After a few minutes spent investigating, she came back downstairs.

"They're gone! They're gone! They took some things, but not all. I suppose they're fleeing before the Russians get here!"

We all hugged and cheered. Heinz danced a little jig, while Horst looked at his father questioningly.

"What is it?" Leo asked him. "Are you just happy, or is there something else you want?"

Horst grinned and asked, "How about some fresh air?"

Jenny gasped. Horst was suggesting that we all go outside. Leo looked down at the ground, pondering Horst's request.

He looked up, a grim expression on his face. "All right. But just for a minute. The Nazis may have fled, but we don't want to take unnecessary chances. Who knows what the rest of our German neighbors would do out of fear or desperation? I don't want to have survived this long only to be killed in the last days of the war."

We opened the door to the apartment and climbed the stairs to go outside. Horst almost skipped as he went, while Heinz walked cautiously, as if he were afraid that his newfound freedom would be snatched from him. Jenny walked beside me with tears in her eyes. She had been outside many times, but the boys and Leo had become virtual prisoners, unable to leave the apartment for fear of arrest and the deportation that would follow. Because of her fake papers and position as a maid in the Nazi district office, Jenny could come and go at will. She had been the family's connection to the outside world. But the two boys and Leo were isolated, unable to leave the apartment.

Leo, Horst, and Heinz poked their heads through the front door. Jenny and I looked out from behind them. The scene outside was one of total chaos. Before the war, Lorenzstrasse had been a quiet, tree-lined street in a peaceful community. Now it was a hellhole. Everywhere, we saw soldiers, guns, and military vehicles. Hitler Youth roamed the streets, armed with Panzerfäust antitank weapons and rifles. These boy soldiers seemed very enthused by their impending assignment to fight the Russians and defend the fatherland to the last man. We could hear the *boom boom boom* of Russian artillery, coming ever closer.

After getting our fill of this scene of impending destruction, we went back downstairs. As night drew on, we endlessly discussed the impending arrival of the Russians and what the consequences for us might be.

"Will the house be destroyed?" Jenny worried. "If they shell indiscriminately, we might be buried under the rubble!"

"We can only speculate and hope for the best," Leo said. "There is no way of knowing what will happen until it happens."

Eventually, the conversation returned to me and my recent experiences. Horst took the lead in questioning me. "You've had your rest, Dago. Now tell us what has happened to you. How have you survived the past few years?"

So I started from the beginning. I told them about being on the run, living underground as a U-boat, a Jewish refugee who had escaped the mass deportations. I told them where I had gone after our sabotage attempt at the weapons factory. I told them about Paul Richter, the blind Communist, and about the black market trade in ration cards and identification papers. I told them how I had nearly been taken by the Gestapo on several occasions, and about Günther and how we had impersonated SS officers. About marrying Ilse to save her from deportation. I told them about living alone in the woods and about being so hungry that I ate pigeons and about the hand wound that almost killed me. I told them about the country doctor who didn't bother to use sterile instruments.

They sat silent, engrossed, as I told them how Anni Kusitzky and Ilse had hung my swollen hand over my head to help it heal. I told them about how, when I was finally recovering, the Gestapo had stormed our hiding place and arrested us, taking us to prison. About how Ilse and Klaus had been deported while I was thrown into a cell and tortured. I told them about the bombing raid and the prison gate and about making a key from a lead pipe and how this led to our eventual escape.

But before anything else, I told them about the beginning; about myself, my parents, and the Gestapo . . .

Here I am in 1997 at a monument in Berlin that represents Jews being shipped to extermination camps. At rear is a commemorative tablet listing transport numbers, dates, destinations, and number of people. My parents were deported to Trawniki, Poland, on transport no. 11, March 28, 1942. There were 974 people in this transport.

2

THE GESTAPO ARRIVES

FOR MY FAMILY, 1942 was the year in which we could no longer deny that a storm was brewing, a storm that would darken the skies of Germany's Jews. Hitler was now putting his final plans for the destruction of the Jews into action. Prior to this, we had stuck our heads in the sand, hoping that the rumors were untrue. There had been no shortage of threats and rumors: rumors about oppression, rumors about arrests and abductions. Our lives were consumed by rumors and up until then, we had closed our eyes to them. This was the tragic mistake made by many Jews, one that would allow Hitler's storm to spread throughout Germany until, ultimately, we would all feel the destruction.

By this time, conditions for the Jews of Germany had deteriorated drastically. We were not allowed to use public telephones or, except under special circumstances, public transportation. We were required to give all winter clothing, blankets, and coats to the authorities, who shipped them to the troops at the Russian front. Tobacco, milk, eggs, fish, radios, telephones, and many other products were forbidden to Jews. Jewish children were banned from attending public schools. Jews were not allowed to own pets. The list continued to grow until anything like a normal life became impossible.

But by March 26, the rumors and threats had become a reality.

For us, as well as many thousands of other Jewish families, the shape that reality took was in the form of a visit from the Gestapo.

On that day in 1942, I was sitting with my parents in the small kitchen of our Berlin apartment at 70 Koepenicker Strasse, eating lunch, when we were startled by a loud, insistent knocking.

"Herr Lewin? Open the door at once!" The voice was imperious and brooked no delay. We were all a little slow to react. It was unusual for us to have visitors at all these days, and even more so for them to come at mealtimes. I looked at my mother. Her hair was, on this day like all others, piled up in a bun.

"I'll get the door, Mutti," I said. "You sit."

I walked down the hall to the door and, with some hesitation, opened it.

Two men, both dressed alike in long, dark leather coats and wide-brimmed hats, stood there. Their facial expressions were as much alike as their clothing, both of them harsh and frowning, without the slightest trace of warmth. Not saying a word, the taller of the two immediately pushed past me, forcing his way into the apartment.

The Gestapo were the Nazis' secret police force. The mission of the Gestapo was, first and foremost, the elimination of certain sections of the German population, especially the Jews. The Gestapo planned and executed campaigns that eventually transferred millions of Jews, from all over Europe, to slave labor camps or death camps. They were the elite of Germany's police organizations: highly professional, totally ruthless, and completely loyal to Adolf Hitler.

"Herr Lewin?"

My father appeared from behind me. As he caught a glimpse of the two men, his face lost color, becoming ashen against his salt and pepper hair.

One of them said, "Herr Lewin, we are here to assist you."

This, I later learned, was an infamous Gestapo tactic. Rather than upset the intended victims, the Gestapo would assure them that they had their best interests at heart and that they wanted to help the Jews in these troubling times.

My father continued looking at them, silent.

"You have nothing to worry about, Herr Lewin. We are merely relocating you. You and your wife and son have ten minutes. You must each pack one suitcase."

My mother appeared, moving up behind my father. She started screaming, "What's going on? What's going on? What are you going to do to us?"

The Gestapo agents told us that we must hurry, that we must grab our belongings and prepare to depart. Faced with the prospect of being forced from her home, required to instantly abandon all that was familiar and beloved, my mother soon became frantic.

"Where are we going?" she wailed, "What's going to happen to us?"

She ran back and forth in frenzy, vainly trying to decide what to take and what to leave behind. My father, on the other hand, tried to remain stoic throughout the entire episode. I suppose he might have been trying to project an attitude of tranquility to reassure us, but the ashen color of his face told of the price he was paying for remaining calm.

The Gestapo watched us closely, stone-faced and businesslike. Like most German Jews, we were familiar with the reputation of the Gestapo. Whatever they might say and regardless of what claims they might make, one thing we could be sure of was that they had not come to help us. This day was a culmination of events that had been many years in the making, a day that every German Jew knew, in his heart, must come.

Johanna and Leopold Lewin, my parents. Berlin, 1921.

The Gestapo knew their business and the goal of that business was the obliteration of our race.

What made them most terrifying was their businesslike demeanor, the everyday, conversational tone of their voices. They certainly knew that they were likely sending us to our deaths, but they showed no more emotion than most men would show while taking out the trash.

The business of rounding up Jews was now a well-practiced routine. Before Hitler's rise to power, the Jewish population of Berlin had numbered around 165,000. By 1942, emigration, deportation, and outright murder had decreased that number to around forty thousand. The Gestapo had perfected their techniques and carried out the deportation of Jews with typical German efficiency.

I walked into my parents' bedroom to find my father grabbing suitcases from a stack neatly piled beside the armoire. My mother was crying and her eyes were darting back and forth, back and forth, looking for a place to begin.

She screamed again and ran to her little freestanding jewelry chest. She didn't have much, nothing very expensive, but everything she had was a gift of the heart, given to her by my father on special occasions. Whimpering, tears streaming down her face, she pulled out symbols of their love. There was a necklace, a few pairs of earrings, and a ring or two. She put each of these into a small cloth drawstring bag and sighed loudly as she placed it in her suitcase.

A moment later, I felt the presence of the Gestapo men behind me. They had closed the front door and followed us into the bedroom. They could have been statues, their expressions devoid of any human emotion. But now, seeing my mother in hysterics, they grew impatient. The face of one of the agents reddened, becoming suffused with blood as his temper flared and he began shouting:

"*Schnell*! *Schnell*! You must hurry! Further delay will not be permitted!" I watched in horror as my parents forced themselves to continue their terrible task.

My mother darted over to the dresser, yanked open a drawer, and rifled through it. She searched frantically through each neat pile of clothing. Back and forth, from the armoire to the dresser she ran, pulling out the drawers, anxiously looking at all the clothes, letting out a heartbreaking wail every few seconds, beside herself. She would throw an item into the suitcase, then take it out again screaming "Oh no!" and would run to put it back in the dresser drawer.

Then I felt a powerful hand grip my shoulder.

"You! You too must pack your bag. You must be ready to go or suffer the consequences. We will not wait for you. Go!"

My father looked at me as he handed me the third empty suitcase. Again, he said nothing. His eyes looked glazed and heavy. He just stared at me, holding my glance for a moment, then nodding his head. I felt, in that instant, that I understood why my father was acting in this manner. He had given up.

He was in an impossible situation. I believe that he knew of the fate that awaited us. He was much too intelligent a man to accept their tale of "relocation." Cooperating calmly with the Gestapo was therefore unacceptable. And yet, if he fought back, he would be placing my mother and me in mortal danger. That was also unacceptable. He was trapped and he knew it. It was the only explanation for his uncharacteristic apathy.

I walked out of the room and turned down the hall, moving toward my bureau. The second Gestapo agent followed me, his boots clicking loudly on the wooden floor. I opened the drawers, took out a few pairs of underwear, socks, and a couple of long-sleeved shirts and put them into my tiny suitcase. Then I retrieved my toothbrush and a bar of soap and put them with my other belongings.

I walked back down the hall and turned the corner, back into my parents' bedroom. Catching sight of me, the first Gestapo man yelled, "Enough is enough! It is time to go!"

My mother wailed, "But I haven't finished! I can't possibly be finished! I haven't decided what to take!" The Gestapo man walked over to her suitcase. "You're done. Don't worry about it." He shut her suitcase and clicked the locks shut. My mother began screaming anew.

Already in her coat, she walked two steps over to me and looked into my eyes. "Isn't there anything we can do?" she asked. "No, Mutti," I said gently, "there isn't." I took my mother by the hand and led her out of the apartment, with the second Gestapo agent following close behind. As we walked out, he shut the door behind us, giving us no chance for a last look at our home.

Many people have wondered why the Jews did not leave Germany when the persecution began, but in fact many Jews did leave. My father had himself sought to emigrate, trying first at the Bolivian consulate and again at the consulate of Chile, attempting to get visas for our family. On the occasions when I would accompany him, lines of desperate Jews would stretch around the block several times. It was not uncommon that a husband would wait in line for eight hours and then be relieved by his wife, who would stand in line while the husband went home to sleep.

Eventually, other countries stopped accepting applications for emigration. Unless one had relatives in another country willing to accept responsibility or had exceptional financial abilities, emigration was no longer a viable means of escape. We were trapped in Germany and the only way the Nazi government would allow us to leave would be in cattle cars or coffins.

The German government did everything in its power to keep the eventual fate of the Jews top secret in order to avoid widespread panic. They wanted to prevent a public outcry from Germans of good will and from citizens of other countries. The Nazis went to great lengths to assure Jews that they would be safe in the "resettlement" areas, even persuading them to bring along their valuables, ostensibly to help them start new lives. In reality, they would steal everything of value that we possessed. Nothing of consequence escaped their grasp. They shaved the hair from the heads of dead Jews to be used for industrial purposes and removed gold fillings from their teeth to make trinkets and jewelry for the wives, daughters, and girlfriends of high-ranking SS officers.

One possible avenue of escape had been presented to us some years earlier, when my father's older brother, Benjamin, visited us in Berlin.

Uncle Benjamin had shocked my father's family in Kovno by leaving home at the tender age of eighteen. Somehow, he managed to make his way through Europe to the United States. There, he became a very successful restaurateur in New York City. He married and had a son, Stanley.

Around 1934, Benjamin decided to return to Kovno, with the goal of becoming reconciled with his father and the rest of his family. His visit was successful, and on his way back to New York, Uncle Benjamin stopped in Berlin to consult a famous specialist about a heart condition. He also used the opportunity to pay us a visit.

Seeing our apartment was something of a shock for Benjamin. He was wealthy, and we were living in very modest circumstances. My father had recently started his business in a basement shop and money was tight.

Uncle Benjamin insisted on taking me shopping. He hired a car with a chauffeur. I'd never been in a private car before, much less one with a chauffeur. We drove to one of the largest and most famous department stores in Berlin—Hermann Tietz. I suppose the car must have likewise made an impression on the management, as they provided a special representative to make the rounds with us.

After an extended shopping spree that exceeded my wildest dreams, the store provided a van and delivered all the merchandise to our apartment on the same day. My parents were aghast as the deliveryman brought item after item after item inside our tiny apartment. They berated my uncle: "This is not necessary!" "He does not need all of this!" and finally, "We have such a small apartment here on Paul Singerstrasse 38, where will we be able to put all of this?"

My uncle just smiled and ignored them. Then he sat down and told my father that we must all emigrate to New York, where he would help us resettle. He said Germany was becoming too dangerous for us to remain. We must allow him to sponsor us to come to America.

My father would not hear of it. He and my mother were absolutely opposed to the idea. "Absurd," they said, and Uncle Benjamin left.

Benjamin wrote my parents again, urging them to consider emigration. Again they said no.

Then, in 1936, Benjamin wrote that a friend was coming to Berlin for the Olympics and that he would carry a message for us. Benjamin's friend arrived and told us that Benjamin still begged my parents to reconsider. If they couldn't come themselves, Benjamin at least wanted them to send me to America. Benjamin would take care of me, adopt and raise me.

But again my parents refused, this time due to the whitewashing that occurred in Berlin prior to the Olympics. Hitler wanted to show the world that Germany had a change of heart and no longer mistreated its Jews. It was a lie, of course, but my optimistic parents couldn't see that. They thought things in Germany were looking up for the Jews. But soon after, things became worse than ever.

It wasn't until after Kristallnacht, the Night of Broken Glass (November 9–10, 1938), that my father realized Benjamin was right. But by then, Benjamin had died, and his wife wrote us a letter saying she could not fulfill the promises that Benjamin had made to us. It was too late for us: escape was no longer an option.

Down the staircase we went. We saw one of our neighbors watching us through a crack in her door, but she didn't try to help us or say anything to us.

Apparently, the Gestapo did not fear an escape attempt, as they allowed my father to lead the way. As we descended, my mother calmed down a little. She was no longer crying, though her cheeks were still stained with streaks of tears. We were picked up by an army truck with dark khaki canvas covers. Two grim-faced SS guards, weapons at the ready, stood at the tailgate waving, motioning for us to get in the truck. When we approached, the guards took our suitcases and loaded them. They stretched their hands down to help each of us into the truck, shouting, "Hurry, we have lots of places to go."

The truck had benches running its full length on both sides. In front of us, we saw about ten Jewish men, women, and children already sitting on the benches. We knew they were Jewish because each of them wore the Judenstern, the yellow, star-shaped badges sewn on the outer clothing of every Jew in Germany. Behind us, the tailgate was closed and the engine started. The truck began to move.

We were sitting very close to each other, huddled with our families for the small comfort that closeness could bring. Some of the people on the truck were holding hands. I stayed quiet, listening to the other people talking, my mind surprisingly clear.

The people inside the truck were asking each other, "Have you heard anything? Do you know where we're going?" Everyone asked, but no one had any answers. The women were crying and sadness was etched into every face.

My father put his arm around my mother and the three of us sat there, asking questions and being asked. As the truck moved along, it stopped several times to pick up Jews walking along the street. Whenever the Gestapo saw someone wearing a Jewish star, they grabbed him. It was like dogcatchers catching dogs. The Jewish animals were being netted and dumped into trucks for processing.

One man tried to run. Guards ran after him, shouting, "Halt! Stop or we will shoot." I could hear them, but I couldn't see anything because of the truck's fabric cover. They must have recaptured him fairly easily, because only a few minutes passed before he was back in the truck and we proceeded onward, to meet the fate that our Nazi government had decreed for its despised Jewish population.

3

DEPORTATION

THE SS TRANSPORT TRUCK wheeled to a stop in front of the Levetzow-strasse synagogue in the Moabit district of Berlin. Parts of the building had been blackened by the fires of Kristallnacht, the night when many of Berlin's synagogues had been burned down by rioters. I had never had cause to go to the Levetzowstrasse synagogue before. My parents were not overly religious. Although they were proud of being Jews, our attendance at synagogue services was limited to occasional visits at the Oranienburger Strasse synagogue, the largest and most beautiful in Berlin.

The SS soldiers opened the gate and helped us step down out of the truck. At this stage, the soldiers were still polite. As they led us into the synagogue, we could see other trucks unloading yet more of our fellow Jews. Once inside, it became obvious that the Nazis had turned the synagogue into a massive collection point. We were told to go into a large room, which was already packed with hundreds of people.

My mother was still anxious, overwhelmed by the stress of not knowing what was going to happen to us. By now, it was well into the afternoon. We sat there, watching, waiting, and talking.

Afternoon turned into evening as they fed us, giving us soup, some bread, and ersatz coffee. People lay everywhere, covering the floors in the big hall and along the corridors of the synagogue. And alongside each person, whatever belongings they had managed to bring were stacked. Some had suitcases, others had paper cartons tied up with strings. Still others had cloth bags and backpacks. There were all manner of containers into which they had stuffed the essence of their lives. The bags and boxes took up so much room that the Nazis were hard-pressed to find space for any more people.

We spent that night on the floor of the synagogue. The Nazis had given us a small amount of straw to lie on. *Like pigs*, I heard someone say.

To say that the talk that night was uniformly negative would be an understatement. It was clear that nothing pleasant awaited us and there was wild speculation everywhere. There were some people who said, "Maybe it's not so bad. Maybe they're just sending us to the East to work and help the German war effort." By then, the war was in full swing. It had started September 1, 1939, with the German invasion of Poland.

At one point during the evening, an older woman came up to us and asked if we could make room for her to lie down. To allow someone else in our carved-out little space was actually quite a favor, given the fact that the room was so packed. It was terribly, terribly cramped. Those who were lucky enough to find a bit of floor space could sit or try to lie down. Many could find room only to stand. The entire scene was one of almost overwhelming confusion.

But one look at this woman's face seemed to awaken something within us that made it impossible to refuse her. There was only one word to describe her: alone.

"Yes, please sit down near us," my father said to her. "We will stack our suitcases on top of each other so that there will be room for you."

My mother looked over at my father with loving pride in her eyes. Even in this dire and desperate time, he had not lost his sense of compassion. I felt a great surge of respect for him.

"I am Leopold Lewin," my father began. "This is my wife, Johanna, and our son, Dagobert." My mother and I both nodded and smiled and she did the same.

"I am Minna Schlesinger," the woman began, almost shyly. As it turned out, Ms. Schlesinger lived with her sister in Friedenau, a subsection of Berlin. Neither of them had ever married and so they shared an apartment. She had been walking down the street when she was spotted by an SS transport truck. Seeing the yellow Star of David on her clothes,

Levetzowstrasse synagogue was burned and partially destroyed during Kristallnacht, November 9–10, 1938. The Gestapo ordered the Jewish community to rebuild the synagogue so that it could be used as a staging point for up to a thousand people, prior to shipping them to extermination camps. The building was demolished in 1956.

they simply threw her into the truck and continued on. She had no opportunity to pack a bag or pick up any of her belongings. She had only her coat and purse.

"We will try to help you, Frau Schlesinger," my father replied. "We will be in this together."

We all decided to try to rest. We hoped to find out more in the morning. But sleep eluded almost everyone in the room. There was too much anxiety, lots of moaning and groaning, tossing and turning. People talked for hours about what they suspected was going to be done to us. Many thought we would be used as laborers in the East.

The SS communicated with us by means of a wall-mounted loud-speaker. The speaker now blared out an announcement about organization. Families were to assemble in one area and singles in another. My father looked at Frau Schlesinger, "Do not worry," he said. "We will find you."

My parents and I picked up our suitcases and went to stand with the other families. Soon after, another order was broadcast over the loud-speaker: "Those families whose names begin with the letters *A* through *D* must line up in front of the staircase."

The loudspeaker barked more letters, going down the alphabet. Eventually the letter *L* came up. We looked at each other again, bent to pick up our suitcases, and slowly walked forward to the stairs.

"Get yourselves into alphabetical order!" a Gestapo agent commanded.

We looked at each other. Of course, few people here knew the names of the other families. So we proceeded to get each other's names and then got ourselves into alphabetical order accordingly. Since our last name began with an *L*, we were somewhere in the middle of the line. The room was packed with people. Two or three hundred, I thought, all in various stages of standing or lining up.

A few minutes later, the Gestapo agent ordered us to hand over any valuables we had with us. We were told that we would not need these for our trip and that they would be held by the Nazis, to be returned upon reaching our destination.

I watched uneasily as men and women all down the line began divesting themselves of their personal property. Wallets, watches, jewelry, and furs were all surrendered to Gestapo agents circulating among us with burlap collection bags. I could not help but notice that they made no effort to label the items with the owners' identities. I tried not to think about any of the ramifications of this, but I was becoming increasingly nervous as the thought occurred to me that perhaps where we were going we would have no need of valuables.

We approached a checkpoint, walking over a straw-covered floor. We huddled together, each of us clutching a suitcase in one hand and holding each other with the free hand. There were lots of people in front of us and behind us. My mother sobbed the whole time, as did many of those around us. Father remained stoic, seeming to accept it all.

By this time, I was struggling to contain myself. The months of abuse, the unfairness of being blamed for all of Germany's problems, the slurs and insults, all of this combined with the current situation to drive me almost over the edge. Why were we all accepting this so passively? Why didn't we fight? There were hundreds of us and only a few Gestapo agents. I asked my father why no one was fighting back. "Why?" he said, "They would just shoot us."

I stared at the SS troops with their guns and the Gestapo with pistols under their coats. I could see what was happening at the head of the line. They were separating many of the young adults from their parents, cutting them out like lambs culled from a flock of sheep. Occasionally, someone tried to resist, but the SS troops soon quelled those who tried by striking them with their rifle butts. We could hear the families screaming and crying as they were wrenched away from each other.

I was in a panic. From somewhere deep within me, I felt the beginnings of a rage, rising and spreading through my body like an electrical current, until I thought I would explode. *Oh my God*, I thought, *they're going to separate me from my parents!* I huddled closer to my mother. *Oh my God! Oh my God! They're going to take them away from me!* I had never felt so close to my family, perhaps because I was beginning to realize that I might never see them again. Up until this point, I had been as numb as the rest. Now, for the first time, the reality of our situation hit me. It couldn't be true. But it was.

We reached the front of the line. Heart racing, I clenched my mother's delicate hand, squeezing it. There was a large, sturdy wooden table in front of us, stacked high with files and papers. Behind it sat a stern-looking Gestapo administrator, peering over his glasses at us. To each side stood tall, husky Gestapo men in civilian clothing, dark suits, white shirts, and ties. They wore no uniform, but the pistols poking out of their jackets left no doubt about who they were.

The power of the state was further represented by two SS soldiers and two Berlin policemen, standing on either end of the table. The policemen looked faintly ridiculous in the bizarre, spiked helmets that they all wore. Most of them were too old for the army and were relegated to working the police beat in Berlin. But any thought that these men were not to be taken seriously evaporated immediately upon inspection of the SS troops, several more of whom were milling around, guarding the exits. They all were well-armed, with weapons that had that special sheen that spoke of frequent use.

A Gestapo man came up to us on my side and barked, "Name?"

"Lewin," I said. "Leopold, Johanna, and Dagobert."

He turned to the seated Gestapo agent with the glasses and repeated our names, "Lewin. Leopold, Johanna, and Dagobert." The seated man went through his files and brought out a large, dark yellow index card and a set of papers. These he handed to the standing Gestapo man who had asked us our names.

My jaw was stiff. The ringing started again in my ears. My mother stood, white as a ghost, eyes wide, the tears still streaming down her cheeks. My father looked forward, chin up, eyes full of disgust.

The standing agent examined the card and papers. Without a word, he lifted his eyes from the papers and settled them on us.

"You! You are Dagobert Lewin?"

"Yes," I replied. My mother took in quiet, measured breaths, hanging on every word. My father stayed silent, sternly watching.

"Are you healthy?" the Gestapo man demanded.

"Yes."

"You have no health problems?"

"No," I responded. By now, I was petrified. Why were they asking *me* these questions? Why only me?

He looked down his nose at the wide index card in his hands.

"You completed an apprenticeship in metalworking?" he asked.

"Yes," I said. It was not surprising that they knew this. The German police had files on every person, living or dead. There was an absolute requirement that everyone, Jew or Gentile, register with the local police precinct whenever they moved away from a residence. They had to register again with the police precinct in the district to which they were moving. Anyone who violated this rule was severely punished. I had also had to register for a special permit that allowed me to travel on the streetcars and on the S-Bahn to attend my apprenticeship courses. Otherwise, I wouldn't have been able to use public transportation. All of this registration was accepted as normal in Germany. The German governmental system exerted a cradle-to-grave system of control that never would have been accepted in the United States.

"Tell us briefly about what you did there."

"I am a machine builder," I replied tersely. I had completed a three-and-a-half-year apprenticeship sponsored by the Jewish Community of Berlin. The standing Gestapo man turned around and whispered quietly to one of his fellows. I could not hear what was being said. My mother squeezed my hand. My attention was totally fixed on this Gestapo agent, wondering what he was up to. No sooner had I thought this than he turned around, facing me once more.

"Is this your suitcase?" he asked, pointing to the small leather bag I had placed on the floor beside me.

"Yes," I answered. I had no time to think about the significance of what he was saying. Everything was happening so quickly.

"Take it and follow this officer!" he ordered, pointing to one of the uniformed men standing there.

I stood there for a brief second, listening to his orders. Then he turned to my parents and yelled, "You! Both of you! Follow this policeman!" He pointed to another man on the opposite side of the room.

It took a second for me to grasp what was happening. They were being taken away from me. I was being separated from my parents, and this might be my only opportunity to say good-bye. I immediately stepped over to them. My mother was just beginning to grasp the significance of the Gestapo agent's orders. A look of unspeakable horror came over her face.

She moaned, but now her voice seemed desperately weak, as though she was too frightened and exhausted to say anything. My father's eyes were blank, his face broken, and tears were in his eyes, something I had never seen there before. We all fell into each others' arms, embracing. We gripped each other tightly, as if that would bind us with some type of familial aura the Nazis would be unable to penetrate.

The Gestapo and police had no patience for this. They reached into our huddle to force us apart. The Berlin policeman reached around my stomach, yanking me toward the door. I tried to resist, but I was no match for him. Two others grabbed my parents around their chests, pulling them toward the other door. "Dago! Dago!" my mother screamed in terror, fighting to reach me even as we were torn apart. My father's eyes seemed to cling to me, desperately recording a last glimpse as he was pulled away.

We lost sight of one another as the policeman turned and grabbed my arm, forcing me to turn away from my parents. As I was dragged from the room, I could still hear my mother's screams, a terrible wailing that gradually faded as she was pushed through the other door and taken away.

It was over. Although I could not have known it at the time, I would never see my parents again. Long years would pass before I would discover that my parents had been sentenced to die, to end their days in an SS camp. And I would be alone, left to make my way as best I could. I was ill-suited to survive in Hitler's new Germany. I had no experience in taking care of myself as an adult or in dealing with the hate-filled environment that now surrounded me. But I had no choice; I would have to learn and learn quickly, without friends or family to lean on.

4

GUN FACTORY

THE EVENTS OF THE PAST TWENTY-FOUR HOURS had transformed me from a typical if slightly overprotected German Jewish teenager into a slave laborer for the Nazi regime. The emotional overload was severe enough to throw me into a state of shock. Before that day, I did not believe that there was any power on Earth strong enough or cruel enough to have so utterly destroyed my life in so short a time. I now knew better.

In the Levetzowstrasse synagogue, the policeman who had dragged me to the door consigned me to the care of another, older policeman. "Get out!" he ordered. "Tomorrow, you'll be told where to report. Do not leave your apartment until you hear from the authorities." He slapped a small piece of paper into my hand, which I put in my pocket, not bothering to read it.

The policeman unlocked the door and waved me out. I grabbed my little suitcase and walked out. Everywhere I looked, I saw SS troops. They were taking people from the synagogue and loading them into trucks and furniture vans. Men, women, and children of all ages, the yellow Jewish stars prominent on their clothing, were moaning and crying. I searched the crowd for my parents, hoping for a last glimpse of them, but they had vanished.

Across the street, I could see some German women standing at a distance, watching the proceedings. They made no move to help. They just stood there, watching, smiling as if this was a show staged for their amusement.

One by one, the trucks, now packed to overflowing with people, drove off. It was clear to me that they were being taken to the railroad tracks. There was only one reason why they would be going toward the tracks; they were going to be loaded into cars for deportation. I had heard rumors that Jews were secretly being loaded into cattle cars and shipped out to concentration camps. Now it seemed that the rumors were true.

The reality of the situation, the utter certainty that my parents were being sent into the East, hit me like a sledgehammer. Once gone, I would never be able to get to them. The thought flashed through my mind that I should follow the trucks and try to join my parents, but it died just as quickly. It would have been a futile act, most likely ending in a severe beating or death.

I turned and started walking, relieved to be out of the madhouse, but the events kept running through my mind, over and over. The Gestapo agent with the big, thick glasses separated me from my parents a thousand times. We were forced in opposite directions a thousand times. I felt the shock of outrage and horror a thousand times. I didn't know if I would ever see my parents again.

After about ten foggy minutes of this, I finally reached a streetcar stop. By this time, it was around noon. The streets were busy, full of people going about their daily tasks. While waiting for the streetcar, I remembered the piece of paper I had been handed and fished it out of my pocket. It was a permission slip to be on the street and to use public transportation. Without it, I could be picked up by the Gestapo again.

The crowded streetcar pulled up in front of me. I paid the conductor and found a spot to stand on the back platform. Jews were not permitted to sit and we were only allowed to stand in certain designated areas. I grasped a ring above me and held on with one hand, putting my suitcase at my feet.

Without warning, a pack of six teenage boys barreled onto the streetcar, all dressed in black pants, brown shirts, leather shoulder straps, and black ties, reminiscent of the dress of Hitler's original storm troopers, the SA. These were the uniforms of the Hitlerjugend, the Hitler Youth.

I knew a little bit about the organization. It had started as the Nazis' answer to other youth groups of the day, notably those of the Catholic

Church and the Boy Scouts. They emphasized physical fitness, confor-
mity to Nazi doctrine, and, like all other Nazi organizations, personal
obedience to Adolf Hitler. Gradually, as the Nazis grew in power, the
Hitler Youth absorbed other groups, until it was the largest organization
of its kind in Germany. Membership became mandatory. Youth group
members were educated in Nazi propaganda and underwent paramilitary
training until they were totally indoctrinated with the goal of becoming
thc idcal Nazi.

In the early days, the Hitler Youth were given unofficial permission
to harass and attack Jews, as well as serve as a kind of junior Gestapo,
turning in those they found to be opposed to the regime. Gangs of Hitler
Youth roamed the streets of Germany and no one, particularly Jews, was
safe from threats of vandalism or bodily harm. I had had one personal
encounter with them and it was not a fond memory . . .

Leslie Baruch Brent, Fred Gerstl,
and Dagobert Lewin in soccer garb
in the courtyard of the Judische
Waisenhaus, age thirteen.

From age eleven to fourteen, I had lived in the Jüdische Waisenhaus—the Jewish Orphans' home. Though my parents were alive, I was sent there so that I could continue my education. New laws had drastically decreased the number of Jewish children allowed to attend public school. Within a few years, the law prohibited any Jews whatsoever from going. All that remained were the few Jewish private schools, like the one in the orphans' home.

One day, we had been playing in the courtyard when we heard a very loud noise just outside the gates separating the courtyard from the street. They saw a big crowd of young people, howling like a pack of wolves as they advanced toward us. They were Hitler Youth, outfitted in miniature uniforms and looking for all the world like smaller versions of Hitler's SA troops. Within a few seconds, we could make out what they were screaming. They wanted to see the color of our blood.

Fear spread across the faces of our teachers.

We were ordered to go back inside to our classrooms and wait. Before we could move, the Hitler Youth had shoved themselves against the gate, battering it, trying to break it down. We went back into the school while our principal phoned the police department and told them what was happening. The police acknowledged what was occurring but said they were, unfortunately, too busy to send anyone. My friend Lothar Baruch (Leslie Baruch Brent) and I ran up to the attic of the building to hide. We were terrified.

The Hitler Youth continued their attempts to break down the gate, pounding on it and yelling threats and curses. Fortunately, they were unable to batter it down and eventually withdrew. No one from the police department ever bothered to respond.

The most horrifying part of this was that these were mere children, little older than ourselves. If they could display such savagery, what would their adult counterparts do when the opportunity presented itself?

To my regret, I was soon to learn the answer.

Finally, the streetcar pulled up to my stop. I stepped down and began the short walk to our apartment. I didn't look at anyone. I didn't want to see anyone.

Judische Waisenhaus, the Jewish Orphans' home; courtyard door we used to flee the mob.

In front of me, I heard the creak of a door opening. One of our neighbors, the same one who had watched yesterday while the Gestapo took us, peered out from behind her door. I glared at her, disgusted by her and by the new Germany she seemed to represent. By now, fear of the Nazis and a desire to gain favor with them had neighbors spying on neighbors, children on their parents, and friends on friends. Any behavior that ran counter to the aims of the Nazi Party was likely to be reported and the offender denounced. Many people were eventually arrested as a result—many were executed. It was another sign of the decay that was rapidly destroying German society.

I reached the third floor and our front door. Our apartment. A lump formed in my throat as the realization that I was now on my own, alone, sank in.

I took the old-fashioned winged key and opened the door. I stood in the doorway, breathing deeply, trying to steady myself. I looked to my left, toward the kitchen. The table was set and the half-eaten pumpernickel and salami were still there, waiting for us. Waiting for the family meal that would never happen. The apartment seemed even more quiet and miserable than usual. I missed the sounds of my parents moving about.

Rear gate where the Hitler Youth attempted to break in.

A profound sadness filled me as I walked around our apartment. I put down my suitcase and went into my parents' bedroom. I sat down on their bed, staring at the walls and trying to calm myself. For the first time in my life, I was totally alone. My mother had always taken care of everything for me. I had never made my own dinner. I had never even made a sandwich. I had never done my own shopping or washed my own laundry.

I walked over to the open armoire. As I started to close its doors, I noticed a cardboard box on one of its shelves. I sat down and dumped its contents, an assortment of old photographs, on the bed. I came across a picture of my father at his graduation from the Jewish school for the hard of hearing in Berlin-Weissensee. Both my mother and father had been sent to that school. It was there that they first met, became acquainted, fell in love, and eventually married.

Then I saw a series of pictures of my father at work. The first showed him holding a metal saw, cutting steel. After my father's graduation, he served an apprenticeship in the trade of metalworking. He eventually succeeded in obtaining the rank of Meister (Master).

After working in an established company for a number of years, he had started his own company in the basement of an old factory building. He carried the raw material, mostly steel, down the steps himself. He then carried the finished product back up to ground level, where he sometimes put it in a pushcart and delivered it to the customer. He worked long days and often part of the night to make ends meet in the great depression that had so devastated Germany. Even with his hearing disability, he had worked himself up to a respectable level of business, with fifteen employees and a five-thousand-square-foot factory at Koepenicker Strasse 112, directly across the street from our apartment building. Eventually, he expanded even further, moving the factory to Oranienstrasse.

My father did all this, only to have the Nazi government confiscate it at the end of 1938 when they "aryanized" all Jewish businesses and properties. Jews were now prohibited from owning any business. All Jewish concerns were closed or presented to a non-Jew. My father's business was literally given away, to a man of no special accomplishments or achievement. He was, however, a longtime Nazi Party member.

My father received no recompense for his business. Instead, he was forced to work at a Siemens cable plant, where he was given the post of cable machine operator. It was a repetitive job, requiring no brains. It was a tremendous letdown for my father, who was a man of great intellect, ability, and initiative. It gave me another reason to hate the Nazis, as though I needed more.

I came across a picture of myself as a six-year-old boy in knickers, posing with a big paper cone—a *zuckerhut*. It was customary that on a child's first day of school, his parents would give him a *zuckerhut* full of chocolates and other candy. Then they would have a portrait made of the child posing with the *zuckerhut*. The wish was that the little child's life and schooling would be full of sweetness and joy, just like the candy. A wave of sadness swept over me. My life after that day had been anything but sweet.

I put the picture box away and walked out of my parents' room and down the hall into my bedroom, thinking about my old life.

Bert Lewyn with *zuckerhut*, age six.

Each evening after public school, I did my homework at the kitchen table while my mother made dinner. On a typical night, my father would arrive from work, newspaper in hand. He'd come in and wash and we'd immediately sit down for dinner.

Afterward, my father and I would come into the dining room while my mother washed the dishes. My father would always get the newspaper. He would spread it out and silently read it from beginning to end. Whenever he came to an article or passage that seemed to concern him, he would read it out loud to me.

When I was nine years old, Hitler was about to come into power. Hindenburg was the president of Germany at the time. Hindenburg was quite old, a war hero extremely well known to all Germans. Some said he was a little feeble. Hitler was working furiously behind the scenes to force Hindenburg to step aside and to have himself appointed to take Hindenburg's place. Hitler made adroit use of his Sturmabteilung (storm troopers) in terrorizing and killing his political opponents. On this night, I watched my father's face as he read the paper. The smile that usually decorated his face slowly changed into a scowl.

"Johanna!" he called, as my mother came into the room with some tea. "Listen to this! Look at this rascal Hitler! It appears he may make it to the position of Reichskanzler. But his methods are *verrückt* [insane]. He's crazy! I cannot believe that he will actually become the Reichskanzler. This does not bode well for Germany, and there's no way to predict what will happen to us."

I was amazed at my father's dismay. He never displayed his emotions this way. Something powerful had to occur for him to do this, and it certainly didn't happen very often. My mother sat down at the table. "What's going to happen? What's going to become of us?" Of course, if we had known the answer at that time, we would have left Berlin if we had to walk out.

———————

My thoughts were interrupted by a knock on the front door. I hesitated. The last time I'd opened the door for an unexpected visitor, the Gestapo had barged in.

"Who is it?" I yelled through the door.

It was a messenger from the Gestapo. He handed me an envelope. Inside was a tan-colored card. On it was typed:

> Message: To Dagobert Lewin. You're herewith ordered to report to the Gustav Genschow Waffenfabrik, Address Bouchéstrasse 12, Berlin-Treptow at 7am tomorrow.

After confirming that I understood the instructions, the messenger departed.

Waffenfabrik—a weapons factory. I started seeing new meaning in some of the questions the Gestapo had asked me. Weapons were made of steel. The Gestapo knew I had apprenticed in metalworking. Now it was all very clear. That's why they separated me from my parents. They wanted to utilize my training and experience in metalworking in their weapons factory. And I had no choice except to obey.

The next day, I headed for the factory. The Gustav Genschow Waffenfabrik was in the Berlin Treptow neighborhood on a road that held a combination of industrial and residential buildings. As I neared the factory building, I resigned myself to working for the Nazis. The only alternative was to await arrest and deportation, and this was not a choice that appealed to me.

Arriving on time, I walked up to the gate. A guard was sitting in a guardhouse. As I approached, he asked for my papers. He notified someone inside the factory and told me to wait until they came for me. Then he returned his attention to the entrance gate.

I stood there, watching and waiting. After a few minutes, an older man wearing a white shop coat approached. Once again, my papers were checked and my identity confirmed. He ushered me inside the building,

G. Genschow & Co., Weapons Factory Berlin-Treptow, Bouchéstrasse 12.

where I was interviewed and my picture was taken. I was escorted to the production area to meet the floor supervisor.

A minute or two later, he reappeared with one of the strangest-looking men I'd ever seen. His name was Herr Giertz, and he was a hunchback. He was very short, probably about five foot six, and in spite of the fact that his body was hunched over, he held his head in a very erect position, almost like a dinosaur. He was older, close to seventy, and wore a pair of very thick glasses. He examined me for a minute, peering over the rims of the glasses as he looked me up and down. He dismissed my escort and proceeded to interview me, extracting information about my training and background. "What can you do?" he asked me. "I have had some information about you, but I want you to tell me about your experience and knowledge yourself." He was quite stern and stuck to the facts without much social chitchat. This was not a man overly concerned with being diplomatic.

I went over my background in some detail, telling him about the three-and-one-half-year apprenticeship in machine building that I had served. Giertz was surprised to hear that there were Jews who worked with their hands, but I assured him that I was only one of many. Nazi propaganda made almost all Jews out to be doctors, lawyers, or merchants.

"Come with me," Herr Giertz said. "I will take you around the floor and show you our machinery." He proceeded to walk with me through the rows of machines.

Most of them were in operation. As I looked at the workers, men of various ages, some of them seemed very obviously out of place. A few of them had no idea what they were doing. They moved awkwardly, hesitating as they moved the levers and wheels. There was a bald, heavyset man using his left hand to advance a tool when he was obviously right-handed. They all looked frustrated and unhappy.

After having made the rounds on the floor, Herr Giertz took me back to his little booth. "I'm going to use you as a setup man," he said. A setup man was one who set up the machine in order to allow it to produce a particular part.

"Can you handle the job?" he asked?

Choking back a bitter reply, I said, "I can and I will."

He didn't smile. In fact, I never remember seeing him smile in the entire time I worked at the factory.

"Since you're a Jew, maybe you can get along with your fellow Jews," he said.

Ah, so most of the machine workers are Jews, I thought. I hadn't known that before. Now it was clear why these men seemed so incompetent and unhappy. I thought it was rather odd that I, being just nineteen with no real life experience, would be instructing and helping men twice and three times my age. As I would soon learn, these men were professionals or intellectuals in other fields. They had all been conscripted as slave labor for the Nazi war effort. Some of them were "allowed" to work there because they had a non-Jewish wife, or because they were of mixed Jewish and Gentile parentage. The majority of them had been separated from their families, just as I had been the day before. There were also Gentiles from other countries working there, forced laborers from Denmark, France, Holland, and Belgium. The few Germans who worked there were almost all in supervisory positions.

I began work that same day and continued six days a week thereafter. What I did was simple. The machines on our floor produced mainly machine gun barrels. To be accurate, the gun barrels had to be made to extremely close tolerances. As little as a few thousandths of a millimeter could cause the gun to fire incorrectly. If the machines were not set up properly, the barrels would be too large or too small. It was my job to make sure the machines produced the barrels perfectly. If they didn't, I and the workers in my department would be reprimanded—or worse.

One day, a few months after I started working in the gun factory, two young, grim-looking SS officers appeared in our department. Outfitted in jackboots and the typical black SS uniforms, they immediately went to the back where the top man, Herr Becker, had an office. No one knew what they were doing at the factory, but we were all sure that it meant trouble.

After a few minutes, they emerged with a prisoner. It was Harry Keil. He was handcuffed and looked pale and nervous. Harry was known to be something of a smart aleck, constantly talking back to the supervisors and making sarcastic comments. His mouth had gotten him in trouble before, but his non-Jewish mother had somehow been able to intervene. The rumor was that she had some sort of influence with Eichmann himself and had been able to get him released from jail in the past. Whether she could help him again remained to be seen. Regardless of the outcome, it did drive home the precariousness of our positions. Any of us could be taken away by the SS at the whim of our supervisors.

A few of our bosses were easy to get along with, but most of them saw us as members of an inferior race, not actual human beings. Paul Giertz, my grouchy, hunchback lizard of a supervisor, made complaints all day, every day. According to him, he never made an error. I agreed with him and told him many times that he was something akin to Superman and this always seemed to mollify him. This was my first experience in having to play up to someone, and I was quickly learning that truth did not always equate with survival, at least not in the Third Reich.

During our lunch break, all the Jews sat together on wooden benches at long tables. Everyone had to bring their own lunch. I usually made a sandwich with a slice of cheese and so-called bread. Many referred to these war loaves as "sawmill" breads because of the real or imagined content of sawdust in them.

It was very difficult to get even bread and cheese. Jews were allowed only small quantities of food, about half the rations of non-Jews. Another problem was simply getting to the store. By law, Jews were only permitted to shop during certain hours. My work schedule frequently conflicted with the allowed shopping schedule, and on these days I had to go without. I was hungry all the time; I never felt full. And it wasn't just the food rations that separated the Jews from the Gentiles. Our pay was less than half of what non-Jews got.

The vast majority of people at the factory were middle-aged or older, but there were a few people working there who were about my age. Among them were two Jewish brothers, Horst and Heinz Lebrecht. Both became machine operators, and I was their setup man. Like the other workers, they looked to me for assistance. I became friendly with them, sitting together at lunch, telling stories.

One day, Horst and Heinz invited me to come visit their parents, Jenny and Leo Lebrecht. On the way to their apartment, they told me an extraordinary story about their parents.

For years, the Lebrecht family had been very friendly with the Keil family. Harry Keil was the young man who had been arrested by the SS at the gun factory where we worked. His mother, a Catholic, had been able to pull strings to get him released, not once, but twice.

But Mrs. Keil also had other strings she was able to pull, this time for the Lebrecht family. Mrs. Keil had another friend, a Mrs. Letts, whose husband had been killed when Germany invaded Russia in the early years of the war. Mrs. Letts had a little boy, only five years old. After Mr. Letts died, the boy was evacuated, along with hundreds of other Gentile children, to a small town in the country. Berlin had become a hazardous place for children due to frequent nocturnal bombing raids by the Royal Air Force.

Mrs. Letts worked as a maid in the Nazi Party district office at 3 Lorenzestrasse in Berlin-Lichterfelde. In addition to a salary, her Nazi bosses gave Mrs. Letts the free use of an apartment in the basement of their office building. All this suited Mrs. Letts, until she decided she desperately missed her boy and wanted to go visit him. Her Nazi bosses told her she could not take a leave of absence unless she found a qualified replacement.

Upon hearing this, Mrs. Keil came up with a plan. Jenny Lebrecht would take Mrs. Letts's place as the maid for the Nazi offices. Jenny (and secretly, her husband, Leo) would live in Mrs. Letts's apartment. In exchange, Jenny would forward the salary she made to Mrs. Letts, who would remain with her little son in the country.

As it turned out, Jenny Lebrecht did such an extraordinary job that her Nazi bosses considered her indispensable and never asked again about Mrs. Letts. And so it was that Jewish Jenny Lebrecht (with fake identification papers) lived and worked in the Nazi district office. Leo hid in the basement apartment. It was a perfect setup for them. It also had the added benefit of shielding both of them from the Gestapo. The Gestapo was less likely to look in the basement of their own district headquarters for hidden Jews. Horst and Heinz had their own room rented in another apartment.

My visit with Jenny and Leo Lebrecht was brief but enjoyable. And ultimately, these Lebrecht brothers would save my life, and I theirs.

Four weeks after my parents were taken from me, I finally heard from them. I had just gotten home from work when I discovered a picture postcard, with an illustration of trees and flowers, in the mailbox. I ran my thumb over the picture, caressing it. I turned it over. The writing was unmistakably my father's.

"We have arrived at Trawniki, near Lublin. We are fine and are doing well. Greetings and kisses from your parents."

That was it. Nothing else.

I read it over and over and over. I was elated to get it and excited to hear from my parents. After a few minutes, though, I sat down on the couch in our living room and thought about it. I realized the postcard had been doctored. The surface message of the card could not be true. My parents weren't really "fine." They did not write this of their own free will. If they had, they would have said more, much more. They would have used the opportunity to let me know that they had not been harmed. Therefore, they had either been forced to write the postcard, or it was an outright forgery. Either way, someone wanted me to believe that they were in good shape.

Much later, I found out this was a common Gestapo tactic, designed to reassure anxious relatives at home and defuse rebellious thoughts brought on by worry about loved ones. The postcards also helped Jews destined for deportation get into the boxcars that would ultimately lead to their deaths without objection or resistance, since those who had gone before seemed to be doing well.

I learned that many people had received these cryptic "we're OK" cards. It was just one of hundreds of lies the Gestapo used to lure Jews to their deaths with a minimum of fuss.

I never again received anything from my parents.

5

MOTOR SALES

Shortly after receiving the postcard from my parents, I found myself remembering the woman who had sat with us at the Levetzow-strasse synagogue, Fraulein Minna Schlesinger. I wondered if she was with my parents. Perhaps her family had heard from her. And, though I knew it was preposterous to tease myself with the hope, if my parents had succeeded in helping her perhaps she would have mentioned them in a letter to her sister.

I decided to visit the Schlesingers' home at 5 Wielandstrasse in Berlin-Friedenau. I took the subway from my neighborhood of Berlin-Mitte to Friedenau. Friedenau was a lovely, upper middle-class neighborhood with many grand old apartment buildings. Arriving at #5, I rang the bell.

After a minute, I heard an older woman's voice come over the loud-speaker. It was Selma Schlesinger, Minna's sister. I introduced myself and told her that I had met Minna at the Levetzowstrasse synagogue. Almost immediately, the door to the apartment flew open and Selma lit-erally dragged me inside. She was frantic, almost in tears at the thought of getting news about Minna. She insisted that I tell her everything.

It was my unpleasant duty to tell Selma how her sister had been arrested by the Gestapo. As much as I would have liked to soften the blow, I felt I had to tell Selma that Minna had almost certainly been deported along with my parents. Selma took the news with a grace and strength that I would not have imagined she possessed. She told me that she felt certain that something bad had happened when Minna had not arrived home. Nothing had been heard from Minna for weeks.

Selma asked me if I had heard from my parents and I told her about the postcard I'd received and my suspicion that it was fraudulent.

"Do you have any other family in Germany?" she asked.

"No, I do not, Fraulein Schlesinger," I replied.

"You are all alone?"

"Unfortunately, yes," I replied.

"So sad. And you are so young." She paused, looking at me with a speculative air. "Please, you must stay for dinner. It won't be much, of course, given the rationing, but at least we can continue our conversation." Never one to turn down a meal, I accepted. We spent a pleasant hour eating and discussing what was happening to the world we had known.

As I bid her good night, she asked me to stop by from time to time to visit. I had no difficulty promising to do so. At this juncture, life seemed very difficult and I would be glad of her company in the little leisure time the Nazis allowed me. I had been working ten-hour shifts, six days a week in the gun factory, never knowing when they would suddenly change my shift schedule. I was being ground down by the cycle of work, eat, sleep, and work again. I was miserable, without friends or family, lacking all of those things that make life something more than a burden to be borne.

And so I decided to contact Dr. Finger.

Dr. Finger was a dentist whom my parents and I had seen over the years and with whom we had become very friendly. He was highly respected by his patients, two of whom were German businessmen with influence that reached high into the upper strata of the Reich. He was fortunate in that these men were able to pull strings to protect him and his wife. For now at least, he was able to continue living in his apartment. Hungry for the sight of a friendly face, I went to visit him at his apartment. He was always glad to see me, and I made it a point to visit him regularly.

One day I arrived for a visit. Dr. Finger seemed nervous, pacing back and forth across the floor as if he were being chased by some private demon. I asked him what was wrong and his reply was one I had heard all too often recently.

"Dagobert, it looks as though the Gestapo is closing in on me. I have reason to believe that they will soon deport me and my wife." In those days, few people understood exactly what deportation meant. At best, it was a complete and total disruption of one's life as that person was shipped off to a different area of Europe. But there were rumors of a more horrific meaning to the word, a meaning inevitably defined by the death of the person selected. In the days to come, we were all fated to learn that deportation was just another word for death.

My heart sank. The Gestapo was becoming ever more efficient at deporting Jews. Fewer and fewer Jews remained in Berlin. Although I did not know it at the time, Berlin's Jewish population had by now been reduced to about one-quarter of its prewar size. And this number would have been even smaller had the Wehrmacht not insisted that Jews such as myself, who worked in areas vital to the war effort, be left alone until replacements could be found.

"However," I heard him continue, "some patients of mine, a Christian family, have offered to take us in. Within the next few days, we are going into hiding." I must have looked a little stunned, because Dr. Finger looked at me and reached out to put his hand on my shoulder. "Dagobert, do not fear. We will still be able to stay in touch."

Stay in touch? Was he crazy? He would be in hiding! "How on Earth can we do that, Dr. Finger?" I asked him.

Gentle old Dr. Finger was probably the last man on Earth I would have ever thought of as being knowledgeable about espionage. Regardless of how he had learned the techniques, he was able to show me an exact method that I could use to contact him without danger for either of us.

This method used the general delivery system provided by the post office. The heart of the system was a fraudulent postal ID card, which identified Dr. Finger as one "J. Streich." I was to write a postcard addressed to J. Streich, care of General Delivery. I would then mail it to the postmaster at the district post office. The postmaster would file the card in alphabetical order under *S*. Dr. Finger would come in to check his mail on a regular basis, present his ID, and retrieve any mail that was waiting.

"That sounds good," I said. "And you will write to me under my real name?"

"No," Dr. Finger replied, "I think it best that we get you your own ID. That way, should anything happen, we will still be able to correspond."

I looked at him, perplexed. Anything happen? I was nineteen, unable to conceive of anything else happening more terrible than those events that had already befallen me. I was still getting used to life without my parents and working at the gun factory. With the insane optimism of youth, I thought that surely nothing else could happen to harm me, that I had reached the bottom of the barrel and I had no where to go but up. In this I was horribly wrong, but it would be some time before I would realize it.

Dr. Finger saw that I was concerned. "Just do as I say," he said. "I'd rather get you an ID while I can, just in case.

"So, he continued, "on your cards or letters to me, you must tell me when you want to meet me."

"OK," I began, but Dr. Finger quickly interrupted.

"I think, Dagobert, that we should use some type of code to determine when and where we meet. It may not be safe to put much in writing." Once again, Dr. Finger advised me on how to set up a meeting safely. He instructed me to always meet him at Aschingers Restaurant. This would make it unnecessary to ever write down the name of a meeting place. I was told to write Thursday if I wished to meet him on Wednesday, or Sunday if I wanted to meet on Saturday. The time for the meeting was handled in the same way. If I wanted to see him at four o'clock, I was to write six in the message.

"All you have to do is to write me using my alias and a meeting will be arranged. You must be patient, Dagobert. I probably won't be able to retrieve my mail more than once a week. So don't expect instant results, but at least we will be able to meet safely."

My education in the world of the underground had begun. I dropped my letters to "J. Streich," and picked up mail under my new name of "D. Leo." We met from time to time. More important, I had been introduced to methods that made living outside of Nazi rule possible.

I continued to grow closer to the Lebrecht brothers, talking to them during work and at lunch. We had much in common. Heinz was my age, and Horst was about two years older. One thing I particularly liked about them was that both were even-tempered, patient men. They were supremely patient in everything they did. This was important to me, because hasty people inevitably made mistakes and I was already beginning to think about the Lebrechts as potential partners. Dealing with the Nazis left no margin for error; any mistake could prove fatal, so being patient and methodical were vital to the survival of all of us.

We spent a good deal of time talking about current conditions in Nazi-dominated Berlin, particularly the food situation. All food and most other consumer goods were subject to rationing and were only available with coupons. Jews received roughly half what Gentiles were allowed. Being nineteen years old with a high metabolism, I was starting to get a little desperate over the food situation. While I wasn't actually starving, I seemed to be hungry all the time. I knew that, in the long run, I would eventually become malnourished on the rations I was allowed.

Even at that time, there was a black market for almost everything, including food and ration cards for food. I was slowly becoming educated in underground survival techniques. But to get anything, legitimate or not, one thing was essential: money. Since we could come up with no legitimate way to obtain more food or money, we concluded that we would have to resort to an illegitimate method.

I had never before even vaguely considered committing any kind of criminal act. I was a straitlaced child and my father was rigorously honest, so even thinking about it was difficult. But by now, I was motivated to do something. The Nazis had stolen my family from me, made me a slave, deported my fellow Jews, and were slowly starving me to death. I wanted to do something to strike back, to sabotage their efforts to make slaves of other men.

With these thoughts in mind, we weighed a number of alternatives. We decided to try to dismantle and sell components from some of the machines in the gun factory. Some of these machines were in storage and the parts would, most likely, never be missed. With the money we made, we would be able to buy additional ration cards on the black market.

The plan had the added appeal that we would be damaging the war effort. The machines would be disabled, useless without parts that would be difficult to replace in wartime. Not sabotage on a grand scale perhaps, but nevertheless acts that would damage the Nazi war machine. The downside of the plan was that, if we were caught, we could expect deportation and, very possibly, execution. I refrained from inquiring as to the exact penalties involved.

We decided to do it. Since none of us had any prior experience or qualifications as a thief, we spent quite a lot of time planning our crime. We'd remove motors from machines that were not in use. As it happened, there was no more suitable target for our efforts. The Gustav Genschow Waffenfabrik was owned by IG Farben, a huge worldwide conglomerate. IG Farben had its fingers in many business pies. Although I was unaware of it at the time, IG Farben also made Zyklon B gas for the gas chambers of Auschwitz and other concentration camps.

We were well aware that, if caught, our punishment would be swift and harsh. The Nazis were already using every possible excuse to arrest and deport innocent Jews. I could only imagine what they would do if they got their hands on an actual Jewish criminal. Some of the methods of execution they were employing included hanging by a rope, being impaled on meat hooks, and guillotining. If the Gestapo were involved, the method of death would be irrelevant. Whatever way the end came, it would be certain to be welcomed after experiencing the tender mercies of the Gestapo torture squads.

There was the problem of how to dispose of the motors. Electric motors, like many other goods, were strictly rationed at this point in the war. The motors contained a large amount of copper wire, which was an imported item and difficult to obtain in wartime. I knew that there was a high demand for used motors of virtually any kind. The military had first priority when it came to any type of goods or service, and the civilian population had to make do with what was left.

Because my father had purchased motors from time to time, I was familiar with several small shops that were in the business of repairing and rebuilding them. I started with a shop owned and run by two older men, brothers, who had done business with my father and had eventually become quite friendly with him.

I walked up to the shop, opened the door, and walked in. A secretary was seated at a desk that was dusty enough to match the rest of the office. Under a layer of dirt, which seemed to coat the entire building, motors and switching gears were scattered all around. I walked up to the secretary, but before I got a good look at her, the odor of her perfume hit me like a sledgehammer. She smelled as though she had bathed in a huge vat of the stuff. I coughed as I tried to breathe through it.

"Got a cold, honey?" she asked, looking at me over thick, horn-rimmed glasses. She had a telephone to her ear and was speaking into it in a rather odd, broken tone of voice. I quickly realized this was due to the bits of candy residing in her mouth that she chewed in a circular manner, using her tongue to rotate the pieces like a juggler throwing his balls.

"No, I'm fine, thank you." I wasn't used to having a stranger speak nicely to me. Knowing that it was absolutely illegal to do business with Jews, I had purposely put on an old jacket of my father's, one that my mother had never sewn a yellow star onto.

"What do you need, honey?"

"I need to speak to the owners of the shop."

"What's your name?" she asked.

"Dagobert Lewin. I'm Leopold Lewin's son."

"OK, wait here," she said.

She rose and walked out the door behind her, into the shop. Her moving set in motion a whole new slew of perfume molecules, which promptly came hurtling my way, triggering another coughing attack. After I caught my breath, I was grateful to see one of the brothers emerge without the secretary. He seemed older than I remembered and a bit feeble.

"Hello, young Herr Lewin. What brings you here?" he asked.

After a little small talk, I felt him out on whether he would be interested in the motors. He let me know right away that he could use them and asked me to come back when I had some to sell. Nothing was said about where the motors would come from. Perhaps he felt the less he knew the better. Whatever the reason, it seemed that I would have no trouble disposing of them. I thanked him for his time and left.

I was glad that he hadn't asked for details. I didn't want to tell him anything, and I now felt sure he didn't want to know. Soon, I would bring him one of the motors and see what he would pay. The next night, the Lebrechts and I went about the business of becoming thieves.

I was working the day shift, and they were working at night. During the night shift, there was only a minimum of supervision. There were hardly any Germans there, and the Nazis would trust no one else as supervisors. The Lebrechts were free to work the inside of the building. It was left up to me to work the outside. Sometime during their shift, the brothers disconnected a motor, took it off the machine, and placed it on the floor.

The next night, I arranged my departure so I would arrive at the factory after dark. We had very little time, since the streetcars stopped running at 10:00 PM and I had to be on my way home before then. I got off the streetcar and walked toward the gun factory. An armed guard behind a barbed wire fence controlled access to the main entrance on Bouchéstrasse, but the fence did not completely encircle the building. We planned on using a side of the building that had windows but no doors. This would minimize the likelihood of our work being interrupted. There was almost no traffic on Bouchéstrasse at night, so there was little chance that anyone on the street would see us.

Instead of approaching by way of the main entrance, I stayed on a grass strip that ran under the window we had chosen as the drop-off point. At the appointed time, Horst's head appeared outside the window, gazing down at me. He slung a rope securely around the motor and lowered it carefully until it was far enough down for me to grasp. I signaled to him that I had it, slipped the motor into a rucksack, and was on my way within minutes. No one had interfered or even seemed to notice.

I walked to the streetcar stop. When the streetcar came, I got on, entered the platform, and let the pack rest on the ledge in back of me. As soon as I got to my apartment, I hauled the motor upstairs. Very early the next morning, I took it to the shop.

All had gone well. The shop owners were as good as their word and paid on delivery. The Lebrechts and I divided the money in two parts, half for me and half for them. I was taking the greater risk and did most of the work, so they agreed that this was a fair division of the spoils. We repeated this scenario at least ten times over the next few months. It was only possible while the Lebrechts were on one shift and I was on the other. Every so often our shifts would change, and in those periods our crime spree came to a halt. But the administrators never seemed to notice that the motors were gone, and there was never any hint of repercussions.

Because of the chronic shortage of manufactured goods, the value of the motors was much greater than it would have been in normal times. For the night's labor, we received enough cash to keep us all in food for approximately a month. And we deprived our enemy, in a small way, perhaps, of tools he needed to make his weaponry. Even more important, I had become familiar with another way of surviving in what had become a brutal world.

6

ILSE

Sᴜɴᴅᴀʏ ᴡᴀs ᴍʏ ᴅᴀʏ ᴏғ ʟɪʙᴇʀᴛʏ, the only day I was not expected to report for work. On this particular Sunday, I decided to drop in on Selma Schlesinger. I continued to see her from time to time, and she would mark the occasions by making dinner for us both. I would bring some type of foodstuff from my newly augmented, criminally derived stores, and we would eat and talk. She treated me like a son and I, hopefully, provided her not only with emotional support, but also a little help in the way of household maintenance—changing light bulbs, repairing the plumbing, etc.

One evening, I was standing on the top of a ladder in the living room, repairing a chandelier. I heard a knock on the door. Selma, apron wrapped around her ample midriff, ran to the door, her thick heels clicking on the wood floor. I wasn't much interested in who it might be. I thought perhaps it was the couple that shared her apartment, but the voice I heard next got my attention. It was the voice of a girl.

Opportunities to socialize were rather limited at that time, especially if one was a slave laborer. The only young women I came across were those taking the streetcars or the ones I happened to pass on the streets around my apartment. The yellow star sewn to my clothing was enough to cause anyone passing me to immediately avert their eyes. So the melodic sound of a young woman's voice, just a few feet away from me, was enough to give my own heart a jerk. I listened in, while trying hard to look like I was concentrating on the quirks of the chandelier.

"Ilse, darling!" I heard Frau Schlesinger say. "I'm so glad you are here!"

Hmm. So the girl's name was Ilse. I wondered what she looked like. I didn't want to seem obvious, so I kept my attention fixed on the chandelier.

"Hi, Tante Selma. Thank you so much for inviting me," the young woman said.

"Dago!" Selma called. "Please come down, dear Dago. I want you to meet someone."

It is difficult to look graceful while backing down a ladder, but I gave it my best. I turned around and saw a young woman dressed all in white, wearing what looked like a nurse's uniform. *Yes, she must be a nurse*, I thought to myself, as I looked up and saw a white nurse's cap. She was very pretty, with reddish hair. She was about my height, a bit on the plump side, with a pleasing appearance. Her hair was very shiny, brushed up underneath her cap, and the figure underneath her uniform seemed well shaped. *What a beautiful girl*, I thought.

"Dagobert Lewin, I would like for you to meet my niece, Ilse Perl."

I smiled and extended my hand to her. "I am very pleased to meet you," I said.

"And I, you," she said with a smile. We both stood there staring at each other, smiling. Frau Schlesinger cleared her throat and declared, "Well, that said, why don't we move into the living room?"

Without hurrying, I escorted Ilse and Frau Schlesinger into the living room, where we ate dinner. We talked for hours. I told Ilse about my work in the gun factory, my childhood, and my family. I told her how my parents had met after they had come to Berlin to attend a school for the hard of hearing.

Ilse talked about her work as a nurse at the Jewish hospital. So far, there had been no definite indications that she was in danger of being deported. The hospital was still being allowed to continue operating with Jewish personnel, under the guidance of the Jewish community leaders. These men reported to and received instructions from the Gestapo.

Dagobert Lewin in front of the Jewish Hospital in 1995.

Ilse told me that the Gestapo ruled the hospital by proxy. They had appointed a Jewish manager, a Professor Lustig. Lustig had become a tool of the Gestapo and had a tremendous amount of power granted to him. Many of the patients of the hospital were privileged Jews who were allowed to remain in Berlin because of some special circumstance. For example, the families of decorated Jewish WWI veterans were characterized as privileged and had not been deported up to now. Jewish wives or husbands of Aryans were also in this category.

Other patients at the hospital were those Jews in Gestapo custody who had fallen ill. It seemed absurd that the Nazis would make every effort to cure whatever illness their victims might have before deporting them to their doom, but it was just one of the many strange idiocies of the Third Reich.

I had been to the Jewish Hospital a decade or so before, when I was eight. I had a middle-ear infection that wouldn't go away and the doctor, Professor Lachman, put me in the hospital. The infection didn't respond to drugs and antibiotics were unknown at that time, so surgery was my only option. Luckily, the doctor was able to remove the infected matter and I soon recovered.

My parents were especially troubled by the fact that there was something wrong with my ear because both of them were hard of hearing. Their speech was normal, but they had to read lips and use sign language in order to completely communicate. Both had learned how to read lips and to sign at the school for the hard of hearing. It was at that school that my parents had met and fallen in love. They married in 1921, when my mother was twenty-four and my father was thirty.

Ilse listened to me with great interest. We talked for hours, long after Frau Schlesinger gave up and went to bed. After a while, Ilse turned to me and announced, "I have a child, Dagobert. A little boy, only five years old. His name is Klaus."

I was dumbfounded. In those days, being a single mother was almost unheard of. So Ilse's revelation was something of a bombshell, as it did not seem possible that someone my own age could have a child.

"Are you married?" I asked her, my eyes wide with shock.

"No," she responded softly. "I did not marry Klaus's father." She paused and then continued, "Klaus lives in a children's home while I work. He is a lovely little boy with beautiful brown hair. He's a very sweet child and I am very proud of him. He's my pride and joy."

"Oh," I began, trying to put words together that would make sense and not reveal how surprised I was. "How wonderful." I took a deep breath. What else could I say?

Ilse stood up, abruptly ending the evening's conversation. "Well, Dagobert, it was a pleasure meeting you," she said, extending her hand. "Perhaps we shall meet again one day."

I stood up. "Yes, yes," I said, my voice stumbling a bit. "I have really enjoyed the evening."

"Since my auntie has gone to bed, I will see you to the door. Then I'll clean up a bit and leave myself," she said.

I rose, grabbed my sweater, and walked with her to the door. Ilse opened the door, turned to me, and smiled, nodding a good-bye. I pantomimed tipping my hat, joined her in a polite smile, and left. My jaw fell open for my entire descent of the apartment building's stairs. I simply could not believe it. A mother. Pretty young Ilse was a mother. And yet, she was only a year older than I.

I was woefully ignorant about children or parenthood. I didn't know a soul anywhere close to my age who was a parent. And here was this pretty girl, practically the first I had ever talked to or flirted with, and she was already a mother! I barely knew how babies were made. I had only the most rudimentary, nebulous idea.

In those days, the times, circumstances, culture, and politics all combined to create an atmosphere of fear for the Jews, which made it difficult to pursue the ordinary activities of teenagers. Girls and boys were heavily segregated in the circles in which I traveled, so the opportunities to meet girls were fairly limited to begin with. And because of German law, I was not able to attend a "normal" school. This, of course, is where most young men first meet young women.

The orphan's home where I went to school had very few girls attending and none of them lived on the premises. Once I began my metal-working apprenticeship, it was even more difficult to meet anyone. In those days, metalworking was definitely a male-dominated enterprise, and you simply did not find females hanging out around technical schools.

Orphans' Home, Berlin-Pankow.

My father worked incessantly, and my mother never went out without him, so there was little chance of meeting people through their activities. As the Nazis grew in power, our friends became fewer. For Jews, every aspect of life was becoming more difficult. More and more laws were enacted that restricted our movement and therefore our ability to work. Obtaining food, clothing, and other necessities for sheer survival became our obsessions. For Jews in Nazi Berlin, the joy of living had long since fled. So meeting Ilse had been something of a landmark for me, the first enjoyable experience I had had since my parents were deported.

Monotony ruled for the next few weeks. I worked nearly all the time, on one shift or another. When I did have free time, I would search for food, go to Frau Schlesinger's for dinner, or (on rare occasions) see the Lebrecht family.

In late June 1942, that simple rhythm changed. I returned home to my parents' apartment and climbed the steps, anticipating the comfort of my bed. It had been a hard day at the gun factory, and I was totally worn out. I was looking forward to the only luxury I had in my life, the total relaxation of deep sleep. As I stumbled closer to my front door, my half-open eyes glimpsed a piece of paper taped to the door. It was from the police.

I grabbed the sheet, ripping it off the door. The light in the apartment hallway was too dim to read by, so I took out my key and opened the door. Stepping in, I hit the door with my hip, shutting it with a bang. I drew the paper closer to my eyes and read, "You are hereby served notice that you are required to vacate this apartment permanently by 10:00 AM tomorrow."

Going limp, I let my body slide down the wall, landing on the floor. I drew my knees up to my chest and read the notice over and over again. "Vacate . . . permanently." I had heard of this happening to other Jewish people. Many of them. It had become commonplace for the Nazis to confiscate the apartments of Jews and give them, furnishings and all, to Nazi Party members.

I had thought that nothing else could go wrong, but this knocked me down to a new low. They were taking my parents' home away from me! The only reminder of them that I had left were these walls and the memories they contained.

"By 10:00 AM tomorrow" meant that I had no time to plan anything. There was no time to figure where I would sleep the next night. No time to try to save anything substantial from the apartment. I had no idea where I could go or how I would survive.

I laid there on the floor of the hallway and closed my eyes. How much more could I take? But as the minutes passed, I realized that I didn't have time to wallow in self-pity. If I wanted to survive, I had to get moving. My mind raced: I had to find a place to stay. Otherwise, I would be sleeping in the streets tomorrow night. That would be the ultimate indignity, and I would not allow it to happen.

Where to go? Where to go?

I thought about Frau Schlesinger. Perhaps she would take me in. I had visited her twice since the dinner with Ilse. Selma still had no word from her sister. During these last two visits, I had briefly met the couple who sublet a room in her apartment. They were nice, though quiet. They didn't come out of their bedroom much.

Yes, I'd go to Frau Schlesinger's. Perhaps she could help me. But in those days, very few people had telephones, so I had no way of contacting her. I had no choice except to arrive unannounced.

I went to the closet and pulled out the same suitcase I had packed when the Gestapo had taken my parents away, months before. It was the only suitcase I possessed and it would have to do. I sat on the edge of the bed and tried to think. What should I take? I looked around at all of the things in the apartment. I wasn't overly sentimental, but as I looked at each object, they all seemed to hold memories I didn't want to part with.

No, Dagobert, I told myself, *you must be practical.* Yes, that was the right way to think. Clothes were of first importance. I had to stay warm. I went to my bureau and took out a few sets of underwear, sweaters, socks, and the like. I threw these into my suitcase. I took my toothbrush and toothpaste, my comb, and a bar of soap. With clothing and toiletries in the case, I looked down and realized I had very little space left for anything else.

As I thought about leaving, I was almost overwhelmed with grief. The suitcase seemed the heaviest burden I had ever carried. I walked over to a picture of my parents and lifted it in my hands, caressing the corner of the frame. *This is it,* I told myself. *What I take with me in this little suitcase may very well be the only things I will have to remind me of life here with my parents.*

I took the frame with a few other pictures and placed them in the suitcase. Then I went over to the dining room cabinet and took out a fork, a knife, and two silver spoons. One spoon was engraved with my name, the other with JOHANNA, my mother's name. These would be small enough to fit in the suitcase, practical enough since I would need them to eat, and the engravings would never let me forget the life I was leaving behind.

I looked out the window and saw the first rays of dawn breaking over Berlin. Closing the suitcase, I locked it tight. I put the little bit of food I had into my lunch bucket, lifted it and the suitcase, and walked out of the door. I was never to return.

I took the S-Bahn as far as possible, then walked the rest of the way to Frau Schlesinger's apartment. By then, the sun was climbing into the eastern sky. I stood before the apartment buzzer and hesitated, hoping that my surprise appearance wouldn't frighten her. I had no choice if I wanted to keep the few things I still possessed from being stolen. I had to put them somewhere; taking them to the gun factory was an impossibility. More important, I needed a place to sleep tonight.

I knocked lightly and held my breath. "Please answer the door," I prayed. The thought of Frau Schlesinger not allowing me to remain was making me very nervous. I had to have a place to stay. If this didn't work out, I might find myself homeless, and that would be more than I could stand.

"Yes?" I heard a low voice ask. It was not Frau Schlesinger.

"It's Dagobert Lewin," I answered.

"Who?"

"Dagobert Lewin."

"Oh yes! You are Frau Schlesinger's friend."

After a little more back and forth, the door opened and I was allowed in. I was greeted by the couple that rented from Frau Schlesinger. When I asked to speak to her, a somber look came over their faces. For a few seconds, they said nothing. Then, to my shock, they informed me that Frau Schlesinger had been arrested by the Gestapo two weeks ago. In what was by now a well-practiced routine for them, the Gestapo agents arrived without any warning, told Frau Schlesinger to pack one bag, and hurried her onto an SS transport. Like many thousands of other Jews, she probably would never be seen again.

God, not again! I thought. I was having trouble standing. My stomach started to rebel as the gorge rose in my throat, and I fought to keep it from showing. Slowly, I regained control of myself. Not trusting myself to speak, I stood mute, waiting for my new benefactor to take the lead.

"We haven't heard from her since then. Because we aren't Jewish, they told us we would be allowed to continue living in her apartment. We feel terrible about this, but we ourselves have nowhere else to go right now. We haven't able to contact her niece to tell her what has happened. Is there anyone else we should try to contact or anything else you think we should do?"

Startled, I realized he was asking me a question and I needed to respond. "No. I don't know of anyone else you should talk to. I suppose her niece Ilse would be the one who would know."

"You are welcome to stay here with us if you need to," he said somewhat awkwardly.

It took me a moment to realize that he was sincere. There were very few Germans who would have anything to do with Jews in those days, and it took me by surprise. I thanked him and shook his hand.

"Why don't you take Minna's old room?" he said. "We could use help with the rent anyway. And it would be nice if you continued doing a few things around the apartment like you did for Frau Schlesinger. I am not at all handy myself, nor is my wife. You could help us keep the place going until the Schlesingers come back."

Help until the Schlesingers came back? Almost involuntarily, my face twisted itself into an incredulous glare. I caught myself just in time and smoothed the look from my face, hopefully before he noticed. This poor, gentle fool actually believed everything would come up roses for the Jews! Perhaps he had not allowed himself to think more negative thoughts, or maybe he had really bought the Nazi line about Jews only being "relocated" to the East. *Well,* I thought to myself, *maybe I should try to believe it too.* I looked up at both of them and allowed the corners of my mouth to rise a bit in acknowledgment of his hopeful outlook.

"Yes," I said, "I'll be happy to help until they come back. Thank you for letting me stay here with you."

I looked at the clock and realized that I needed to leave immediately or I would be late for work at the factory. I went into Minna's room and, without bothering to turn on the light, I placed my suitcase on the floor. There was no time for inspecting right now. I turned, closed the door, bid good-bye to the couple, and left.

I walked out of the apartment and made my way to the Gustav Genschow Waffenfabrik. *Yet another one gone from me,* I thought, as I moved toward my place of work. *There is no one left.*

I later learned that both Minna and Selma Schlesinger had been killed in concentration camps: Minna at Trawniki in March 1942, as she was on the same transport as any parents, and Selma at the Majdanek camp in Poland.

7

MARRIAGE

Shaking only a little, I said, "I do."

This was in answer to a question I never expected to hear at the tender age of nineteen. It was something along the classical lines of "Do you, Dagobert Lewin, take Ilse Perl as your lawful wedded wife?"

The events that led up to my answer had begun only a few short weeks ago. After moving into Schlesinger's apartment, my life, at home and at work, gradually assumed as much of a state of monotony as was possible for one expecting disaster every minute. I came home each evening, exhausted. I would be greeted by the resident couple, who would hand me a note with household chores to do and then retreat back into their bedroom. I would eat what food I had available and proceed to do whatever it was that needed doing, usually some sort of repair.

After a week or so, the requests slowed down. There wasn't much more to fix. The apartment probably hadn't run so smoothly in years.

One evening, after I returned from work, the door to the apartment creaked open. *Aha*, I thought to myself. *I know what will be next on my repair request list—oiling the door hinges.* I decided to go ahead and take care of it before they asked and started walking toward the cabinet where I thought I'd find the proper oil.

As I approached the cabinet, I heard footsteps shuffling through the door. The footsteps were distinctive. They were Ilse's.

She stood before me, as beautiful as when I had first met her. Milky white skin, shiny auburn hair, looking radiant. Once again, she wore her white nurse's uniform.

"Ilse," I exclaimed, unable to hide my delight at her presence. "Hello!"

"Dagobert?" The look on her face told me that she had come here to grieve, expecting to find an apartment occupied only by memories of her beloved aunt. My presence here suddenly seemed invasive, almost sacrilegious, as if I had intruded on a very private moment. It made the next few minutes that much more difficult.

"Uh, I guess you were not told that I was living here," I began, trying to explain my presence there.

She continued to stare at me, surprise written large on her face.

"Let me explain," I said, desperately trying to head off the explosion that I felt sure must be imminent. "Two weeks ago, the Gestapo confiscated my parent's apartment. There was a note on my door telling me to be out by the next morning. I didn't know where to go, and I thought of your aunt Selma. I had visited her a few times since I met you here, and she was always very kind to me. I hoped she might let me stay here for a while, until I could find another place."

Ilse continued to stare dead straight at me.

"So the next morning I packed my suitcase and came here. The couple who were living with your aunt invited me in. Once I got here, they told me the terrible news, that your aunt had been arrested. Of course, I was horrified. But then, they asked me if I could stay here with them. They needed help with the rent, and they also needed someone who could take care of the place, make repairs and the like."

There was silence for a few seconds and then Ilse spoke. "So you're living here, Dagobert?"

Somehow, her question made me feel guilty, as though I was being accused of a crime. I tried to respond casually, but I couldn't help feeling as though I had done something wrong. "Well, yes. I guess you could say that."

"I see," she said seriously. "So this couple invited you to live here?"

"Umm, yes, they did," I said, waiting for the fireworks to start.

There was silence again. Ilse seemed to be pondering the situation. Finally she spoke again. "Interesting."

And that was all she said. She walked over to the sofa, rubbed her hand over it as though she were inspecting it for damage and sat down, a thoughtful expression on her face. I didn't know what to do, so I walked over and sat in a chair across from her, awaiting the verdict.

Finally she said, "Well, I guess it's fine. I suppose it's for the best."

Upon hearing this, I nearly jumped for joy. I had been afraid that she would ask me to leave, and I had nowhere else to go.

Ilse continued, "It is sweet of them to think that my aunties will be coming back. Yes. It's a sweet thought."

I nodded in agreement, feeling a bit foolish. I thought I had best make some conversation, lest she think the situation over and change her mind. "And you, Ilse? How are you? I am so terribly sorry about your aunt Selma. So very sorry. I know what it is like to have someone you love taken away from you."

Ilse looked at me up and down. She rose and said, "Yes, Dagobert, I guess you do. It is terribly hard, really, isn't it? To have them gone. *Poof.* Almost as though they never existed." She paused again and looked at me. "Actually, Dagobert, I am glad you are able to stay here. My aunties would also be happy, I think."

I was relieved that Ilse felt this way. I dreaded her disapproval, which would have meant my immediate departure.

"And you, Ilse? How are things at the hospital?"

"They are fine, thank you. Tensions are mounting all the time. It is very worrisome. But at least I still have a job, and Klaus is still safe."

Klaus. The mention of her son brought back the memories of our last conversation.

"Where is Klaus staying now?" I asked. "Is he with you at the hospital?"

"Oh no," she responded. "I live in a dorm with the other single nurses. There is no room there for a child; they would not allow it. He is living in a children's home where he is very well cared for. The women who work there are very fond of him and extremely kind. I am lucky to have them."

"That's good."

"Of course," she continued, "I don't know how long we will remain lucky. Since I am a nurse in the hospital, I have some degree of protection, but I doubt it will last forever. I am terrified by the thought that our special status will end."

We continued to talk for a while. Ilse told me she had come to see her aunts' apartment and to fetch a few things of sentimental value. It was quite late when we finished talking, and we were both very tired. Ilse said she would sleep in Selma's old room and then leave in the morning. And so we bid each other good night. I retreated into Minna's room, where I usually slept.

I had been asleep for a few hours when I became aware that I was not alone. There was someone in the bed with me, someone warm and soft. Through the first foggy minutes of awakening, I recognized Ilse's form, her body outlined in the moonlight. It was like a dream. I awoke in the early morning, feeling exhausted but satisfied. I turned over in my bed, sheets rumpled, blankets half on the floor.

Ilse was gone. Gone from the bed, gone from the room. I threw on my clothes and went walking through the rest of the apartment. She was nowhere to be found. I was shocked, but I had no choice except to go on with my day. After a quick breakfast, I departed for the gun factory.

The following evening, the door to the apartment swung open to reveal Ilse, along with someone I had heard about but never met. His name was Klaus and he was five years old.

With no mention of the activity of the night before, I walked with Klaus over to the sofa, sat down beside him, and tried to make small talk. He was a very nice-looking little boy, with dark brown hair and sparkling brown eyes. He was obviously quite intelligent.

I talked to him about the children's home, his friends there, and other matters of great importance. I was pleased with myself for being able to communicate with him at all. I had never held a conversation with anyone so young before. An hour or so later, Ilse announced it was time for them to go home. She smiled at me as she took Klaus's hand and led him out the door.

I just stood there, confused. Ilse had said nothing about last night. Not having any other choice, I spent the next days as normally as I could, thinking often of Ilse. I could not help but wonder about her reasons for acting the way she had. I had a feeling that there was more to this than met the eye. She had never impressed me as being the impulsive type, and her behavior baffled me.

Later, I would discover some of the implications of our night together. For now, I was content to experience the changes that she had initiated. I felt like a different person, as if I had matured overnight and had somehow crossed through a mysterious barrier, to emerge on the other side as an adult.

On June 30, 1942, on my way to the gun factory, I passed a news-stand and noticed a headline: JEWISH SCHOOLS CLOSED FOR GOOD! I stopped abruptly and stared at the headline. I felt my stomach turn over. If there had ever been any doubt in my mind that the Nazis sought the destruction of Germany's Jews, it was now gone forever. What was happening to the Jews was unbelievable. What else could they do? They had arrested and deported most of us already, and now they were forbidding those who remained any education whatsoever.

Education has always played a major part in the survival of Jews everywhere. Education was the means by which Jews, as well as other peoples, could rise above a subsistence level existence to obtain security for family and self. Education and study were urged on every Jewish child as the most worthwhile activity they could undertake. It was almost holy. The closing of our schools was a message from the German government: they were telling us that this was the beginning of the end.

It was therefore not surprising that this was the chief topic of conversation during lunchtime in the gun factory. This latest attack on our civil rights did not bode well for our future. "They want to get rid of all of us," said one of the men who worked on my floor. "They're going to take everyone. No one is safe." Anxiety levels ran extremely high. Everyone was so tense that it was hard to concentrate on our work. We were all living with a constant outpouring of adrenaline, wondering who would be the next to go. It was enough to send anyone over the edge.

One measure of how seriously the Jewish community took this news was reflected in the suicide rate. After the news became common knowledge, there was a radical increase in the number of suicides among Berlin's remaining Jews, especially those who had already been arrested and were awaiting deportation.

Ilse had told me that the Jewish Hospital was being flooded with attempted suicides. She said it had become a depressing place to work because of it. Doctors and nurses debated endlessly whether they should save these people, or whether it was more humane to let them die. If the doctors had possessed crystal balls with which to view their futures, the debates would have been short and sweet.

There are no words to describe the daily horror life in Berlin had become. Some of those intending suicide took overdoses of Veronal, a sleeping pill. Poisons were traded at extremely high prices on the black

Entrance to Weissensee cemetery, where the majority of Jewish suicides were buried. The inscription on the memorial plaque reads: REMEMBER ETERNALLY WHAT HAPPENED TO US. DEDICATED TO THE MEMORY OF OUR MURDERED BROTHERS AND SISTERS. 1933–1945 AND THE LIVING WHO HAVE TO FULFILL THE LEGACY OF THE DEAD.

market. Sometimes they worked, and sometimes they didn't. Other poor souls threw themselves over the balcony at the Levetzowstrasse synagogue, where my parents and I had been taken. They preferred to fall to their deaths rather than wait to be deported.

Over the next few months, Ilse would occasionally come to see me at her aunts' apartment. She was becoming more and more concerned about her and Klaus's safety. She and the other nurses could be arrested at any time. It was hard to know what to do and, in any case, our options were limited.

Then, one day in the fall of 1942, I received a letter at Frau Schlesinger's apartment. It was from Ilse. *This is peculiar*, I thought to myself. We usually communicated in person. I wondered why she would be sending me a letter. I went into my room and sat on the bed, quickly running my finger under the envelope's crease to open it. It was only one page. I took it out and read:

"Dagobert," she wrote, "I have contracted typhus from a patient and am now in the hospital myself. I will probably be here for a long time. Please come and see me when you can."

Typhus. How horrible, I thought to myself. She must be very sick. Typhus was an extremely contagious, lice-borne disease. It typically appeared in areas devastated by war or famine. The mortality rate ran as high as 20 percent, and death from it was excruciatingly painful.

A few days later, I awoke, got dressed, and went straight to the hospital. Before being allowed to see her, I was made to put on a hospital coat and mask. Ilse looked very sick, very weak. But upon seeing me, her face brightened a bit and she managed to hold a short conversation. "Dagobert, I am terrified! I think that, as soon as I am well, I might be deported. There is talk that they are going to arrest all of the single nurses at the hospital. It is so awful!"

I tried to reassure her. "Just rest," I told her. "You need your strength to get well."

Soon after that, the nurse told me I had to leave and allow Ilse to sleep. "I'll be back next week if I can," I told her.

And so, after another week at the gun factory, I returned to see Ilse. I came back a few times after that. Each visit was very short. Each conversation covered the same subject: fear. Fear that she would soon be deported.

A couple months later, Ilse was feeling much better physically but remained too weak to be released. As her release date approached, she continued to go downhill emotionally. She was terrified, but there was nothing to be done.

"Dagobert," Ilse said, "this is very serious. Single nurses with children are going to be scheduled for deportation. Children without two parents are also being deported. Klaus and I are in great danger."

I didn't know what else to say. We had discussed the situation many times and each time I had tried to make her feel better. I told her to concentrate on getting well, but there was little I could do to comfort her. Now the situation was different. She was nearly well. Her fears might well become reality.

"Dagobert," she continued, "please help me. Please help little Klaus and me."

I continued to look at her without saying a word.

"Dagobert. Please marry me."

I gasped.

"Dagobert, it is my only hope. If I am married, I might be able to remain in Berlin. If I am a married nurse, I won't be scheduled for deportation, at least not immediately."

Suddenly, I had trouble looking Ilse in the eyes. The end of the bed attracted my attention and I stared at it, speechless.

"You would be saving my life, Dagobert. Saving Klaus's life."

I tried to concentrate on breathing. My head was swimming, my thoughts churning frantically, making me dizzy. *Marriage? Me? Married?* The ringing in my ears began again. I was only able to comprehend about one word in three, as she continued to plead.

"Please, Dagobert? Help Klaus and me."

Klaus. Mention of that little boy made my heart stir. And all of a sudden, my brain began to work again. *You have the opportunity to help her,* I told myself. *To help Klaus.*

I turned back to Ilse and looked at her desperate face. There were tears streaming down her cheeks.

Dagobert, I told myself, *this is the right thing to do.*

She continued, "Being married might also help you, Dagobert. Who knows what will happen to the Jews working in the factories? Even though you are helping the Nazi war effort, one day they may decide to deport all of you. And they might begin with single people like yourself."

I thought about this. She could be right. I finally spoke, "So, Ilse, how do you propose we go about this?"

Her eyes brightened. "I know exactly how. I already have it all worked out. The nurse on this floor is a friend of mine. I have asked and she has agreed to let me leave for a few hours to go and get married. Then I would come back here for the rest of the prescribed hospital stay."

Hmm. She had it all worked out. She had done the research. Obviously, a methodical woman. Ilse continued, "That way, when I am

Certificate of my marriage.

released, I will be married. They will not be able to take me away with the single nurses."

The next day, on December 11, 1942, I went to the hospital. I had just been switched to the night shift at the gun factory, so I was able to go during the day. Once there, I helped Ilse get ready, and we left for the Standesamt. This was a registry office that performed weddings, among other public services. There, in a matter of two hours, we waited in line, did the proper paperwork, and went through the wedding ceremony. All very perfunctory, with very little said by either one of us. It was not exactly how I expected my wedding day to be. But then again, nothing in my life was turning out the way I expected.

After the deed was done, we returned to the hospital, where a few of Ilse's nurse friends greeted us with congratulations. It wasn't possible to obtain a wedding cake, so we celebrated by consuming a huge bowl of ice cream. I stayed with Ilse in her room into the evening, until it was time to go to work at the gun factory.

While at work, I pondered the monumental event that had taken place that day. Regrettably, there were no monumental feelings to accompany it. I was married. I was a husband, practically a father. But it was all very otherworldly, as if it had happened to someone else. Maybe it wasn't a marriage made in heaven, but I had done a good deed for a good person and her child. And for that, I was happy.

In the next few days, Ilse was released from the hospital. Now that she was married, she was not allowed to continue living in the single nurses' dorm at the Jewish Hospital. We would have to find somewhere else to live.

Living together at her aunts' former apartment was also not an option. A few weeks earlier, the Gentile couple who lived there with me announced that they would be moving back to the wife's hometown in the countryside. They were fearful of being in Berlin during the war, fearful of food shortages. They were fearful of the bombings that had begun and only threatened to get worse. For these reasons, they abandoned the apartment and left for the country. Since I was a Jew, I would not be able to live in the three-bedroom flat without other Aryans in residence. That was now forbidden.

So the timing of the wedding and subsequent moving in with Ilse turned out to be a godsend for me. Ilse found a room for the three of us at Grabbeallee 27. We rented it from a woman who was a night nurse at the Jewish hospital. She and her husband welcomed the extra money, and she even offered to watch Klaus while Ilse and I were at work during the day.

This was a very exciting prospect for Ilse. She had longed to live with Klaus again, but she had been forced to let him stay at the children's home because she had no one to care for him during the day.

The next week, Ilse and I went to the children's home, retrieved Klaus, and moved him into our room at Grabbeallee 27. Ilse and I went to work while Klaus stayed with our female landlord. And somehow, we eked out a decent semblance of a family life.

So things continued, until one day a few weeks later when lightning struck us for the second time. In this case, however, the lightning bolts were not the less painful version generated by thunderclouds. Instead, the dual lightning bolts of the SS, in its Gestapo incarnation, came hammering at my door once again, seeking the destruction of myself and my new family.

On this day, we heard the now-familiar pounding at our door, accompanied by the insistent demand for immediate entrance. The Gestapo once again ordered us to pack our bags for instant departure. We were arrested pending deportation. Our crime, once again, was in being Jewish and thereby impeding the progress of the Reich toward the ultimate goal of becoming *Judenrein* (cleansed of Jews).

We were taken to Grosse Hamburger Strasse, a collection point for Jews being deported. As we entered the building, we were instructed to get in a line. I thought we were done for and on our way to the boxcars to be taken to the East.

"Papers!" the Gestapo agent standing beside the line barked.

I stood beside Ilse and held her hand tight. She held onto Klaus.

I admit to being overwhelmed with fear. My mind was filled with the memories of one year ago. Like today, a family of three—two parents and a son—walked slowly to the head of a line where their fate would be decided. Tears welled up in my eyes as I remembered it. And then the irony sank in. A year ago in a line much like this one, it had been I who was the young boy walking with his parents. Now I was a parent, walking with another little boy, Klaus.

This was my new family, and though I was only nineteen, I was the head of it. I clung to Ilse and Klaus as we ventured forward. As before, a table stood in front of us with a Gestapo agent sitting behind it. As soon as we got to the head of the line, Ilse produced her *schutzkarte*, or protection card. This had been given to her by the director of the Jewish Hospital, Dr. Walter Lustig.

Dr. Lustig had a special relationship with the Gestapo. They depended on Lustig to keep the hospital running, and Lustig depended on them to protect his doctors and nurses from deportation. Lustig knew that the Gestapo was rounding up Jews throughout Berlin. He also knew he couldn't afford to lose his staff. No staff would mean no hospital. So Dr. Lustig arranged with the Gestapo to give certain hospital employees *schutzkarten*, or protection cards. These cards allowed the employees to purchase ration cards and, in the event of an arrest, would temporarily protect them and their families.

I held my breath. The Gestapo agent glanced hard at Ilse's *schutzkarte* and looked all three of us up and down. He grunted, mumbled something I didn't understand and pointed his finger to the door. Ilse and I looked at each other hopefully. We looked back at the Gestapo agent.

"*Raus!*" he yelled at us. "*Schnell!*" I looked again at Ilse, my heart bursting with relief. He was telling us to *Get out! Fast!* I bent down, picked up Klaus, took Ilse's hand, and we walked out the door, just as we had been ordered: fast.

Once we got outside into the fresh air, we hugged and held each other close for a moment or two. Thankful. So thankful. For as strange as our marriage had been, prompted by the terrors of Hitler, I had to admit to myself that it was wonderful not to be alone. And I also had to admit that Ilse's predictions had been correct. Our marriage helped not only her. It had also, at least for now, saved me.

For a brief period of time, we went back to Grabbeallee 27. Back to work. Back to family life.

The level of fear in the hospital's rumor mill escalated every day. Ilse came home with new stories about how the protection cards would be canceled soon, and how Dr. Lustig was going to have to choose more hospital employees for deportation. Ilse and I talked about our urgent need to make a move. We both felt the same way. We could not afford to tempt fate again. We could not count on being released another time. We had to make plans to go into hiding. Frankly, I doubted my ability to take care of myself, much less an entire family.

But we had no idea how soon we'd need to make that move. In a few weeks' time, we would have no choice but to run for our lives.

8

FACTORY ACTION

By EARLY 1943, Nazi persecution of the Jews had reached a fever pitch. The war was in full swing, with German tanks rolling across Europe, crushing everything in their path. As their military successes continued, the government's policies toward the Jews became increasingly harsh. A year earlier, on January 20, 1942, the infamous Wannsee Conference had taken place to establish the Endlösung, their horrific "final solution" to the "Jewish Problem."

On February 27, 1943, the day seemed fated to be like most others. The alarm clock buzzed, I woke and ate, then readied myself for work. Ilse had already gone to work, dropping Klaus off at the babysitter. I looked out the window. The weather appeared fine, and I readied myself for one more day of routine.

I shrugged into my windbreaker with the Judenstern, the yellow Star of David that alerted German citizens to the fact that a Jew walked among them. Gulping down my breakfast—bread with artificial margarine and chicory, the coffee substitute—I prepared my equally meager lunch of black "sawdust" bread. Someone had given me an apple the day before, so my lunch today would be a treat.

I left the apartment and, as usual, I got to the streetcar stop as quickly as possible. The less time I spent on the street, the less exposed I felt. I stood there amid the other travelers, still waking up, my mind blank. The streetcar arrived within minutes. I paid the fare and entered, ignoring my fellow passengers. By this time, I was used to being persona non grata. No German in their right mind would have stooped so low as to talk to a Jew. I was rapidly getting used to being invisible.

When the streetcar pulled up to my stop in Berlin Treptow, I got off and started walking toward the gun factory, carrying my lunch in a paper bag.

I had only walked a couple of blocks when I saw Heinrich Schultz, a man who worked in the gun factory with me. Heinrich wasn't Jewish, but he was made to work in the factory because he limped and therefore couldn't serve in the army. One of his legs was shorter than the other, and he wore a shoe with a sole that was three inches thick to try to compensate. It allowed him to walk but gave him a noticeable bob.

By this time, the demands of war required that all German men of fighting age serve in the military. But Germany also desperately needed factory workers to produce the guns, tanks, and aircraft that were its only hope of ultimate victory. To fill the gaps in personnel, German women, prisoners of war, volunteers from the occupied territories, and slave laborers (my own category) made up as much as 70 percent of the workforce. Prisoners and foreigners filled the unskilled positions. Anyone suspected of sabotage, or of simply failing to work hard, were dealt with by the Gestapo.

Heinrich himself was something of a loner. He lived close to the factory with his wife and baby. For reasons I didn't understand, he seemed comfortable talking to me, and we eventually became quite friendly. In those days, physical fitness was given a very high priority by the Nazis, and it was the wish of every man and boy to live up to the Aryan ideal of being the athletic soldier-farmer. Perhaps his physical disability made him feel inadequate. In a society that had adopted an official policy of euthanasia for those judged unacceptable, his fears may have been justified.

Whatever the reason, Heinrich spent more time with me than any self-respecting German would. I had even been to his apartment once.

"What a surprise to see you, Heinrich! How are you this morning?" I asked.

But my banal greeting died in my throat as I caught the intense, troubled look on Heinrich's face. Prior experience, learned slowly and painfully since my parents' deportation, indicated the presence of danger and warned me not to reveal any sense of alarm.

"What is it, Heinrich? Tell me, what is wrong?"

He looked at me, concern plain on his face. Very quietly, he whispered, "Dagobert, turn around. I've just finished my shift. They are loading the Jews onto trucks."

Shocked, I could only stutter. "Whaaat?" It appeared that a day I had long dreaded had at last arrived.

"They are loading the Jewish workers onto trucks. I saw it just now as I was leaving the factory. You must turn around and leave! Leave, I tell you!"

I literally felt the blood drain from my face. We had all known that this time would come, but it was still a shock to realize that the game was over. I didn't know the details, but I sensed that there would be no more reprieves, no more delays. Our time had come, unless we moved quickly.

Keeping my face carefully blank, I said nothing. I turned and walked away, not even thanking him. I could think of nothing except getting myself and my family to safety. My mind raced and I had to fight to suppress the fear that threatened to overwhelm me.

Unbeknownst to me, the Nazi government had made the decision to remove the last of the Jews from Berlin. The Nazis had instituted a Fabrikaktion, or factory action. Munitions workers, such as myself, who had previously been judged as too important to the war effort to dispense with, were finally being rounded up and sent to the rail yards to be transshipped to the death camps.

It is hard for the average person to comprehend the intensity of the Nazis' desire to do away with the Jews. There were constant arguments between the army and the Gestapo over what had priority for shipment on the trains. The Gestapo used the trains to send many thousands of Jews to concentration camps. But the Wehrmacht also needed the trains to transport men and matériel to the eastern front. In spite of the fact that millions of German soldiers were facing defeat and death on the eastern front, the trains hauling Jews to the death camps never stopped.

Over the next few months, more than twenty thousand Jews would be deported from Berlin and by May of 1943, Berlin would be declared to be Judenrein (cleansed of Jews). In July of the same year, laws would be passed stripping any remaining Jews of the protection of the courts and placing any Jews still in the Reich under Gestapo jurisdiction.

This was all still in the future. At that moment, all I could do was keep walking. *Calm, calm*, I told myself under my breath. *Panic and die! You have to appear as if nothing is wrong or you'll draw attention to yourself.* Where should I go first? What should I do? One thing was for sure: once they realized I hadn't shown up for work, the Gestapo would be hunting for me in all the familiar places. I couldn't afford to make any mistakes.

I walked quickly back toward the streetcar. By chance, I looked down and caught a glimpse of the ever-present yellow star sewn on my jacket. It would take only one observant Nazi to see the star and arrest me. It was firmly attached, as was required by law. My mother had sewn it on over a year ago, before she had been taken. All Jews hated these badges. Not only were we forced to wear them, we also had to pay for them.

I darted around the corner into a nook behind a building and took out a pocket knife my father had given me for my birthday. As quickly as I could, I cut the thread loops attaching the yellow badge to my jacket. Gradually, I was able to pull it off. I quickly stuffed the star into my pocket.

I started walking again. Slowly, the significance of what I had just done sank in. I was no longer marked. By simply removing a patch on my clothing, I was no longer pinpointed as an outcast. I would have expected to feel elated by this, but the truth was that I now felt like even more of a pariah.

As long as I had worn the star, even though I was a despised member of a despised race, I was still part of the official establishment, part of the system. I had an apartment, a job, ration cards, etc. Now, by taking off the yellow star, I had instantly become an outlaw, someone outside the bounds of society, who would be ruthlessly hunted and, eventually, executed.

My Judenstern (Jewish star). Every Jew
above the age of six was required to
wear it sewn to their outer garments.

I had to think. *Ilse.* I needed to go and warn Ilse. She and Klaus would also be in danger. I had to tell her what happened. Our time was up.

I made my way to the streetcar. As I walked, I was passed by a convoy of green, khaki-covered trucks, the same trucks that had transported us after we were arrested. Now those trucks were carrying more Jews to meet their fate.

As I waited for the streetcar, I tried to calm my racing mind, to force myself to think rationally about my options. It would be hard enough finding a place for myself. How in the world would I find a place for three refugees, one of them a child?

Stop it, I told myself. It was pointless to think about being alone. I had made a commitment, and, for better or for worse, I would live up to it. That would be what my parents would have expected of me.

I had been brought up to be a decent person. My father's family was a very close-knit one whose members looked out for each other. Before the beginning of the war, my father had written to his family and told them about the dire circumstances we were living in under the Nazi regime. They did not hesitate to send regular packages of food. Once every three to four weeks, they would send salami, breads, cheese, and some clothing—sweaters, gloves, and so on.

Everyone helped. Life for them in Kovno, Lithuania, was also diffi-cult. But since Lithuania was primarily an agricultural country, the Jews there were better off than the Jews in Germany. They didn't have the terrible food shortages that we'd experienced in Berlin. This all changed in 1939, when the German army occupied Lithuania. The persecution of the Jews began immediately.

Although I was afraid, full of doubts and anxiety, I remembered my father's family and their legacy. I couldn't turn Ilse and Klaus away. My duty was clear and I would live up to the roles of husband, surrogate father, and protector. I had to keep myself alive to protect my family. So it would be.

The streetcar arrived and I boarded it. I arrived at the right stop and walked briskly toward the Jewish Hospital. Once inside, I quickly went to Ilse's floor. She seemed startled when she saw me.

I took her by the arm and led her into a corner, where, in as few words as possible, I explained how the rest of Berlin's Jews were being rounded up and how I had escaped only by chance.

"Oh, Dago!" she exclaimed, terror in her eyes. "What are we to do?"

"I don't know yet, Ilse, I don't know. I thought about it long and hard on the way here, but I'm just not sure yet."

"Klaus!" she whispered with alarm. "I must get Klaus!"

"Yes," I told her, putting my hand on her arm to try to calm her. "Go and get him, but then leave the apartment building at once."

"But, Dago, our things! Can't I go into our apartment to get our things?"

"Ilse," I said a bit impatiently, "when they discover that I have not shown up for work at the gun factory, they will surely go to the apartment."

"But our things, Dagobert! Can't I go quickly now? I will just throw the little we have into a suitcase."

I looked at her. Her eyes were pleading. "Well, I think it is dangerous," I said, "but if you insist, then go. Just hurry. And say nothing to anyone!"

"Very well. Where will I meet you?" she asked.

"After you get Klaus, kill some time walking. Then meet me at Alexanderplatz in three hours," I replied.

"Three hours?" she asked, "Where are you going, Dago?"

"I'm going to try to find a place for us to stay, Ilse." I looked at her and tried to smile. "Just do as I say. Leave here at once and pick up Klaus. Pack a small, inconspicuous bag with our things, and then meet me at Alexanderplatz next to Aschingers Restaurant. Do not go back to the apartment after that. Do not come back here. The Gestapo will be looking for me and possibly you as well."

I turned and hurriedly walked off her floor and out of the hospital. Where to go?

I tried to think of the non-Jews I knew. The only ones who came to mind were those who had worked with me in the factory. If we were to have any chance of surviving the next few days, we had to stay with a non-Jew.

I thought about the men on my floor, those who weren't Jewish, but I didn't think I dared trust any of them enough to ask for help. Then it came to me. Heinrich Schultz! The man with the short leg who had told me not to go to the factory today. He was concerned enough to warn me then. Perhaps he would be willing to help me now. At least it was a plan.

Heinrich Schultz lived in Neukölln, a working-class neighborhood. Most of the neighborhood consisted of tenement buildings, usually covering all four sides of a city block. These tenements had inner courtyards where one would often find workshops and small factories. There were *kneipen*, or little bars, on nearly every street corner. During peaceful times, they dispensed the local beer, piles of typical Berlin food like sausages, sauerkraut, potatoes, ham, and pork chops. During wartime, they served what they could. As I walked past, I remember thinking that it might be a long time until I stopped into one again.

Finally, I reached Heinrich's apartment. It was on a quiet side street, just below street level. Not quite a basement apartment, but you had to walk down a few steps to get to it.

I knew where he lived because I had visited him, his wife, and their toddler during my days at the gun factory. His apartment was small, but everything was in its place and it was so clean that it virtually sparkled. His wife was at home most of the time, taking care of their child and the apartment. She also spent quite a bit of time caring for Heinrich.

He not only had a short leg but also had other afflictions that prevented him from doing certain basic things for himself.

Heinrich worked in a special department in the gun factory where the work did not require standing on one's feet all day. He sat and checked the manufactured parts with gauges to insure that the dimensions were exactly as specified.

He had invited me to visit him one Sunday a few months earlier. This was an unusual invitation, because I was Jewish and he, of course, was not. It was rare for a Gentile to want to spend time with "vermin" like me. Heinrich had said he wanted to introduce me to his wife, Hilde, and his young daughter, Inge. I was struck by how excited he was for me to meet them. He was obviously very proud of his family. He beamed at Hilde and complimented her in my presence. He emphasized how hard she worked to keep their house running and how much he appreciated all that she did for him.

The other unusual thing about Heinrich was that he was very proud of his friendship with me. He was excited to have Hilde meet me and talked very enthusiastically about how much he had enjoyed his conversations with me at the gun factory. We had these opportunities for discussion whenever he found parts that were suspect.

If he found faulty parts, he would question the supervisor responsible for the team that made them. Sometimes he would skip the supervisor and come directly to me. I would have to go to his desk to arrange for a replacement part to be made.

During these conferences, Heinrich would be eager to talk about subjects having nothing to do with the making of gun parts. Even at an early age, I seemed to instill a certain confidence in people. They would confide in me about things or people with whom they had problems. Heinrich often would ask my opinion regarding his wife's relatives, people I had never met. He felt they were not treating him right, that they looked down on him because of his disability. Heinrich wanted to know what I would do if I were in his place.

So as I approached the door, I thought about old Heinrich. He was a kind man, a bit befuddled, but proud. I prayed he would be kind to me now.

I opened the exterior door to his floor and walked into a little hallway, turned left, and rang his doorbell. *Please be here*, I thought. *Please don't turn me down.* I wasn't worried that he would betray me to the Gestapo. If he had any anti-Semitic feelings, he would never have warned me not to go to the factory that day.

The door opened and there stood Hilde, his thirty-year-old wife, wearing a floral kitchen apron, a dark skirt, and sensible polished shoes.

"Herr Lewin!" she exclaimed, consternation covering every inch of her face. "I'm so surprised to see you! Are you all right? What brings you here?"

"Hello, Frau Schultz. Is Heinrich at home?"

"Yes, yes. Come in. You must please come in."

I stepped inside. Hilde asked me to come and sit at her kitchen table. She'd go get Heinrich from the bedroom.

When Heinrich limped in, he looked pleased but worried. He took my hand and shook it and then sat himself across from me at the table.

"Dagobert. You're here. Are you all right?"

"Yes, Heinrich, my friend. I am doing OK. Thank you so much for helping me escape today. You are the only reason I am not on a train bound for the East right now. I can never thank you enough. "

"Do not worry, Dagobert. I know you would have done the same for me. But you haven't answered my question. Why you are here? I'm glad to see you, but why have you come? Surely not merely to say thank you?"

This didn't sound very inviting to me. My heart started to pound. This had to work. He must help us!

"Heinrich, I come to you in great need of help. I was dearly hoping that you might allow my wife, Ilse, her son, Klaus, and I to stay with you for a while. At least until we can make other arrangements."

Heinrich took another deep breath and looked somberly at Hilde, who was standing by the sink, drying dishes and listening. Hilde looked back at him sadly. I could guess what was coming.

"You have been a good friend to me, Dagobert. I have enjoyed the times I have spent talking with you. However, and it makes me very sad to have to say this, I do not think we will be able to help you. Our apartment is very small, just two rooms. It would be impossible for us to add three people here and have that go unnoticed. I do wish I could help you. I truly do. But I cannot. It would endanger my family too much. I hope you can understand."

I looked down at the table and moved my finger in a circle over a small corner, drawing an invisible pie over and over again, then bisecting it, over and over again, nervously. I was dejected and terrified. What would we do? Where could we go?

We had, within the space of one day, become nonpersons, living on the run. Before today, we had been leading horrible lives, but at least we had a place to live and food to eat. What would we do now? I braced myself to get up and say thank you and to leave. But to my surprise, Heinrich motioned me to stay.

"I think, Dagobert, that I may know of someone who might be able to help you. We go to the same doctor, and I've talked to him a few times in the waiting room there over the last few weeks. He's told me that he is in need of money and was asking my advice. He wants to take on a renter or two. They'd have to live in a spare bedroom in his apartment and he'd live in the rest, but he works during the night, just like me, so he wouldn't be around much."

I thought about this. I was elated to hear he might have a plan, but there was one extremely important question. "Heinrich, why do you think he would rent to Jews? Are you sure he is not anti-Semitic? If he was, he could turn us in. He would be applauded, and we would be deported."

Heinrich responded, "Well, I'm really pretty sure it would be all right. He has tried to rent it before but has not had any luck. It is not the most beautiful apartment, from what I gather. He is desperate for the money, Dagobert. It wouldn't make sense for him to turn you away or turn you in if you were giving him what he needs so badly."

This sounded better to me.

Heinrich continued, "I believe he has also mentioned that he has a cousin who married someone Jewish, though I'm not sure how that would have come up. But I distinctly remember him saying that matter-of-factly, with no malice or prejudice in his voice. So I'd think it would be worth a shot for you."

I let this sink in. Not the most beautiful apartment, Heinrich had said. I could only imagine what that might mean. I was a little bit of a fanatic when it came to cleanliness, but I was in no position to be picky. Heinrich's voice broke into my thoughts.

"Why don't I contact him for you, Dagobert? I could say that I heard of a Jewish couple with a small child who have money. They desperately need a place to stay. What about it? Do you think it will be all right for you? You three could stay with us tonight—only tonight—and then hopefully, by tomorrow after work, I could get you an answer. Do you have money to pay the rent?"

I sat there, still looking down at the table. Do I have the money to pay him rent?

I thought about it. Ilse and I had just quit our jobs. There would be no more money coming in for our family, no matter how little it might have been. Now that we were going underground, there would be no more ration cards that could be obtained legally. Ilse's protection card would be voided, of course. Just surviving was going to be difficult.

I looked up and saw Heinrich and Hilde looking anxiously at me. Do I have the money, they want to know? I thought it over.

"Yes, Heinrich. I have the money. It will not be a problem."

I left Heinrich's apartment and went to Alexanderplatz to find Ilse and Klaus. After a few minutes I located them sitting on a bench beside a storefront window. Ilse was obviously scared and trying not to show it.

It was pitch black outside, with the only light coming from the very small streetlights on the sidewalks. Berlin was in blackout mode, trying to make itself disappear into the night to protect itself from Allied bombings. All windows were covered at night. Cars and streetcars covered most of their headlights, except for a small slit to allow for vision.

Berlin, with a population of more than four million, was one of the greatest centers of industry and commerce in Europe. It was the sixth largest city in the world and contained a plethora of prime industrial and military targets, as well as being the center of Germany's war effort.

All three branches of the German military were represented in Berlin, as well as more than ninety military headquarters, barracks, depots, and miscellaneous buildings of various sizes. Berlin was also a major rail hub, with twelve main lines converging on the city.

Berlin had factories for producing radios, radar equipment, generators, ball bearings, and innumerable other vital components for military equipment. It was also an important center for aircraft production. Hundreds of aircraft were produced each month, including bombers and fighters. The city was a prime military target and by March 1943, large-scale Allied air attacks had begun.

Daytime bombing was carried out by the US Air Force. Hundreds of B-17 and B-24 heavy bombers would contest with single- and twin-engine German fighters and batteries of antiaircraft guns in desperate battles that would ultimately decide the fate of Germany's factories and, therefore, the course of the war itself. The air battles continued after dark, with the British Royal Air Force continuing night missions. By March 1943, Berlin had become a city under siege, with the thoughts,

Industrial complex of Agfa, IG Farben, and Gustav Genschow weapons factory.

hopes, and aspirations of the entire population totally controlled by the course of the war. It was not a comfortable environment, and for me, it was about to become much less so.

I smiled and took both Ilse and Klaus by the hand and began making them walk toward the streetcar. Ilse looked at me tentatively, seemingly wondering what was going on. "Don't worry," I said. "Just come." We had to move quickly.

Our journey on the streetcar was made in silence. We did not want to talk publicly about what we were doing. We couldn't talk about who we were or where we were going.

Ilse, Klaus, and I arrived back at Heinrich's apartment and settled in for the night. Heinrich had visited his friend and confirmed that the room was available. The next day, I left for his friend's apartment, hoping to strike a deal.

Our future home was in a working-class neighborhood called Kreuzberg. It was a bleak place, with little in the way of trees or grass. The buildings were old and decrepit, dating probably to the late 1800s. There was none of the unique architecture common to other parts of the city; it was strictly a working-class environment.

The apartment was on the fourth floor of a four-story building. The stairs were narrow, with a landing between each set. There was no natural light. One low-wattage lightbulb flickered from an exposed socket on each floor. The place smelled a bit from strange cooking odors, none of which were recognizable.

Well, it's better than nothing, I told myself. *It's the only option you have.*

I took a deep breath and knocked on the door, praying to myself that the man would not be as bad as this apartment building would lead me to think. Hopefully, the current resident was just in need of money and wouldn't care who I was or what I was.

After I knocked a second and then a third time, the door sprang open. Instantly, the smell of stale beer permeated the air, almost before my eyes got a chance to focus on the human specimen before me.

He wore a dirty white undershirt with his soiled pants hiding only a small part of his rather hairy body. It was no surprise to look down and see a half finished bottle of beer in his hand.

"You must be Herr Lewin," he said immediately, in a much more polite tone than his dress would have led me to expect.

"Yes, I am," I replied, wondering at the incongruity of this man. If he's happy to see me, then why didn't he present himself a bit better? The least he could have done would have been to throw on a clean shirt. *Oh well*, I thought, *don't look a gift horse in the mouth.*

"You are the one Heinrich told me about, the one who wants to rent a room?"

"Yes."

"And you have a wife and a son?"

"Yes," I heard myself say, still not used to the concept of marriage. "My wife's name is Ilse, and our son is Klaus."

About this time I began to notice that he was still resting against his door, beer in one hand, not letting me in. I began to get a little nervous. Perhaps this wasn't going to go as planned. Perhaps it wasn't a done deal. *This must be my interview*, I thought. *I have to make it beyond this point or we might be out in the cold.*

"Heinrich has said many nice things about you, Herr Braun."

"Yes, well, yes," he replied rather magnanimously.

An awkward silence followed. We were still standing there where we had begun, in the dreary, dimly lit hallway, Mr. Braun leaning against the doorframe.

"Have you got the money?" he asked, taking another sip of beer.

Well, at least he got to the point, I thought, still very nervous. He didn't seem overly interested in striking a deal, which worried me. He was fairly polite, which was a plus, but the manners seemed a little out of character.

"Don't you think it would be a good idea to talk about this inside?" I asked, leery of the fact that he didn't seem to understand how dangerous this situation really was. I was supposed to be in hiding here, that was the hope. How could my presence here be a secret if the whole building knew he was renting to someone?

"Well, yes, I guess you can come in," he said, gulping the last sip of beer in his bottle.

He moved slightly aside so as to leave barely enough room for me to get past him. My first sight of the apartment wasn't much. In a typical Berlin arrangement, from the front door one walked into the hallway. To the left, I could see a door leading to a kitchen. To the right, there was a hallway that led to other rooms.

I followed him as he walked into the kitchen. The kitchen was sparsely appointed, equipped only with the essentials. There was a free-standing stove with gas burners, a cast-iron sink, and one cabinet with upper and lower shelves. There were a few pots and pans in the open cabinet, as well as a few plates and some silverware. The room looked fairly clean, though there wasn't much there to dirty in the first place. There was also a small table with a few chairs. I looked at him, waiting for him to sit and to offer a place for me to sit, but that was not to be. He started talking, standing in the middle of the room, with me standing in front of him.

"So I asked you, do you have the money?" he demanded.

"I have three hundred Reichsmarks that I can pay now, and I may be able to come up with another three hundred later in the month," I told him, lying.

He looked at the floor, a bit of a scowl creeping across his face. I hope I hadn't just made a mistake. "What do you mean you only have three hundred? Heinrich said you had it all," he muttered.

"Well, that is all I have right now, but I do expect to have more, as I just told you. It is most likely that I will have more money," I said, praying that this would work. "I can assure you that if we move in with you, we will be no trouble. We will cause you no problems. I would appreciate your helping me, and I will show you my gratitude later on," I told him, still trying to negotiate. I just did not want to pay his full price.

"I really expected more than that, especially since I will be taking a great risk, having Jews here," he said, now looking me in the eye.

Another awkward pause followed. I could not figure out what to say, so I guessed that silence might be my best tool.

It was. "All right, fine," he said. "I need the money, so I'll let you stay. You'll have to be very quiet so that no one will suspect that you are here. I don't want to see you when I'm awake. You must stay in your room. I work mostly at night and sleep during the daytime, so you will have to be very quiet or I will throw you out," he said, seeming to swagger with bravado.

"That will be fine," I replied. "Can we move in tonight?"

"Yes," he said curtly. "But you must pay me now."

"First, I'd like to see which room we'll be staying in, please," I requested. So far, I had only seen the kitchen. I needed to see the rest.

He walked me down the hall and into a small room with a double bed and a very plain closet, half with a hanging rod and half with drawers. There were old-looking blankets on the bed. The walls were plain, absent of any attempt at decoration. "'This is it," he said. "If you want it, give me the money."

"Well, we want to be able to use the kitchen. We have a small child and we'll need to be able to cook some simple things," I said.

"That's OK, I never use it anyway," he said.

And that was that. I reached into my pocket and handed him the wad of 300 Reichsmarks I had separated from my wallet before I arrived here. I did not want him to see the rest of the money. I needed to keep that to myself as long as I could. I still had a bit of money left over from my black-market motor escapades, between 500 and 600RM. And then there was always my belt buckle, a last present from my father, which was worth more than it seemed.

9

THE DRUNK

I RETRIEVED ILSE AND KLAUS from Heinrich's apartment and took them to our beer-soaked accommodations at Herr Braun's. As I led them up four flights of dark, dreary stairs, I didn't look back, at either Ilse or the past. Ilse would be less than thrilled with the facilities, but it was the best we could do, at least for now. I was just thankful to have someplace, anyplace, to go.

Approaching the door, I knocked lightly. Braun appeared, still attired in his undershirt. I mumbled a greeting and walked in, dragging Ilse and Klaus in behind me. I introduced him to my family and then beat a hasty retreat, leading Ilse and Klaus down the hall into the sparse little bedroom.

We walked into the room and I closed the door behind me. Klaus immediately mounted the bed and started jumping up and down, while Ilse just stood there, staring at the little room, looking deflated as she pondered what life would be like in our new home.

I leaned against the wall, looking at her, waiting for her to say something. She put down the packages she was carrying and walked around the room, running her hand over the bed blankets and then on the sides of the armoire. She opened the armoire and looked at the drawers and spaces for clothes. Then she turned away from me and, after a moment, turned back. Smiling a tense little smile, she said, "This will be just fine," but it sounded more like she was trying to convince herself. *It would have to be*, I thought. There was no other choice.

We didn't talk much that night. Ilse got Klaus out of his clothes and into his pajamas. She undressed herself and, without a word, climbed into bed, putting Klaus beside her. At the moment, there was nowhere else for him to sleep.

I got into bed myself. Saying good night, I rolled over, facing away from Ilse. We would have lots of time to talk in the morning, and it appeared that we would need it. I knew Ilse was less than pleased with the living conditions, but there was nothing to be done. The reality of our situation was that we could live here or in a concentration camp.

Klaus tossed and turned, trying to sleep. He was having a tough time trying to adapt to the rapidly changing conditions in our lives. I hoped that his childhood would not be completely lost. My thoughts wandered and I began thinking of how, even as a child, the specter of the Nazi Party had affected my life. This particular specter took the shape of my best friend, Rolf Fehrer.

Rolf was a boy my own age who lived in our apartment house at 38 Paul-Singer-Strasse. He had the Aryan looks so dear to the Nazis: tall, with blue eyes and light blond hair. We attended the same public school, were best friends and constant playmates. Like myself, he was an only child.

Rolf and I did everything together. We played soccer, studied for school, and visited each other's families constantly. My family lived on the third floor, and he lived on the fourth. Only at school did we allow other boys to come into our little circle, but at home we were inseparable.

As our friendship evolved, our parents also became friends. Mr. Fehrer was very tall, well in excess of six feet. I thought he must be the tallest man in the world, certainly a giant compared to my own father, who was of average height. Mr. Fehrer had the gift of gab and always seemed able to talk to me about subjects that I found fascinating.

Mrs. Fehrer was also Aryan through and through, the very picture of a Teutonic woman. She was tall and blond, extremely well organized and correct. She and my mother would often swap tips on cooking, baking, and washing. As my mother did not have many other friends, she cherished her conversations with Mrs. Fehrer.

Around the time I turned ten, the N.S.D.A.P. (National Socialist Deutsche Arbeiter Partei, or Nazi Party) had grown in popularity to the point that it was influencing the thoughts and behavior of the general population. Unbeknownst to us, Herr Fehrer had joined the Nazi Party.

One day, Herr Fehrer asked us to come see him at his apartment. Rolf and Frau Fehrer were also there. Herr Fehrer greeted us as usual, but once were inside the apartment the atmosphere became inexplicably tense. Herr Fehrer seemed cold and distant, as if he were conducting a meeting in an official capacity. I glanced at his lapel and saw he was wearing the Nazi Party button with the *hakenkreuz* (cross with hooks), also known as a swastika. I had never noticed him wearing one before.

He was very short with us and very bitter, making no attempt at the usual social platitudes. "I have to ask you, from this point forward, not to visit us again," he began sternly, squinting as he eyed my parents and myself. "You are not to talk to us and not to talk to Rolf. Likewise, we will not talk to you. We will not have anything further to do with you."

My parents and I were shocked, speechless. I heard my mother gasp, and she hurried to the couch to sit, as though she needed it in case she fainted.

My father walked forward, toward Mr. Fehrer. "Why?" my father asked. "What is going on? Why are you doing this?"

"I have joined the party," Mr. Fehrer declared. "It is the official policy of the party not to have anything to do with Jews. You Jews brought on the downfall of the German people after the Great War. You and Jews like you around the world have carried out an international conspiracy to destroy Germany by extracting huge reparations that we cannot possibly pay."

In my absolute shock, I gathered that he was blaming us for the Treaty of Versailles, which made Germany entirely responsible for all damage done in World War I. I had recently learned a little about the war in school. In 1921, the Allies had decided that Germany would have to pay war reparations in the amount of 132 billion marks in gold, an enormous amount, at that time equivalent to about $31 billion. Prewar commercial agreements with other countries were canceled. Foreign financial holdings were confiscated and the merchant marine was reduced to less than one-tenth of its prewar size, while the Allied countries were granted most-favored-nation status in the German marketplace for a period of five years.

In addition, the German currency suffered horribly from inflation. At one point, it took literally billions of marks to equal one dollar. Boxes full of marks might buy a loaf of bread. Under these circumstances, food riots occurred. Attempts were made at stabilization, and, for a time, Germany's economic picture improved. But when the New York stock exchange crashed in October 1929, the effect on the German economy was horrendous. Unemployment rose dramatically, foreign trade dried up, and the number of bankruptcies increased daily. By October 1931, there were more than six million unemployed in Germany.

Under these circumstances, the population became desperate for economic relief and some people were open to the ideas of anyone promising a better tomorrow. Along with the Communist Party, the Nazi Party grew in popularity. Hitler blamed all of Germany's problems on the Jews and the treachery of the German government. He promised that, once the Nazis were in power, the Jews would be eliminated and prosperity would return to Germany. By 1932, enough people believed him to make the Nazi Party the largest in Germany.

Of course, at my age, my understanding of the country's financial picture was extremely limited. I could only listen in shock as Mr. Fehrer continued, "You have bled the German people. It is you Jews who have brought on the inflation that almost destroyed the Fatherland. Now that I know the truth, I want nothing to do with you. I want my family to have nothing to do with you. We do not want any type of relationship with Jews whatsoever."

I stood where I was, my face drained of color, staring at Rolf. Although I knew he understood the situation no better than I did, he was trying to appear very strong and stern, adopting the attitudes of his mother and father. He refused to even look at me, though I was desperate for a sign that our friendship would continue. I could not tell whether he agreed with his father or whether he was merely going along with this out of fear or respect. Whatever the reason, the result was the same. I was losing my best friend.

I heard the word "but" come out of my father's mouth, as he tried to reason with Rolf's father, but Mr. Fehrer would have none of it.

"The Führer is going to see to it that you Jews will be removed from Germany and my family welcomes this," Mr. Fehrer said, in a taunting tone of voice.

My father wanted to discuss it further, but Herr Fehrer refused. He would say no more. My mother and I were stunned into complete silence. There was nothing we could do to change Mr. Fehrer's mind. With nothing left to say, Herr Fehrer practically threw us out of his apartment.

When we returned to our apartment, my mother began sobbing uncontrollably. I was angry and confused. How could the Fehrers be so easily influenced by Nazi propaganda? How could they believe that garbage? My parents and I tried to discuss what had happened, but the discussion did not get very far. None of us could comprehend it.

Up until this point, we were not really aware of the tremendous power of the Nazi movement. It was almost impossible to believe that the absurd Nazi propaganda could influence intelligent people like the Fehrers.

We should not have been so surprised. Newspaper articles were now universally influenced by Nazi theories and though some articles objected to their doctrine, it was not long until those voices were silenced. All articles, comments, and opinions in the newspapers were singing from the same sheet of music, one written by Hitler's Minister of Propaganda, Dr. Joseph Goebbels. But until we witnessed the turnaround of the Fehrer family, none of this had really sunk in. Until this point, our lives had been unchanged, with my father still running his business and me still in public school.

Prior to this day, Herr Fehrer had showed nothing but admiration for my father. He had complimented my father for being such a hard worker, persistent despite the extremely difficult economic conditions.

I did not sleep well that night. I had run headlong into a brick wall called reality and I was having a hard time accepting it. I told my father that I would like to have a private conversation with Rolf and have him tell me whether he entirely agreed with his father. I could not imagine that he did. It was almost impossible for me to believe that my best friend now thought so poorly of me or believed that I could be part of some secret international conspiracy.

My father discouraged me strongly. "I don't want you to get into any more trouble, Dagobert," he said. "We are in enough trouble already."

That was the beginning of the end of my "normal" childhood. Things were never the same again.

———————

Now I lay on the bed, remembering that day as I looked at little Klaus. Klaus had probably never had a real friend in his life. He was only five, but at this moment, I could not foresee a time when he would have that chance. He had been forced to live in a children's home so his mother could work. Now he was living in a drunk's apartment where he was not allowed to speak loudly, much less socialize with other boys and girls. And to top things off, I was supposed to be the father figure in his life. Me, a father, who had never before had a relationship with a woman, much less been responsible for a child. I had no idea how to be a father. I felt as though I was playacting, trying to survive.

In the morning, I gave Ilse and Klaus a daylight tour of the apartment. I showed Ilse the kitchen, the tiny bare room that served as Herr Braun's living room, and the single small water closet that would have to serve all four of us. The place was nearly as miserable in the day as it had been in the dark of the night, with bare walls and an absolute minimum of furniture. The furniture that was there was old, decrepit, and ugly. Worst of all, the place had a horrible stench. From what, I did not dare even imagine.

We spent most of our time sitting on the bed in our room, trying to be as quiet as possible so as not to alert the neighbors that we were there. When Braun was gone, we did not allow ourselves to talk at all. When he was present, we spoke only in whispers.

As bad as it was for Ilse and me, it was a living hell for Klaus. Like all five-year-old boys, he instinctively wanted to run and play, which made for a noisy situation. Trying to restrain him was difficult and demoralizing. We simply could not let him make noise. Almost every neighborhood had at least one individual who made it his business to report "suspicious" incidents to the Gestapo. We could not chance the Gestapo discovering us, or even a visit from the regular police.

Virtually every day, I had to discipline Klaus in an effort to keep him quiet. I tried to talk to him, but it was useless. He was five years old and incapable of understanding the danger he was putting us in. More often than not, our only choice was to hold him down, covering his mouth with our hands. We tried to hug him while we did this to take some of the sting out of it. We all hated it, but it was life or death.

On those rare occasions when we left Braun's apartment, we dressed Klaus as a girl. This was a necessary precaution because if someone happened to see that Klaus was circumcised, we ran the risk of being reported. Luckily, his voice was still high and his mannerisms still child-like enough. We bought a dress on the black market and forced him to wear it. At first, he complained bitterly. He didn't want to dress like a girl. But he accepted it after Ilse and I firmly told him that he had no choice.

Life with Herr Braun and his beer turned out to be worse than I could have imagined. That first day with Braun had been only a small indication of how severe his problem was. We quickly learned that he was a complete alcoholic. He could easily drink ten or twelve bottles of beer in one sitting. Then he would rant incoherently, sometimes coming to the door of our room and banging away until I opened it.

"You Jews don't know how to have fun," he'd babble. "Why don't you come out and have a few beers with me?"

"Maybe later," I would say. "We're a bit busy right now."

The next day he would remember none of this. Like many alcoholics, Herr Braun would occasionally begin cursing and arguing with whomever he found himself. We, of course, were usually the whomevers.

"Why don't you go out and get a job?" he'd yell at me. He obviously had no understanding of the situation we were in. I couldn't apply anywhere for a job. They'd ask for my papers and I'd be arrested. Right now, as far as the rest of the city was concerned, Ilse, Klaus, and I did not exist.

One day, I finally discovered the source of the stench that I had noticed when we first moved in. Herr Braun had indulged himself in a particularly spectacular drinking session. I happened to be walking out the door when I noticed that he was finishing up his bout with the bottle by urinating all over the living room floor, immediately prior to passing out. After these disgusting occurrences, the whole place would reek for days.

Life was wretched for the three of us. Ilse and I were tense, but we tried not to fight; we were determined to do what had to be done, to get through this period. One thing we could not avoid was disciplining Klaus. We just had to control his activities because if we couldn't, we felt sure we would have been discovered. But this did not change the fact that we were punishing him for acting like a normal five-year-old, and that was hard to bear.

We had a few arguments with Braun and more than once he invited us to get out. But we couldn't leave until I found other quarters, so somehow I always managed to calm him down so that he relented. At night, we would all go out for some fresh air and to forget, for a few minutes, the mind-numbing misery of our self-imposed isolation.

Food was a big problem. Usually, I would go out alone to buy the small amount of food we could afford. I went out of my way to avoid meeting anyone from the apartment house. Most of the time, I managed to avoid them.

One day, Ilse told me that she wanted to go out and take Klaus with her. "He does nothing normal. He hasn't been outside for weeks, except to go out in the street at night. I need to get him into the fresh air, to feel the sunshine. Let us go for the bread today."

It was risky, but it was also true that Klaus had been cooped up much too long. I agreed.

I sat for two hours, worried, waiting for them to return. When they did, Ilse had a strange look on her face, as though something important had happened.

"What is it? Are you all right?" I asked.

"Yes, yes, Dago. We are fine."

"What happened?" It didn't take any keen powers of observation to see that something was bothering Ilse.

"Something wonderful, Dago. Something hopeful. Klaus and I were on the U-Bahn, standing because the benches were full. Klaus started crying that he was hungry. I tried to comfort him, telling him we were going to try to buy bread. I bent over to give Klaus a hug when I felt something touch my coat pocket. I nearly jumped out of my coat. I thought someone was trying to steal from me! I turned around and put my hand in my pocket. And you know what?"

"What, Ilse? Did someone steal our ration cards?" I asked.

"No, Dago. I put my hand in my pocket and felt something soft. I took it out and looked at it. Sandwiches! Sandwiches, Dago! Wrapped in brown paper. Salami sandwiches!"

"What? How did they get there?"

"I gasped when I saw them and put them back in my pocket. I looked down the row of benches and saw an old woman gazing up at me from her seat. There were tears in her eyes, Dago, and a sad little smile on her face. It was her, Dago. She heard Klaus and took pity on us. Somehow she must have got behind me and slipped her sandwiches into my pocket. It is a miracle, Dago! Such kindness! I cannot believe it!"

"So what did you do?"

"I tried to speak to her, but she put a finger to her lips, motioning me to be quiet. I mouthed 'thank you' to her and then tried very hard not to cry. I still feel overwhelmed."

I silently thanked our benefactor as we ate. We gave one of the sandwiches to Klaus and Ilse and I shared the other. I hadn't tasted anything that good in a long time. It tasted all the better because of how we got it. At a time when so many were struggling just to survive, such acts of kindness had become extremely rare.

Life went on with little in the way of change, until one day, I suppose as a result of complaints from neighbors, a police patrol appeared at the door. Braun was away at the time; only Ilse, Klaus, and I were home. The police rang the doorbell and knocked heavily on the door, but we didn't dare open it. Looking through the peephole, we could see two policemen standing there, demanding entrance. We kept very quiet, trying to give the impression that there was no one in the apartment.

To our extreme dismay, Klaus chose that moment to let out a hearty cough! Ilse immediately fell over him, putting her hand over his mouth, almost suffocating him. He squirmed and writhed, but she kept her hand there, holding him close and trying to calm him. I looked over at her. "Did they hear him?" I mouthed silently. She shrugged her shoulders, trembling with fear. If the policemen had heard noises inside, they would likely break down the door to gain entry into the apartment!

Several minutes passed. We stood there in terror. At last, we heard the sound of footsteps moving away from the apartment door. They were leaving!

I bent over, picked up Klaus, and carried him into our room. All three of us lay down on the bed and held each other. "We have to do something," I whispered to Ilse. "This apartment is too dangerous. It's only a matter of time until we are caught."

I closed my eyes and tried to think of where we could go. Who would help us now?

I decided to try contacting Dr. Finger, the old dentist who had taught me how to use the mail service as a covert means of communication. I had not heard from him for months. I hoped his plans to avoid being deported by the Gestapo had been successful. We would soon know.

I wrote to him as "J. Streich" and explained the situation I was in. A week later, he responded, setting up a meeting with me at Aschingers Restaurant. When we met, he told me about a family that was known to be opposed to the policies of the Nazi regime. The family surname was Kusitzky and they lived in Lübars, a small town near Berlin. Dr. Finger's hosts had suggested I contact the Kusitzkys and explain the situation. They assured him that I could speak frankly with the Kusitzkys.

That afternoon, I went back to Braun's apartment. Back to Ilse. I told her about the Kusitzkys. The next day, I left her and Klaus at the apartment and made my way to Lübars.

10

REFUGE

THE KUSITZKYS' HOME was at 206 Benekendorffstrasse in the town of Lübars. The house was situated on a hill that rose gradually from the street and overlooked the surrounding area. As I looked at it from the road, I estimated it to be between 100 to 150 feet away, with the nearest neighbors at least that far. This was much better for anyone who needed privacy and would certainly be much safer than the crowded conditions in most apartment houses.

This was the first freestanding house I had ever visited near Berlin. I had lived in the big city of Berlin for all of my nineteen years, where almost everyone lived in apartments. My only experience with a house of any kind had been the huge home my maternal grandmother, Henriette Wolff, had at 10 Tilsiter Strasse in Heidekrug, East Prussia. I visited it during the summers of my early childhood, before the Nazis took power.

A simple walkway paved with fieldstones led from the street to the house. Fruit trees were growing along the borders of the property and along the walkway that led to the front door. As I walked up it, I noticed large beds of vegetables and flowers of various kinds, all bearing evidence of painstaking care.

As I walked farther and looked ahead, I was able to pick out some details. It was two stories high, with a steep gable. It appeared to be made out of stone on the bottom, red brick and stucco in the middle, and wood on the top. There was a prominent chimney in the center

The Kusitzky House in Lübars. The upper
window is the room in which I was hiding.

of the house. It seemed well built, though only about thirty feet wide,
resting on its grand little hill.

I walked around to the side of the house, up to the front door, and
hesitated. There was no way of knowing if the residents would be truly
sympathetic to my situation, or whether Dr. Finger had got it wrong
and I would be greeted by people only too happy to do their duty to the
Fatherland by turning me in. Whatever the truth was, I had little choice.
I had to take the chance. I looked around and familiarized myself with
the way I had come up from the street, in case I needed to depart in a
hurry. By now, it had almost become second nature to plan for disaster.
Survival demanded it. No matter where I went, the possible need for an
escape route was foremost in my mind.

I rang the doorbell and waited. Very soon, the door opened. A woman
stood before me, of medium build, with straight black hair combed back
and tied into a bun. She wore very simple clothes with a striped apron and

a pocket on the side. She wore not a stitch of makeup, with a decidedly non-Aryan looking pair of dark eyes and a straight nose.

"Yes?" she asked, looking me up and down.

Before she could say anything else, I blurted out my name: "I'm Dagobert Lewin," I said and mentioned the name of the family who were hiding the Fingers.

"Ach, so! Please come in!" she said, her face lighting up with excitement. "I am Anni Kusitzky. Come this way," she beckoned.

She led me into a small but well-organized kitchen. There was a large hearth in which a fire crackled. Pots and pans were hanging on the racks above the hearth and along the wall, creating a very cozy effect. There was a sturdy wooden table in the center of the room, with containers prominently displaying flour, sugar, and other essentials.

"Please sit," she said, as she turned around and, to my astonishment, put down what looked to be a plate of homemade cookies. She then poured two cups of ersatz coffee and came and sat down, putting the plate of cookies in front of me.

It had been a long time since I'd had anything like cookies and I gulped them down. I was very, very hungry. Flour was practically impossible to obtain in quantities large enough to make decent bread, much less sweets. How could she have so much flour, I wondered?

The deprivations created by the war were felt in every area of society, but nowhere more than in the food supply. Only very basic items, such as low-quality bread, a few eggs, and occasionally a small amount of meat were available to the general population. On rare occasions we could acquire beans and some vegetables. More often than not, our meals were a watery soup, made of whatever ingredients we could come up with.

Living in hiding with Ilse and Klaus, I had to purchase ration cards on the black market for three people. They were not always available, and sometimes we came close to starving. Even if I could get the cards, the food itself was expensive. On the black market, where you could buy food without ration cards, it was even worse. An egg went for twenty Reichsmarks. One pound of butter cost five hundred. I was still buying illegal ration cards with the money I'd made from the sale of the motors stolen from the weapons factory.

I would purchase the ration cards through some contacts that I had made before my parents were deported. There was a trade in the illegal cards even then, because Jews were legally allowed very little food, far less than the general German population. Those Jews who had the money and black market contacts bought ration cards. There seemed to have always been a black market, not just for food but for a huge variety of items—clothing, gold, diamonds, passports, identification papers—anything and everything.

Anni noticed I was hungry and she looked at me somewhat sadly. "You must have not had much to eat recently," she said.

I finished chewing the cookie that was in my mouth and looked up at her. "Yes, you're right. I have had very little to eat for a long while."

"Tell me about your family and your background," she said.

I had nothing to lose in divulging my background. She already knew I was Jewish and living illegally. She had all the ammunition she needed to call the Gestapo, if that was her intent. As my father told me long ago, "You can't trust everybody but you have to trust somebody." So I decided to tell her what she wanted to know. "I am Jewish. I was born in Berlin. My parents, Leopold and Johanna Lewin, were deported by the Gestapo a little over a year ago. The Gestapo forced me to work in one of their gun factories."

"And you are married?" she asked.

With only the briefest hesitation, I said, "Well, yes, I am."

"When did you get married, dear?" she asked, almost maternally.

"Not too long ago, actually," I replied. "Ilse and I have been married just a few months."

I stopped and continued looking at her, thinking she would respond. But she didn't. I decided that I should continue.

"So, I worked at the gun factory until the end of February. One morning, as I went to work, I was warned that the Gestapo were loading Jewish employees onto trucks for deportation to the camps. So it was that morning that I ran from the factory and started my life as a nonperson, running from the Gestapo. My wife, Ilse, and I, together with her son, Klaus, went into hiding in Berlin."

"Your wife, you said her name was Ilse?" she asked.

"Yes, exactly. Ilse," I responded.

"And she has a little boy, yes?" she asked.

"Yes. His name is Klaus."

"Please, please tell me about the little boy. I am very interested in him," she said.

"Well, Klaus is a very nice little boy," I began, feeling awkward.

"How old is he?" she asked.

"Five."

"And he is with Ilse, your wife, right now?"

"Yes. We have been living with a man in Berlin. Unfortunately, though, we now feel we are in great danger by living there. He is an alcoholic and this makes it difficult to remain unobtrusive."

"Hmm. Awful!" she exclaimed.

"We try very hard to be quiet and to live unnoticed, but his drunken escapades have provoked our neighbors until they have become angry and suspicious. The police came to the door two weeks ago. We stayed very quiet and eventually they went away, but I know it won't be the last time they come."

"You think the neighbors know this drunk man is hiding Jews?" she asked.

"No, I don't think they know that we are there. But I do think that his behavior is so bad that they have begun complaining to the police. So it is only a matter of time before they complain again and the police return. If the police come into the apartment, they will find us and we will be sent to the camps. That is what we fear. It is a very, very dangerous situation."

"Yes, I can see that," she said.

"This is why I am here. We are desperate for a new place to live, even for a short period of time. I am hoping that you can help us."

"Hmm," she said and rose from her chair. She started to walk a bit around the kitchen.

"Dr. Finger's friends told you about us, didn't they?" I asked, wondering why she seemed a bit surprised.

"Well, yes, they did tell me a bit," she said. Then she paused.

I was very worried. Something wasn't right here.

"You see," she began, "I had told them that I wanted very badly to help a child. I want very much to help a little boy or girl. But I am not sure that I can hide all three of you."

"Oh," I said dejectedly. I didn't know what else to say.

She looked at me sadly, seeing the expression on my face. "Let us wait until my husband comes home before we make any decisions. In the meantime, tell me more about yourself."

And so I described my father's large, close family in Lithuania, my mother's family in Heidekrug, and how I had visited them when I was very young. I told her how my father's business had been taken away from him and how Nazi law made living in an orphan's home my only means of obtaining an education. I described my metalworking apprenticeship, where we lived, and so forth. She listened, rapt.

"Tell me about the people who referred you to me," she inquired.

This was an interesting question. I was aware that she knew these people very well. I, on the other hand, did not know them at all; I had only heard about them through Dr. Finger. But I described them as best as I could. I had the feeling she wanted to test me to determine in her own mind whether I was telling her the truth.

When I finished, I sat there and looked at her, waiting for another question. She smiled softly and took a deep breath.

"I have great sympathy for your plight, Herr Lewin. I hope, though, that you will understand that I cannot make a commitment to you without first talking to my husband, Alex Kusitzky."

"Yes, of course," I answered, quite worried. I wanted some comfort, some definite assurance that we could come here. But there was no choice except to wait.

Almost immediately, I heard footsteps behind me. I spun my head around quickly, with a start. In the doorway to the kitchen stood a man. He was about my size but very muscular. He had blond hair and wore heavy thick glasses. He acted very surprised to see me.

"Alex," Anni immediately began, rising to her feet. "This young man is Dagobert Lewin. He is here for our help." Anni told him a few things about me and why I was there.

"Dagobert, would you please tell my husband what you have told me? Please tell him every detail. Spare nothing."

And so, I gathered, the test of my honesty would continue. I was more than glad to oblige. It was a fair request.

As I spoke, Alex just watched me, listening. He was not a long-winded man. Alex said little and when he did talk, he spoke in a sort of monotone, using short sentences.

Anni and Alex then turned to each other and began to talk about the situation while we sat around their kitchen table. They were right in front of me; I could hear everything they said. They talked about basic considerations—where would they put us, and how they would go about helping us. They pondered aloud the logistics and practicality of letting three new people into their house, one of which was a small child.

There was a small pause. I held my breath as their audible conversation died and they seemed to communicate silently, as people who have been married for a long time sometimes do. Finally, Anni turned to me and smiled.

"We will help you, Herr Lewin. We are happy to help all three of you for now."

My heart jumped with joy. I smiled and my eyes became watery. I was so thankful that I was sure that both of them could read this on my face.

Up until this point, Alex Kusitzky had remained mostly silent. But now, he began to speak.

"However, Herr Lewin, I do not feel it would be safe to have all three of you hiding here for a long time. I think it will be best if you and your wife make other arrangements and leave the child here. This way, the child will be safe and will live in a stable situation."

I looked at him, surprised.

He continued, "You see, Herr Lewin, we feel strongly that what the Nazis are doing to the Jews is a violation of all we believe in. We have been watching the government's actions, and we cannot sit idly by and allow them to proceed. We are not the only people who feel this way. There are others in our church who feel as we do. Most people are afraid to do anything that the Nazis would object to, because they fear the consequences. But we feel so strongly about this that we are quite willing to take the risk, as we are convinced we are doing what God would expect of us. That is why we are not only willing but anxious to help you. I wish we could tell all three of you to stay here indefinitely, but I do think it is safest if we permanently hide only the child."

My emotions about this were mixed. On the one hand, I felt like kissing his hands. After all the years of Nazi persecution, I had never once heard anyone make statements like that. German society of that time had been so thoroughly deluged with anti-Jewish dogma that all I recalled were degrading, condemning comments about Jews from all kinds of people.

———————

The source of much of the Nazi propaganda about Jews was the work of Dr. Joseph Goebbels. In March 1933, Hitler had appointed Goebbels to the position of Reich Minister for Public Enlightenment and Propaganda. Much of the ideology of the Nazis was based on the idea of a pure-blooded "Master Race" whose members were tall, strong, and healthy, with blond hair and blue eyes.

Goebbels himself had been rejected for military service during World War I because of a crippled foot, the result of contracting polio as a child. Some feel he was tormented by a sense of physical inadequacy and these negative feelings were made worse by his diminutive frame, black hair, and intellectual background. Bitterly aware of his deformity and fearful of being regarded as a "bourgeois intellectual," Goebbels overcompensated for his lack of resemblance to the Nordic type by attempting to be the perfect Nazi and by the intensity of his commitment to Hitler and the Nazi Party.

Like Hitler, Goebbels believed that Jews were the primary enemy of the German people and the reason for their failure to dominate Europe. He became a relentless Jew-baiter, demonizing Jews as shadowy figures working behind the scenes in international financial circles and allied with the "Jew-Bolsheviks" in Moscow, in his mind the chief cause of Germany's disgraceful defeat in World War I.

———————

So to hear Germans talk about Jews in any type of positive way was as shocking as it was welcome. And I was happy that they were willing to take care of Klaus. At least he would be safe. But the question of what would happen to myself and Ilse remained up in the air, not to mention how Ilse would feel leaving her child with people she didn't know. But Anni Kusitzky seemed to be reading my mind.

"Herr Lewin," she began, "I think it would be best for all of us if you and your wife lived here with us and the child for a week or so. This way, the child will get used to our home in the presence of his mother. And as well, I am sure that your wife will want to be certain of the atmosphere she is leaving him in."

Her husband interrupted, "You see, Herr Lewin, my wife and I have a son of our own. His name is Heinz. But we were not able to have more children, and we had always wanted them. So by leaving Klaus with us, you will not only be helping Klaus. You will be giving us some of what we have yearned for all these years. Another child."

I let this sink in and then decided that now was the time to speak. "I cannot begin to tell you how grateful I am to both of you. I can only hope that God will give you a just reward. I hope that someday I will be able to pay you for your kindness."

That having been said, Anni spoke up and said, "Let's eat. Though I didn't know we would be receiving a special visitor, I think I have enough food prepared to feed us all a nice dinner. Please stay with us. I know you must be very hungry." After the months of deprivation, I certainly wasn't about to turn her down.

For me, the food that she had prepared was a feast. Mashed potatoes, beef, carrots, bread, butter, and finally kohlrabi cooked with ham. I had never in my life eaten ham. At that moment, though, I was so hungry that I could not have cared less what was in the kohlrabi dish.

As I ate, I wondered how they could obtain this much food. The carrots, potatoes, and kohlrabi might have come from the garden I'd passed on the way up from the street. But the bread seemed to be of a much better quality than one could buy on ration cards. And the beef! Even non-Jewish ration cards did not allow that much beef for one meal. And this was a meal she had prepared for two people, not three.

Finally my curiosity got the best of me. "This is all so delicious, Frau Kusitzky. It seems that you are blessed with more and better food than others in Berlin."

It was then that Alex piped up. He explained that he worked for a butcher and so had access to a variety of meats. His boss allowed him extra rations of the beef, which he then traded for items like flour, butter, sugar, even clothing.

"This is certainly a wonderful position to be in," I said. "I'm very happy for you."

Anni then spoke, "You know, Herr Lewin, you are the first Jew that we have ever met. We did not even think about Jews until the Nazi regime came to power. They certainly have brought the Jewish people to the forefront of the public mind. All the discussions and reports and statements about Jews make them out to be evil, almost subhuman. We know that most of what has been said is just a hate campaign. We've heard rumors that the Jews are being mistreated, arrested, beaten, and killed for no reason at all. We don't want that to happen to you or your wife and son."

"Thank you very much, Frau Kusitzky," I responded. "I do not think there are words to describe how very grateful I am to you and Herr Kusitzky."

We continued talking late into the evening about matters in general, but mainly about my own circumstances and what would happen to the Jews in Germany. The Kusitzkys told me they were devout Catholics and that they knew the Nazis were persecuting Catholics who did not agree with Nazi policies.

Finally, we found ourselves still sitting around the dinner table at nearly midnight. I was so tired I could barely move. Anni noticed my exhaustion and immediately stood up. "You must sleep here tonight. Here with us," she said.

Through my mental fog, I thought about her proposal. I had not planned on being away from Ilse and Klaus the entire evening, but at this time of night, I didn't have much choice. There were no trains or buses running that could take me back to Berlin. Ilse and Klaus were back at the apartment, and there was no way to contact them. So I meekly nodded my head and smiled.

"Let me take you up to your room," Anni beckoned and led me out of the kitchen and up a narrow flight of stairs. "Here is the bathroom," she said as she pointed to a door at the top of the stairs.

Then Frau Kusitzky opened up a section of wall paneling that I could now see was also a door. Behind the paneling were stairs leading to the attic. We walked up those stairs and into a room under the eaves of the roof.

"I hope this room will suffice," Anni began. "Our son, Heinz, sleeps here when he is home, but that is rare these days."

The attic was a bit chilly, but it contained a bed big enough for two, with a bedspread and plenty of blankets. I lost no time in lying down, feeling completely safe, at least for one night. I fell asleep immediately.

By the time I got up, Alex was already gone. Anni demonstrated her skill as a cook once again by feeding me a breakfast consisting of eggs, homemade bread, butter, something like grits, sausage, and fruit. I thanked her for the offer of help and told her I would return later that day with Ilse and Klaus.

As I walked away from the Kusitzky's home, I couldn't help but think that perhaps my luck was changing. German propagandists made every effort to portray Jews as fiends whose fondest desire was to destroy Germany. To find a couple who could think for themselves was the best of luck. I tried not to think about the fact that the stay for Ilse and I would be only temporary. I'd just have to deal with that later.

I made my way to the Lübars station and then back into Berlin and to the apartment for what I hoped would be the last time. I walked up the flights of stairs and then rang the doorbell. Braun, drunk as ever, answered the door and let me in. I nodded a curt hello to him and went into our room. I told Ilse about the Kusitzkys, that they would keep us for a while and were willing to keep Klaus for much longer, if she felt comfortable with the idea.

Ilse paused and mulled this over. I could see that she was not at all happy with the idea of leaving him. "At least we'll be able to stay there for a while to get to know them," I said. She nodded in reply.

And so we packed our two little bags. Into one, she put Klaus's things. Into the other, she packed what few possessions she and I had managed to hold on to. I had very little, only an extra sweater, some basic toiletries, and the spoons I had taken from my parents' apartment.

When this was done, I went out into the apartment to make sure Braun was asleep. I had no patience for a shouting match, especially now, when we had a real chance at obtaining safety.

Luckily, Herr Braun was in a drunken stupor and would not be getting up for anything short of an air raid. And so with that, I picked up Klaus, Ilse picked up the bags, and we walked out into the early morning fog, toward what we hoped would be the start of a new life.

11

KUSITZKY

I watched Ilse's face as we walked up the path toward the Kusitzky house.

"See, Ilse, isn't this nice?" I asked, hoping she would share my enthusiasm for the place.

As we walked, I realized I how little I knew about this woman I called my wife. We hadn't talked much about her background. I knew that she had been born in Bismarkhuette, Silesia, a region which had been controlled first by Germany, then Poland, then Germany again.

Was she well off there? Were they poor? *Strange*, I thought to myself. *How strange that I didn't know even this simple bit of background information about someone who was my wife!* But then, everything about our lives was strange. No part of our lives during this war was even close to normal.

We arrived at the front door and I knocked a few times and waited. Soon, the door opened and Anni stood before us, beaming.

"I'm so glad you are here," she said. "You must be Ilse!"

The corners of Ilse's mouth lifted in a tight little half smile. She was obviously tense at the idea of leaving Klaus alone with strangers. I considered saying something to try to reassure her but decided against it. I did not seem to have the knack for soothing Ilse's upset feelings, and I would probably end up adding fuel to the fire. Silence was definitely the safest course to steer.

Ilse nodded a greeting, saying, "Yes, I am Ilse and this is my son, Klaus."

Klaus was now bubbling over with excitement. "Hello," he said. "My name is Klaus!"

Anni giggled. I had to admit to myself that his childish energy was quite refreshing. As frustrating as it had been when we needed him to be quiet at Braun's apartment, here, in this bucolic setting, Klaus's enthusiasm seemed welcome and appropriate.

Anni reached down and took Klaus's hand. "I want you to come inside and to see my house," she said. "I have a surprise for you inside."

"A surprise! Yay!" Klaus practically screamed. Ilse and I looked at each other. It was a good thing we were going inside. His joy was gratifying, but none of us wanted the neighbors to hear him.

Ilse and I followed Anni and Klaus into the house. Ilse looked around, interested in the house where her son would be living.

"Come this way, both of you," Anni beckoned. We walked with her into the kitchen where Klaus was sitting half on, half off a chair at the table. The nature of his surprise was revealed by the cookie sticking out of his mouth.

Anni seated Ilse and me at the table and set three plates laden with food before us. I looked over at Anni. She seemed pleased to be able to feed us, knowing how hungry we were.

We spent the rest of the afternoon and evening in our room, relaxing and getting settled. Ilse didn't say much to me, but she did talk to Klaus off and on. We went to bed very early, happy to be sleeping in a clean room, far away from the stench and stress of our former landlord.

The next morning I awoke early, before sunrise. I dressed quietly and left a sleeping Ilse to go downstairs. Anni was already up and seemed delighted to see me. She greeted me warmly and presented me with a hot breakfast. Then she sat down next to me and started to indulge in what I discovered was her favorite pastime: talking.

She talked. And talked. And talked.

Anni seemed to have an unquenchable desire to communicate about all kinds of subjects. She talked about the weather, she talked about her town of Lübars. She especially wanted to discuss her own family, in particular her son, Heinz. I had never met anyone before who seemed so starved for a friend to talk to.

Alex and Anni Kusitzky in front of their house.

Anni would even talk about people she didn't personally know, but knew of. For example, she went on about a former girlfriend of hers who had married twice. This was considered a sin by Anni's standards. She devoted considerable time to a description of this woman's morals, her high living with her poor husband's money, her flirting with strange men, and her readiness to accept favors from casual acquaintances. Anni felt all this was something to be avoided and even condemned.

Throughout the conversation, I would nod my head empathetically. I said "ah" and "my" and "really" when I felt she needed something more than a bob of the head to acknowledge her.

From time to time, she would ask for my opinion about the people she described to me. It all added up to a tremendous urge to talk about a huge variety of people and things. I wondered whether Alex, her husband, spent much time in these types of conversations. I knew he was a man of few words. Maybe he was unable or unwilling to discuss these things and this was why Anni was so pleased to have my full attention.

I was beginning to wonder what had happened to Ilse. I had gotten up very early, but it seemed like Anni and I had been talking for hours. Where were they? Fortunately, Anni eventually ran out of steam, saying she needed to go tend her garden. With as much grace as I could muster, I thanked her for the wonderful conversation and went to check on Ilse.

When I got upstairs, I opened the door, worried about what I might find there. I saw Ilse and Klaus, cuddled together, she sitting on the edge of our bed and he in her lap. She was rocking him, and they were singing together. I paused, just looking at them. It was so very, very sweet. Something they hadn't been able to do at Braun's, I reminded myself. It warmed my heart to watch them. It also made me miss my own family. Terribly.

I tried very hard not to dwell on my parents' fate, but of course, this was impossible. If I made the mistake of thinking too much about what had happened to them, I became virtually incapacitated. I would get so worried and angry that it would soon be difficult to function. So I tried to think about them and their fate as little as I could.

It was impossible to do this all the time. I could usually hold off these thoughts during the day. At night, though, it was a different story. I was plagued with nightmares. I often awoke in a great sweat, having had yet another dream in which my parents were cruelly torn away from me by the Gestapo. Sometimes my dreams would be of them being badly mistreated in some distant location. Eventually I would awake and realize that it was just a dream. The horror of it was that there was no way to know if the dream was true.

It was just too dreadful to comprehend—too disabling. And so I squelched my imagination as best I could.

We stayed at the Kusitzkys', all of us, for the next three weeks. Then an unexpected development disturbed our arrangement. Alex had learned from coworkers, several of whom lived in the same neighborhood, that policemen were patrolling the Kusitzkys' street and other nearby areas. They would stop at random, asking questions about escaped prisoners and admonishing the residents to report any suspicious-looking men, especially young men.

Prisoners had escaped from a concentration camp in Sachsen-hausen, near Oranienburg. Lübars, located near the S-Bahn line and roads leading toward Oranienburg, was among the areas under sur-veillance by the police. As if that were not enough, Alex also said that there were rumors that an army deserter was hiding somewhere in the Lübars area.

All of this was too much for Anni. She was usually calm and collected, but the prospect of having the police come to her house to ask questions completely terrified her.

It became clear to me that I had to take the initiative and remove myself from the scene. The risk of discovery for Ilse, Klaus, and me was too great. With me gone, the danger to Ilse and Klaus would be greatly reduced. There were many women with small children who had fled Berlin to escape the ever-increasing bombardments by American and British warplanes. A single woman with a small child, as was the case with Ilse and Klaus, was less likely to arouse suspicion.

I explained all of this to Ilse and the Kusitzkys. Anni and Alex readily agreed, but Ilse became silent, as if I had somehow insulted her.

After a short discussion, it was decided that I would leave in the morning. We went upstairs to our room, with Ilse continuing to say nothing. I closed the door to our room and began to walk over to the bed when Ilse hissed, "How could you do such a thing to me?"

I looked over at her, speechless. "What? What are you talking about?"

"How could you just inform me, in front of the Alex and Anni, what your plans were? Why didn't you discuss them with me beforehand? Does my opinion count for nothing? Does the fact that we are married count for nothing? Am I to be treated as though I were just an appendage?"

Shocked, I just stood there, like a deer caught in the headlights.

Ilse raged on, "How could you fail to talk to me about this first? Aren't I more important than Alex and Anni?"

My own temper started to flare. I was doing what was best for all of us! It was not as if I looked forward to leaving a safe, warm house for the streets of Berlin. How could she question my judgment like this? "I was only trying to do what was best for everyone!" I yelled.

She burst into tears, crying in frustration.

I wasn't going to take this. Handling this type of conflict was something I had no experience in, and my natural defensive mechanisms asserted themselves. "That's the way it is going to be, Ilse," I said. Then I climbed into bed, turning away from her to face the wall and closed my eyes.

The next morning I woke up very early, before it was light. I was still indignant about yesterday's dispute. Ilse was asleep, turned away from me and curled into a fetal position. Klaus slept on his little cot, separate from our bed.

I got dressed and stuffed my toothbrush, soap, razor, and blanket into my attaché case. I'd need all of these in Berlin. It would attract attention to be seen filthy and unshaven, and that could be dangerous. The blanket, of course, was important in case it got cold where I was sleeping—and who knew where that would be?

I walked out of the room. If Ilse heard me, she gave no sign.

I went down the stairs and decided to leave a note for the Kusitz-kys. I went over to the little kitchen cabinet where they kept a pad of paper and wrote:

Dear Herr and Frau Kusitzky,
    I have come to the decision that I have to leave. I feel it is safest for all of us if I do not stay here for too long a period at one time. I hope to be back in a few weeks. I cannot thank you enough for everything you have done for Ilse, Klaus, and myself.

Dagobert

Leaving the note on the kitchen table, I picked up my jacket and walked out the door.

Dawn was still breaking and visibility was poor, which is exactly how I wanted it. I wanted to leave the house very early so as to avoid being seen walking away from it.

It was a long walk. It took me about an hour to get to the S-Bahn station, giving me ample time to think about the night before. I eventually came to the conclusion that I had acted childishly. But it was hard. I was only nineteen and I had never even had a girlfriend, much less a wife and son. How was I supposed to act? How was I supposed to know what to do?

I now regretted leaving without making things right with Ilse. But in my ignorance, I wasn't even sure how to go about it. I still felt that I was in the right, and that got in the way of any impulse I might have had to apologize.

Perhaps my parents had disagreements from time to time, but if so, they never had them in front of me. As it was, I had no idea how to have an argument of this type, much less a relationship. It seemed I would have to learn the hard way.

As I boarded the S-Bahn for Berlin, my mind turned to other, more immediate concerns. The most important of these was trying to come up with a place to stay. I was returning to a city where I had no family and almost no friends. I wished I could return to my parents' apartment, but of course that had been confiscated by the Nazis long ago. The other places I had stayed were out, for one reason or another.

The only possibility that came to mind were the Lebrecht brothers, my friends and coworkers from the gun factory. I hadn't seen them since before the Fabrikaktion, and I had no idea whether they were still in Berlin. My hope was that they and their parents still lived in the apartment under the Nazi district headquarters building. Perhaps they could help me out for a night. I knew that the apartment was on Lorenzstrasse, since I had been there before when I worked in the factory.

The only trouble was that it was still morning, still during business hours. Nazis would be going in and out of their district headquarters building constantly. I could not risk going there now. I would have to wait until about 6:00 PM, when everyone went home for the day.

I had to kill some time. I walked the streets of Berlin, going nowhere in particular. My new life as a "U-boat" was simultaneously nerve-racking and boring.

What do homeless Berliners do? I wondered. *Were there homeless people here? There must be*, I thought to myself. But one never saw them. There was no such thing as a bum lying on the sidewalk; the Berlin police would never have allowed it. Perhaps there were shelters set up for those who were less fortunate? I didn't know, but I could never go there in any case. They would ask for identification papers and that would be the end of me.

After hours of seemingly endless roaming, 6:00 PM came. At last it was time to make my way toward 3 Lorenzstrasse and the Lebrechts.

When I first caught sight of the building, I was immediately impressed by the workmanship. It was quite grand, made of gray, weathered stone with rows of windows on every floor. Wide stone steps with stone rails led up to the fancy wooden doors. The doors were about ten feet high with ornamental leaded glass. And of course, the obligatory Nazi flag hung from a flagpole attached at an angle to the building. It seemed monstrous. Not a very welcoming sight.

I waited across the street from the building for quite a while as people poured out at the end of the workday. I tried to look natural, tying my shoes, looking around as if I were waiting for a friend. It is amazing how awkward and self-conscious one can feel standing alone with nothing to do.

I waited a few minutes to make sure that no one else came out. Finally the building seemed empty of occupants. Wasting no time, I crossed the street and ran up those grand steps into the building. Nothing had been locked. I found a set of stairs going down into the basement, at the end of which was a door. I was sure this must be the entrance to the Lebrechts' apartment.

I took a deep breath, knocked on the door, and waited.

"Who is there?" a female voice, presumably Mrs. Lebrecht, called out.

"It's Dagobert Lewin," I responded.

"Who?" she asked.

"Dagobert Lewin."

A moment passed in silence. Then all of a sudden, the door was flung open. Mrs. Lebrecht was there before me and literally yanked me into the apartment, almost slamming the door behind her. As I looked around, there seemed to be no one there but her.

No sooner had this thought crossed my mind than Heinz, Horst, and their father, Leo, appeared. I was thrilled to see Horst and Heinz alive and unharmed.

"Dagobert! My friend! What a surprise to see you!" said Heinz. "How are you?"

"What brings you here?" Horst asked.

"Well," I began, "I'm all right, but I've also been better. As you might guess, I'm illegal now. A U-boat."

"Yes, yes," Heinz replied. "A U-boat. Just like us. You hide underground and only surface once in a while."

"And what have you been doing?" Horst wanted to know. "Where have you been?"

"Well," I began, but then I looked around and decided that it would probably be a good idea if we got more comfortable. I wanted them to feel relaxed when they heard my plea. Jenny Lebrecht must have read the look on my face, because she lost no time in suggesting that we all sit down. I gladly obliged.

"On the day of the factory action, after I was warned not to go to the gun factory, I made my way to the Jewish hospital to tell Ilse what had happened. She went and got Klaus while I tried to find a place for us to hide."

"Klaus? Ilse?" Jenny asked.

Apparently the Lebrecht boys hadn't told their parents about my marriage, so I proceeded to fill them in on my new life as a husband and father.

"And where are they now?" Jenny inquired.

"I'll get to that in a moment," I responded. I cleared my throat and then continued. I told them all about living with Braun, about the dirt and the stench and how he urinated all over the floor.

"How disgusting!" Jenny exclaimed.

"Yes, yes, it was," I responded. Then I told them about how the neighbors had complained, how the police had come and we'd barely been able to keep Klaus quiet. Lastly, I told them about the Kusitzkys and how nice they were, but how afraid I was of staying in one place for too long.

"So that is why I am now back here in Berlin," I said.

"And Ilse and Klaus?" Leo asked. "Where are they?"

"They are still in Lübars at the Kusitzkys'," I replied. "Ilse wasn't ready to leave Klaus yet."

"Uh-huh," Leo said. Then he got to the question that most concerned me. "So where are you staying in Berlin, Dagobert?"

I paused and looked around. A lot rode on the next minute or two and I was very nervous. I took a deep breath and said, "Well, that is something of a problem. You see, I don't have anywhere to stay. I really have nowhere to go. I was hoping that you might allow me to stay with you until I could find another place."

Leo and Jenny both frowned as they looked at each other. They turned and looked at their sons, both of whom had nervous looks on their faces as well. All four of them kept glancing at each other. The trouble was, no one would look at *me*.

"I was hoping that you might be able to give me some suggestions as to what to do. I really do not know where else to turn," I almost begged.

Still no one spoke. Then I heard Leo sigh. He had stopped looking at his wife and sons and had fixed his attention on a blank spot on the wall. Finally, he turned to me with sad eyes.

"Dagobert," he began, "I wish we could help you, but we can't. It is just too dangerous. We can't risk having someone other than Jenny go in and out of this apartment. Her Nazi employers think she lives here alone. They do not know and cannot know that Heinz, Horst, and I are here as well. It would look far too strange to have a young man traipsing in and out of here."

His words struck me like a blow from a club, instantly throwing me into a state of deep despair.

Leo continued, "Since you are already here, I suppose it will be all right for you to stay with us tonight. But unfortunately, we must ask you to leave early tomorrow morning, before the Nazi offices fill with workers. And we must ask you not to return. I know it seems cold of us, and I feel awful about it. But there just is not enough food for all of us here. We are already all living off black market rations and the little Jenny can salvage from the Nazi offices."

"But I could get money to pay you," I interrupted, pleading. "I could get money and ration cards so that there would be more food for everyone."

Leo and the rest of his family looked dejected. "No, Dagobert," he said, "that will not work. As I said, the greatest problem would be for you to be seen walking in and out of here. It is too great a risk. It would look too suspicious to have a young man visiting an older woman who is supposed to have no family. We cannot have it."

My face fell as disappointment and fear sunk in. I had nowhere to go! What was I going to do?

Jenny put her hand on my shoulder, "Dagobert, I am so sorry. We all are. We would love to be able to help you, but it just isn't realistic. Forget about the problem of you being seen. Forget about the food issue. Just the fact that our tiny apartment is right below the Nazi offices makes it very, very dangerous for us. The boys and my husband must be totally silent day and night. No one can ever hear them! No one can ever suspect that they are here. Any noise could create suspicion that might mean the end of all of us."

Leo interjected, "I am so sorry that we cannot be the generous people we were before the war. We deeply regret not being able to help you. If there was any way that we could help, we surely would." He paused, and then continued, "Besides, Dagobert, you are a very clever young man. Our sons have told us of your creative escapades with them. You are a survivor. You will find a solution."

His last note of confidence did little to boost my outlook. It was hard to feel optimistic when I had no idea what I should do next. I had only one night of security. Come tomorrow morning, I would be homeless and alone. And while Leo's comments about my cleverness were flattering, I could not help but remember that the SS transports were full of clever people who nevertheless were headed east toward an unknown fate.

12

BLACK MARKET

I slept that night on the Lebrechts' floor, though not very soundly, knowing that tomorrow I would be wandering the streets of Berlin again. I was becoming a human Flying Dutchman, forever on the move.

What made life hard to endure was not just the lack of a place to call home. There was also the danger of running into Gestapo agents or Wehrmacht patrols, who would be curious as to why an able-bodied man was not in uniform. There was also the chance that I could meet some old friend or acquaintance who might gossip to the wrong person. Informers were everywhere, some of whom were in the pay of the Gestapo and others who denounced people to curry favor with the authorities. Every apartment complex, every factory, practically every building in Germany had its share of informers.

Under these circumstances, it was almost impossible to keep anything hidden from the Nazis, which is why there were so few successful acts of sabotage. The Reich had its share of internal enemies, but most of them did not live long enough to do much damage.

As long as I was on the streets, especially during daylight hours, I was exposed to the danger of arrest. It was imperative to stay hidden as much as possible. I wracked my brains, trying to think of anyone I might stay with. I made one vain attempt and visited a distant relative by the name of Bukofzer. Although sympathetic to my plight, they were afraid of being denounced for harboring a Jewish fugitive. If discovered, they would certainly have been arrested themselves. They allowed me to stay one night and then I had to move on. I did not count it as wasted time. You never knew who might be willing to offer aid—and although I had no way of knowing at the time, Herr Bukofzer's sister, Susi, would be of great help to me in the future.

The next day I was on the move again, walking the streets. A sense of hopelessness threatened to overwhelm me and I had to concentrate on remaining calm. I could not allow myself to fall apart now.

After wandering aimlessly for a few hours, I stopped for a moment and leaned against a streetlamp. By chance, I was in front of a theater that I had visited several times in the past. The concerts I had attended there had been one of the greatest joys of my life. I stepped back toward the curb so that I could read the billboard announcing who was playing. It was Will Glahe!

Glahe was a band leader who was a favorite with teenagers in Germany. He played all kinds of swing and jazz, including some American music. At this point, musicians could still get away with performing American music, although it was later made illegal. On impulse, I checked my wallet. I still had a little bit of money left from the sale of the electric motors, enough to buy one of the inexpensive tickets.

The theater would be a perfect place to hang out for a few hours. Nazis abhorred jazz music, which was supposedly contaminated by "Negro" influences. Theater houses that featured jazz musicians were therefore avoided by party members. Also, there should be a large crowd of young people, which would allow me to sink into the background. And, I rationalized, it would get me off the streets for a little while.

I had a few hours to kill before the concert began, so I found a cafe that did not require ration cards and went in to have a chicory coffee and a piece of imitation cake. All the while, I kept my attention focused on the room, looking for Gestapo. Ilse had told me about *greifers* or "catchers"—Jews who were working for the Nazis, rounding up their fellow Jews.

The catchers bought their own freedom and sometimes that of their immediate families by roaming the streets looking for U-boats. They would see someone they knew to be Jewish and would approach them in a friendly manner, striking up a conversation. The other person would usually be pleased to see a familiar face and would welcome the chance to talk. Being a U-boat, as I was presently learning, was a lonely business. Constantly in fear, constantly on the run, these poor people would be delighted to chat with someone from a happier time.

In the course of the conversation, the catcher would tell the U-boat that he was also on the run, hiding from the Nazis. This would establish a rapport and some degree of trust. The *greifer* would then inquire as to the whereabouts of the U-boat's family and friends. He would ask where the U-boat was staying, whether he had been able to get fake identification and from whom, etc. Quite often, the soon-to-be victim would tell all, thinking that he could trust a fellow Jew.

Within a few minutes, the catcher would signal a member of the Gestapo who was waiting nearby. These people often roamed about, working as a team. The *greifer* would make the first contact and then *whoosh*! The Gestapo would jump in, capturing the U-boat in midsentence. The U-boat would be taken to prison, where he would await deportation or execution.

So I had to remain alert as I drank my chicory and ate the imitation cake. But I tried hard to enjoy both the calories and the opportunity to sit, however tense I felt. I looked around at the rest of the cafe. *This was a good place for someone on the run*, I thought. It was packed with people. Here I could sink into the background.

Picking a table near the rear, I took a seat that gave me a good view of the room. Most Gestapo agents constantly wore their leather hats and trenchcoats, which made them easy to spot. Keeping one eye on the door, I sat near an exit. I had learned that two exits were better than one and that walking was better than running. Simple rules, but they could save your life. My life had devolved into a focus on two principles: avoid capture and stay alive.

I finished the chicory and got up to leave. It was just about time to go to the concert. During the war, concerts often took place during the day instead of in the evening. Most nights, the British had reserved the skies over Berlin for their own use and no one wanted to be caught in the open when the Royal Air Force came calling.

There were already long lines of people when I arrived at the concert hall. I walked into the building's main lobby and went to take my seat. The music was wonderful, mostly jazz with some of the swing music that made young Germans go crazy with delight. But even as I was enjoying the music, I caught a glance of someone who looked very familiar. I could only see his back. It was a young man with flaming red hair, tightly curled. Could it be Horst Dobriner?

Horst and I had known each other for a long time. We had lived together in the orphans' home where, when we took time out from our studies, we played for the same team in the Maccabi Jewish Soccer League. He was a very good-looking young man, exactly my age. He was witty, an outstanding soccer player, something of a poet, and an absolute sports fanatic. If he had escaped deportation, he might be in a position to help me.

We had stayed in touch after my parents had been deported. I visited him occasionally while I was working at the gun factory, but I had not seen him for some time. He knew I had met Ilse but was unaware that I had married her.

Horst and his mother, Frau Dobriner, had been extremely fortunate. Frau Dobriner had been seeing a Gentile man, Erich Ziegler, for years. A few months before the factory action, when it became apparent that huge numbers of Jews were being arrested and deported, Herr Ziegler invited them to move in with him. By failing to register their new location with the police, they became U-boats, living underground. No one, except for a few friends like me, knew where they were.

Ziegler and his son, Oskar, used their ration coupons to keep all four of them alive, though Horst was sometimes able to help a little. Horst had a job in a large factory where he performed menial tasks until he and his mother went underground. At that point, of course, he had to live by his wits like the rest of the U-boats.

At intermission, the lights went on and I was able to get a better glimpse of the redheaded man. It wasn't Horst. But as I sat there, waiting for the second half of the show, I realized that the Dobriners would still be a possible haven for me. I resolved to go there immediately after the show.

After the concert was over, I hurried out of the building. The structure that housed the Ziegler apartment was three stories high, squeezed in on both sides by other apartment buildings. I walked up the steps and inside to the second floor. There on the door in front of me was the name ZIEGLER.

I knocked on the door. After a moment, it was opened by tall, skinny man with brown hair on a head that was rapidly going bald. He had a long, slim, face with a Hitleresque mustache and buckteeth. He reminded me of a rabbit.

"Yes?" he asked.

"Hello, Herr Ziegler, I am Dagobert Lewin. I'm a friend of Horst's."

Ziegler's eyes grew wide and frightened. He looked down at the ground. I immediately caught on.

"Herr Ziegler, is there something wrong? Where is Horst? Is he not here?" I asked, worried about the response.

Ziegler looked at me. "Come in please." I entered, and he shut the door behind me.

"Please come in here," he motioned, taking me into a combination dining room/living room.

Sitting there on the couch was Frau Dobriner, Horst's mother. She was a plump, black-haired woman. Horst's father had died some years earlier, and Frau Dobriner had been faced with the task of raising Horst by herself. She couldn't seem to bring herself to face some of the usual parental tasks, such as attending Horst's soccer games. But she was always friendly and hospitable in earlier days. I had gotten to know her pretty well during the many social visits I had made to their apartment before my parents were deported.

She looked up, saw me, and gasped, clutching her heart. Tears immediately started flowing from her eyes.

"Dagobert! Oh my God! Dagobert!" she exclaimed.

I went up closer to her and sat next to her on the sofa. "Frau Dobriner, I am so sorry to have shocked you so by coming without warning. I had no way of contacting you. What is wrong, Frau Dobriner? Is it Horst? Has something happened to him?"

She reached out and hugged me, pulling me toward her. I remember her body feeling large and soft, like a down pillow.

Horst, like so many others, had been captured by the Gestapo. Herr Ziegler had some contacts in the local police district office and was able to learn that Horst had been arrested sometime in early January. They were unable to learn how the Gestapo found him, but somehow Horst was picked up as he walked down the streets and was hustled into one of the infamous SS transport trucks, almost certainly to be shipped to the camps. So Frau Dobriner had now lost her son as well as her husband.

Fortunately for her, there were no records detailing her move to Herr Ziegler's apartment and it was unlikely that Horst would give her away.

"And what of you? What are you doing here? I am so happy that the Gestapo have not gotten you, too," Frau Dobriner said.

"I am a U-boat. About a month after Horst was seized, I narrowly escaped capture at the gun factory where I was working." Once again, I found myself telling about my brushes with the Gestapo and asking for a place to stay.

Frau Dobriner looked over at Herr Ziegler, then back at me. Unlike the Kusitzkys, she asked that I excuse her and Herr Ziegler so they could discuss it in private.

They excused themselves, leaving me alone. I sat there, heart beating fast, hoping. I was still shaken by what I had heard about Horst. No matter how many times I heard about my friends being taken by the Gestapo, it was still a shock when it happened. People like Horst were more than just bodies being taken away. They were friends and family and therefore important to me. While I could never allow myself to be so emotional as to fall apart over bad news, it still shook me.

Eventually, Frau Dobriner returned with Herr Ziegler in tow. It seemed to me that Herr Ziegler was used to deferring to Frau Dobriner. He looked back at her frequently as he spoke, apparently making sure that he did not overstep some invisible boundary.

"We will be glad to help you, Herr Lewin," Erich Ziegler began. "For a few days, that is. We have a small apartment here, but we can make do for a while to help you out."

Frau Dobriner nodded her head behind him. She obviously had primed her man and had spoken to him about me. He seemed very agreeable and

looked back to her with a loving smile. I was later to learn that Herr
Ziegler relied on Frau Dobriner for direction in many areas. Events generally seemed to turn out the way Frau Dobriner wished in this household.

"Thank you, thank you, Herr Ziegler," I said animatedly.

Herr Ziegler then took a minute to advise me of some of the conditions of my residence. Herr Ziegler's son, Oskar, also lived in the apartment, and he wanted to forewarn me now to prevent any surprises. I was
shown an older sofa in the living room where I would be sleeping and told
that meals would be, at best, on the light side. It seemed to me that Herr
Ziegler was subtly fishing for information about my financial condition,
without being so crass as to come right out and ask. He mentioned that he
had a source for black market ration cards but could rarely afford them.

This intrigued me. I knew of only one place to buy the cards, but
I had a gut feeling that sooner or later the man who was selling them
would be arrested and take everyone he could with him. It was just a
feeling. Not very scientific, perhaps, but the price for making wrong
decisions was excessively high, one I did not care to pay.

Buying black market ration cards was not as easy as purchasing
everyday items. They were illegal and therefore required taking risks.
Secondly, they were expensive. The black market was fueled by cash—no
other method of payment was acceptable. It seemed now that I would
be able to develop a new contact from Herr Ziegler, but that still left the
problem of the money to purchase them. This I had in very short supply.

"Dagobert," I heard Herr Ziegler now interject, "do you have the
money to buy illegal ration cards?"

It was amazing how he seemed to be able to read my mind. I looked
up at Herr Ziegler and could see that he had been studying my face these
last few moments. He was not a good-looking man, or rather, there was
something about him that made me wonder if he were ill. I would later
learn that he had a lung problem for which he received treatment and
special ration cards.

I heard him say again, "Dagobert, my boy. I asked, do you have the
money to buy ration cards?"

I looked at him and gave a weak smile, just barely turning up the
corners of my mouth. I thought about the pittance I had in my wallet.

Barely enough for a drink at a cafe, much less ration cards to sustain one person or a family.

"Yes, Herr Ziegler," I responded. "I have the money."

It was not exactly true that I had immediate access to cash, but I did have the means to obtain it.

That evening, Herr Ziegler's son, Oskar, came home. We all sat around their dining room table, Frau Dobriner, Herr Ziegler, Oskar, and I, eating the meager meal that Herr Ziegler had anticipated. It did not matter to me. I was happy to have any food at all. Having a home where I could eat the food was even better.

After dinner, Herr Ziegler sat me down on the couch in their living-dining room and gave me some fatherly advice. "Tomorrow, Dagobert, about four o'clock, I can take you to a place where you can buy ration cards. You will then be able to have them to feed yourself when you go and also you will be able to help out while you stay here. You will be able to help us as we are helping you. I can also tell you where to obtain identification papers. You'll need these, since you obviously have to move around quite a bit. If you're stopped without papers, you are doomed."

"Yes, I am very interested in everything you are saying. I look forward to your guidance tomorrow," I said, thinking to myself that I would need to have money by four o'clock tomorrow.

And in truth, I was very interested in a source of identification papers. In Germany, life without ID was impossible. A wide variety of papers, permits, and cards were used for work, transportation, travel, or simply walking the streets. Nazi Germany was a police state, and lack of proper papers meant immediate arrest.

"Good. Then it is done. We will both meet here tomorrow afternoon at four o'clock."

That night I slept on their couch. I slept fairly well, except for a few ticklish interruptions whose origins I did not want to contemplate.

The next morning, Frau Dobriner offered me some bread and chicory coffee, which I gladly accepted. Then, excusing myself, I left to begin my attempt to raise some money.

The neighborhood was fairly nice and middle class. Here, as in most areas of Berlin, the residents lived in apartment houses. I had been here several times before, once with my father before he was deported by the Gestapo. I had been back on another occasion while I was working at the gun factory.

I knocked at the door. A moment passed, then the door opened.

"Dagobert! What are you doing here?"

"May I come in?" I asked him.

"Of course, come in."

I walked into the living room.

"Please sit down," he told me. "Can I get you anything? Some tea?"

"Yes," I said. "Thank you. I never turn down anything to eat or drink, especially these days."

So he excused himself and went back into the hallway and down into the kitchen. I waited in the living room, which had been converted into a lavish collection room and personal library.

Before long, Hirschfeld returned, carrying a teapot and glasses. "So, Dagobert. What brings you here?" he asked.

"I'm a U-boat now," I told him plainly.

"I see," he said. There was no need to elaborate. Almost all Jews were, by now, familiar with what this meant.

"I wanted to see you very much, Herr Hirschfeld. I wanted to see you not only for old times sake, but also to see if we could do some business together," I said.

"Hmm. What kind of business? What did you have in mind?" he asked.

"I would like to see if you could help me dispose of something," I said.

"Ahh," he intoned. "And is this something very valuable?"

Seeing that this preliminary sparring could go on for quite some time, I decided to simply show him the item. I extracted a small envelope from my pocket. The envelope contained a stamp, an 1859 two-penny Mauritius, which I knew was worth a substantial amount.

He took the envelope over to a small table and opened it. An expression of delight grew on his face as he examined the stamp.

Herr Hirschfield was a cautious man, not given to overt displays of human warmth. But on this occasion, he was overcome by emotion. He shook his head and I could barely make out that he whispered, "Good for you, Leopold. Good for you."

I found myself getting misty-eyed as I heard him pronounce my father's name. He looked over at me, and in that moment, something seemed to pass between us. After all was said and done, in spite his error in underestimating the danger presented by the Nazis, in the end Leopold Lewin had taken care of his son. He was taking care of me now. And this, both of us knew.

My father had taken two ordinary belt buckles and joined them together in such a way that a small compartment was created between them. One of them was now the front, as in any common buckle. The second now became the back of the buckle.

The back had an opening that was covered with two doors held in place with tiny springs. The compartment could be accessed by simply prying open one of the hinged doors, which would snap shut when released. He placed some of the most valuable stamps from his collection inside and closed the compartment.

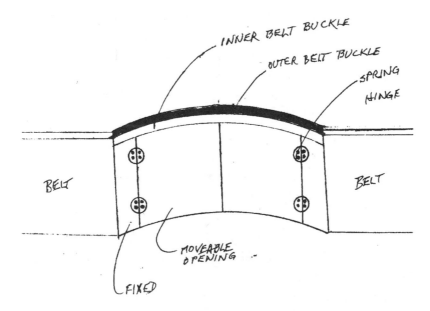

Drawing of the belt buckle my father devised to conceal valuable stamps.

He wore one, and he gave me one. This way, we would always have an emergency source of funds. It was a near-perfect solution to the problem of carrying valuables, as rare stamps could be sold to collectors anywhere and my father's ingenious method of concealment made discovery by a cursory search unlikely. I knew that my father had hidden the rest of his stamp collection in a leather goods store on Potsdamer Platz, but I'd have to wait till the end of the war to retrieve them, presuming both the store and I survived.

"Let's check the catalog to see what it is worth," Hirschfeld said. Rising, he removed a thick reference book from the crowded shelves.

It took him only a few seconds to locate the information we wanted. He moved his finger across the page, reading the description softly to himself and then across to the trading price. He showed it to me.

"This is the trading price," he declared. "I don't know whether I can get the full amount for it, but I will try. I will take it to someone else, whose name I prefer to keep to myself. Come back in three or four days and I will have your money."

Three to four days? *Yes, that probably is realistic*, I told myself. But Herr Ziegler expects me to have money today, and I was penniless.

Hirschfeld was another Jew who had married a Gentile wife. He and my father had been good friends as well as fellow stamp traders. Hirschfeld and I shared a love of music, and he had once invited me over to his apartment to listen to some very rare recordings he owned. So while we were not the best of friends, I felt that I could trust him.

Now he was the only hope I had of obtaining money for the black market cards. I had no choice but to give him the stamp. It was a tremendous trust I was placing in him, and this we both knew.

But there was another problem. I needed money now, immediately. I was not in the habit of asking for loans, but I managed to convince him to advance me a hundred marks. *A fair exchange*, I thought, *for my trust*.

So he gave me the money and I soon left his apartment, leaving the two-penny Mauritius behind.

That afternoon, at four o'clock sharp, Herr Ziegler took me to the Tiergarten park. Ziegler directed me to a bench, where we took a seat and waited. After a few minutes, I noticed a young man looking in our direction. After carefully surveying the area, he headed over to us. He was carrying a green coat folded over his arm, with an attaché case in his hand.

"*Guten tag*, Herr Ziegler," the man said. "It is nice to see you again. Who is the young man with you?" He appeared nervous but under control and seemed surprised by my presence. I guessed that Ziegler had neglected to tell him that I would be there for fear of scaring him off.

"He is a friend of the family," Herr Ziegler said. "He needs your help." We explained that we required two sets of ration cards and settled on a price. Reaching into his attaché case, he took out a paper-wrapped package. As surreptitiously as possible, I handed him the money, which he promptly deposited in his case.

As I handed him the money, I told him that I would be interested in future purchases of both ration cards and identification papers.

"Let's see how this works out. You can always contact me through Herr Ziegler."

He was obviously a cautious man and did not care to provide me with a way to contact him directly. Nothing infuriated the Gestapo like finding black market dealers, since the goods sold in this manner were usually stolen from military and civilian supplies.

Our dealer tipped his hat and walked in the direction of the exit while we proceeded on in the direction of Ziegler's apartment.

Shortly after our arrival, I handed Herr Ziegler one of the sets of ration cards. I hoped to stay with the Zieglers for a while longer, and the cards were my payment. But it was not to be.

The second evening after our trip to the park, Herr Ziegler pulled me aside. He had seemed anxious all day. Never a particularly brave man, Ziegler had hidden refugees only because of Frau Dobriner's wishes. Now he informed me that the Wehrmacht had been conducting unusually heavy patrols in the area. These soldiers were watching people more carefully than was usual, as if they were looking for a particular face.

Ziegler told me that he suspected that someone had seen me enter the apartment and may have informed the Gestapo. After weighing the risks, they felt it was better if I left for a time. Berlin was rife with informants and with Frau Dobriner already living there illegally, they could not chance the apartment being searched.

Reluctantly, I agreed to leave in the morning, even though I had nowhere to go.

Early that next morning, I packed up my few possessions, bid them good-bye, and left. Once again, I was homeless.

At this point, my options were extremely limited. It was much too soon to return to the Lebrechts or the Kusitzky residence, and public parks were heavily patrolled by the SS. I wandered the streets of Berlin, passing first the Nazi district office building near the Lebrecht's hiding place and then past a series of abandoned buildings made uninhabitable by Allied bombings. As I walked, my heart pounded. Ziegler had seen heavy army patrols on this very street. I had to find shelter before curfew or I would certainly be picked up. In my case, an arrest would be equivalent to a death sentence.

I looked around, trying to keep a close watch for military patrols. As I walked, my thoughts returned to the wrecked buildings I had passed. By this time, Allied bombers had devastated large portions of Berlin, doing a great deal of damage to many buildings. Some had burned but remained standing. Other buildings had collapsed, leaving gaping wounds through which lower structures and basements were exposed.

The more I thought about it, the more I considered this as an opportunity. I could hide in the ruins with relatively little chance of being discovered. It was dangerous because the buildings, already weakened structurally, could collapse at any moment. I decided to give it a try. I picked out a building that seemed relatively sturdy and lit a candle I had gotten from Frau Dobriner. I crawled into an opening that exposed steps, which I discovered led to the basement. It was pretty much intact. Like most basements, this one had almost certainly served as an air raid shelter. There were cots, chairs, and tables.

I could not help but notice an extremely unpleasant odor, which was much more intense than the normal musty smell associated with dark, wet places. I didn't like it but decided that I had no choice except to endure it. I examined the cots and picked out one of the least dilapidated ones.

I walked to the entrance to retrieve my bag and get settled. As I approached the stairs, I found the source of the odor.

Before me, partially covered with bricks and stones, was the first corpse I had ever seen. It looked as if the ceiling had fallen in on him and had either killed him immediately or trapped him there to die.

Horrified, I immediately turned and hurriedly walked out of that area and across the basement hall, into another area that had been used as an air raid shelter and thus also contained chairs and cots.

When I found another suitable place, I immediately blew out my candle. Candles were hard to come by, rationed as most things were in those days. I crawled onto the cot, curled up in a fetal position, and tried to get to sleep.

13

BASEMENTS
AND BEDBUGS

I AWOKE THE NEXT MORNING, freezing and alone, except for the company
of a few small beams of sunlight streaming through the cracks. Shaking
the ever-present dust off my clothes, I made my way out of the basement
and onto the streets of Berlin. I spent the day walking the streets, using my
ration cards to buy bread and salami. Having no way to do any cooking,
I was limited to food that wouldn't easily spoil, that I could carry or hide.

For the next few days, I followed this same routine. Nights in the
basement, corpse and all, days wandering the streets, avoiding police
and SS patrols. On the third day, I decided that I needed to move. More
than three days in the same spot was too risky. Prolonged occupation
increased the chances of someone spotting me and denouncing me. I
would then have unwelcome visitors to my little abode, men who would
insist on moving me to an even less desirable one.

Thanks to the Allies, there was no shortage of bombed-out apartment buildings. After returning to Herr Hirschfeld's residence and picking up the rest of my money, I resumed scouting the area until I found
a suitable basement. This became a routine: staying in a building for
three days, then moving on to another. Finally, I judged that enough
time had passed to risk returning to the Kusitzkys.

I had thought often about them and about Ilse and Klaus. I awoke very early one morning, well before sunrise. Brushing myself off, I hurried out of the dark basement to the S-Bahn station, excited at the prospect of seeing my family again.

When I got to the station, most of the people in line were turning around and leaving. When I reached the front, I discovered the reason. On a temporary post in the middle of the walkway, a homemade notice was posted that read: *"Track line interrupted by bombing. S-Bahn will not be running for an undetermined period of time. Will reopen as soon as possible."*

My heart sunk. How was I going to get to Lübars? I looked around to see how other people were reacting when I overheard two men next to me talking. One of them, an older gentleman wearing a brimmed hat, was trying to visit his mother in the northern suburbs. His companion suggested, "Why don't you try taking the busline north, past the center of the city? Hopefully, the tracks near Reinickendorf will be operational. You can catch a train there."

Brilliant idea, I thought to myself. I'll do that and go from Reinickendorf to the Waidmannslust station near Lübars. From there, I could walk to the Kusitzky house on Benekendorffstrasse. I hurried toward the bus stop.

But there was one problem. Daylight. With the S-Bahn closed, there was no way I could make it to Lübars before the sun rose. I couldn't risk being seen. I would have to kill time walking around Berlin and leave for Lübars in the evening.

And so I did. I wandered around until finally, close to sunset, I arrived at the Reinickendorf station. The train was running! I boarded, taking the S-Bahn to Waidmannslust. My roundabout route took twice as long to reach my destination, but it allowed me to arrive after sunset. I walked in darkness to the house, being careful to avoid being seen by anyone on the streets.

My heart beat faster and faster. I couldn't wait to see everyone, to hear voices who wanted to hear mine.

Anni Kusitzky answered the door. "Dagobert! What a surprise! Come in! I'm glad to see you!"

I walked inside. Alex walked toward me from the kitchen, his expression worried. He held out his hand. Before he could speak, I shook it and said, "Do not worry. I will not stay long." He smiled a bit of a guilty grimace and silently nodded his head. Alex was not a man of many words.

Little Klaus came barreling down the steps, looking like a child running into a toy store. "Dago! Dago! You're here! You came back!" I reached down and picked him up, swinging him around. "Yes, Klaus. I'll always come back," I said, feeling surprisingly paternal.

I heard footsteps coming down the stairs. As always, I recognized them. Ilse.

I was kneeling, hugging Klaus. I stayed right where I was and looked up, fearful of the greeting I would get. Would she be happy to see me, or still disgruntled about the manner of my departure?

"Hello, Ilse," I said hesitantly.

She stood on the steps and looked down, blinking her eyes. "Hello."

Putting down the giggling Klaus, I smiled at her and kissed her on the cheek. This prompted only a small, wan smile. She had a hard time looking me in the face.

I suppose it was inevitable that there would be some hard feelings, and I had dreaded having this conversation. Even before I had actually left the Kusitzkys, I knew that sparks would fly on my return. It didn't take a genius to see that I had hurt Ilse's feelings.

In the ensuing conversation, she made it plain that she felt that I had abandoned her and Klaus. It didn't seem to matter to her that the neighbors were keeping a close watch on anyone deemed to be acting in a suspicious manner, or that the sudden arrival of three new faces would inevitably be noticed.

The fact of the matter was that Ilse was scared. I would have had to be blind, deaf, and dumb not to see that she had married me, at least partially, to avoid being alone. She was a young, single woman, with a child, trapped in a situation that could well prove fatal.

I tried to continue the conversation, but Ilse couldn't even look at me. Finally, Anni and Alex got smart and took Klaus upstairs for some cookies.

I now had the opportunity to explain to Ilse how I been living. Although it did not completely satisfy her, at least she understood where I had been and what I had been doing. She broke down in tears.

"I'm scared, Dagobert!" she said. "How can you endure it?"

"I don't know how, Ilse," I said. "The Gestapo have already taken my parents, but they won't get me! I want to beat them. To survive in spite of them. I will not go like a lamb to the slaughter. They are not going to get me, and you should feel the same way."

This seemed to break through her shell, at least partially. "All right," she said. "I'll try."

After that, things seemed to go better. Our marriage may have been one of convenience, but at least we had helped each other along the way. Our biggest problem was in communicating. Perhaps now, we understood each other a little better.

I stayed with Ilse for two more days, talking to everyone and catching up on what they had been doing. Our biggest fear was unexpected visitors. If Ilse and Klaus were seen by anyone, there was a good chance questions would be asked. This could lead to a visit from the Gestapo. To minimize the possibility of being taken by surprise, they had developed a system to alert them when visitors came.

Whenever the doorbell rang, Anni would send Ilse and Klaus to the attic and warn them to be quiet. They had some advance notice whenever someone came to visit because there was a bell mounted on the garden gate. When anyone entered the garden, the bell would ring, and even though it was about 150 feet away from the house Anni would usually hear it. She would then alert Ilse and Klaus.

On occasion, though, Anni would fail to hear the bell and they would have no warning until the person actually rang the doorbell. Then the situation became urgent. Ilse would have to grab Klaus and run up to the attic.

This happened once during my visit. I had not been around when the system was initiated and had not had much practice in implementing it. Anni didn't hear the garden bell, and she went into a panic when the doorbell went off. I had been busy in the living room when she ran in with a wild look in her eyes. "Get to the attic!" she whispered urgently. "Find Klaus and Ilse and get to the attic!"

I threw down what I had been doing and ran around the house, looking for them to no avail! Where were they? I darted into every room, searching frantically. Finally, I was forced to give up the hunt. I ran up the attic steps, trying to not make much noise. As I reached the top of the steps, I sighed. They were already there. Ilse had grabbed Klaus on the second floor and had gone up without me. We huddled there, trying hard to be quiet. It reminded me of hiding at Braun's apartment, afraid for our lives.

Time was passing and I knew that I could not stay with the Kusitzkys any longer. Every day I was there increased the chances that we would all be found out. So the next morning, I woke up before dawn, kissed Ilse and Klaus good-bye, and left for Berlin.

Enough time had passed since I had been at the Herr Ziegler's apartment. Perhaps they'd let me stay with them again, even if just for a few nights.

Arriving in Berlin. I made my way to the Dobriner apartment. They lived quite close to the train station, so it only took about fifteen minutes to reach their apartment. I climbed the steps and made my way to their door. I knocked and Frau Dobriner answered as usual.

"Dagobert!" she exclaimed, smiling. *Good*, I thought to myself. Her smile was a good sign. Perhaps she'd let me stay. She seemed to be in good spirits.

I knew from my past visits that this was not always the case. Frau Dobriner was often very sad. Sometimes she would cry, complaining that she felt trapped in her tiny, miserable apartment. The last time I saw her, she had wept bitterly and frequently over the fate of her son, Horst. She had no entertainment and no way of communicating with anyone on the outside.

Horst's father had died before the war of a rare disease, leaving her with their son to raise. She had never quite gotten over that. She told me about her deceased husband many times, about what a wonderful man he had been. He had been a mathematics teacher in a prominent Berlin gymnasium (high school). She related how proud he had been; several of his graduates had gone on to become well-known scientists and engineers. "He did this only to have died at a young age," she'd weep, sitting on an upholstered chair in her combination living-dining room.

Sometimes Herr Ziegler was present during these conversations about her late husband. He would only listen. He did say on one occasion, "Can't we talk about something else? We already know about your husband and how great he was and successful he was!" Then Frau Dobriner would start crying more heavily and Ziegler would leave the room in disgust. It was during those times that I felt they could both stand a good vacation from the apartment and from each other; neither of which were a possibility.

As I entered the living room now, Ziegler greeted me warmly. "I'll only stay a short time," I assured him, thinking to myself that this had become my standard greeting. They both seemed to be happy to have me in spite of the scare that had forced me to leave weeks ago.

After a bit of small talk, everyone retired to their respective bedrooms. Herr Ziegler and Frau Dobriner shared a bedroom, and Ziegler's son had a very small room of his own. I slept in my underwear on the dingy, upholstered couch in the living room. I had a blanket to lie on, another to cover me, and for total luxury, a pillow.

In the middle of the night, I awoke to a peculiar tickling sensation in my legs. I lifted the blanket and saw a number of little round creatures the size of a pea. Bedbugs, already swollen with blood they had sucked from my legs.

I will skip the gruesome details of how the night progressed. Suffice it to say that, the next morning, I said my farewells to the Dobriners.

"Frau Dobriner, I greatly appreciate the opportunity you've given me in letting me stay here, but the time has come for me to move on for good."

"Why, Dagobert? What is the matter? Did we say something offensive? Tell me."

"No, Frau Dobriner. It's nothing that you've said. I just cannot stand the hordes of bloodsucking bugs that descended on me during the night. I've never seen anything like it before and I cannot take it. You've been so wonderful in helping me, and I very much appreciate it, but I have a great fear of insects."

I went up to her and shook her hand. "Thank you for everything. I wish you well." She just stood there, looking as if I had hit her with a club, mouth open and eyes staring. I turned to the door, opened it, and left. Perhaps I am overly fastidious but, homeless though I was, I would rather face a single corpse in a bombed-out apartment building than hordes of bloodsucking insects. I never went to the Dobriners again.

I decided to shake off my revulsion by treating myself to an imitation bratwurst and beer at Aschingers, the quick-serve, stand-up restaurant. Aschingers was an automat, where you dropped coins into a slot. A circular, rotating dispenser placed the food in front of a small window and you reached into that window and pulled out your food. It was an early version of what would later be called vending machines. There were no tables, only tall platforms where you could stand and eat. I remember my father taking me there two or three times, years earlier, before he was deported by the Gestapo.

Aschingers was safer than other restaurants because people stayed there only a short time. There were always large numbers of people coming and going, which made it easy to blend in. And the fact that you never sat down made it easier to run, if this became necessary. It was cheap, too, and at this stage, any food that could go into the mouth and down the throat was good enough for me. I was too hungry to be picky about what I ate.

Beer was the beverage of choice at Aschingers. I wasn't much of a drinker; it was bitter and I wasn't used to it. But there were times during the war when even water wasn't available, so beer it was. During the war, beer was often composed more of plain water than anything resembling malt liquor. But such was the case with the quality of many things. Beer, bread, they all went downhill in those days.

As I stood there with my beer, I pondered my options. I couldn't return to the Kusitzkys so soon, I couldn't go to the Lebrechts, and there was no way I would return to the bug-infested Dobriner house, no matter how kind they were. I sighed as I realized I might have to sleep in the ruins of buildings again.

I really didn't want to do that. I wanted that strategy to be used only as a last resort, not as my primary residence. Not only was sleeping in bombed-out buildings uncomfortable, but there was also the possibility that an Allied bomb would drop near it, causing the already weakened walls to collapse. I did not care to be buried alive.

So I stood there, sipping slowly, always watching the door for Gestapo, and trying my best to think of another option. *Perhaps Hirschfeld?*, I thought. But no. I couldn't go to him for lodging. Hirschfeld himself was in danger. Even though he had a Christian wife, he was Jewish and therefore could be picked up by the Gestapo. I couldn't risk him having the ability to reveal my whereabouts. It was safer to appear at his apartment erratically. I didn't want him to know anything else about me.

This made me sad. Sad because I couldn't depend on adults who I'd known for so long. Sad because I saw someone like Hirschfeld—a friend of my father's—as being as vulnerable as myself. Also sad because my prospects of finding decent shelter for the evening were dwindling by the minute.

"Heinrich!" I heard a man at the bar call out to another man at the entrance. I turned my head and saw the two greet each other and then walk out of the restaurant.

But watching their encounter gave me a great idea. Heinrich Schultz! Yes! My crippled friend from the gun factory, who had referred me to Herr Braun. Granted, living with a drunkard hadn't been paradise, but it was always possible Heinrich would know of another soul who might take pity on me. Or at the very least, take money from me and give me a bed for the night.

I knew my presence at his apartment would make him and his wife, Hilde, uncomfortable. I could understand that it was frightening to have me—a Jew on the run—sitting at their kitchen table. But I'd give it a try anyway. All they could do was send me away. Actually, they could do much worse than that, but I didn't dream that Heinrich or Hilde would ever turn me in.

So off I went to Neukölln, the working-class neighborhood where the Schultzes lived. I reached their apartment building, walked down the steps to their subterranean floor, and rang their doorbell.

Soon, Hilde opened the door, looking very surprised. "Herr Lewin! You're here again!" she stated.

This was somewhat of an odd greeting. Not exactly a warm welcome. "Yes, Frau Schultz. Sorry to bother you. I was wondering if Heinrich is at home?"

"Well, ah, yes, he is," she said.

I waited awkwardly for her to invite me in. But she made no move to do so. "Frau Schultz, may I speak to him? It will only take a moment."

She paused. "Oh. So you want to see him?" she asked.

Strange! Wasn't it obvious that I needed to see him, if I had taken the trouble to come to his apartment and ask to speak to him? I had to be polite, though. I'm sure she had her reasons for feeling nervous in my presence. Jews trying frantically to avoid capture by the Gestapo weren't exactly A-list guest material. "Yes, if it is at all possible, I would very much like to see and speak to Heinrich. Is it terribly inconvenient? Should I come back another time?"

Hopefully, she would not say yes to this last little nicety. Coming back at an assigned time would make me very nervous.

She paused and sighed. Looking beyond me at a spot on the wall, she grimaced as she pondered the situation. Then she sighed again and said, "Well, all right. You may come in. But just for a moment."

I relaxed slightly and smiled at her. "Thank you so much, Frau Schultz," I said.

It was odd to have to beg to see an old acquaintance, but these were odd times. I walked in and Hilde guided me to the kitchen table. "Please sit down. I will get Heinrich."

Heinrich soon limped into the kitchen, dragging his foot behind him. He looked more worried than pleased to see me. *I obviously could not come here again after today*, I told myself. These people are too nervous about my presence.

He walked into the kitchen and sat down. "Dagobert, what a surprise to see you again! How are you?" Heinrich asked. His welcome seemed forced.

"Good to see you too, Heinrich. I am all right. I wanted to thank you for referring me to Herr Braun a few months ago. We stayed with him for a while. I am so very grateful to you for your help."

"So you did stay with him? Good. I have not seen or talked to him since I last saw you," Heinrich mentioned. I thought to myself that Heinrich certainly wasn't missing anything by Braun's absence. Nothing at all.

"Heinrich, I have come here again in hopes that you might have someone else to recommend to me. I need a place to stay."

"Have you come from Herr Braun's?" Heinrich asked, seeming a bit perplexed. I tried to put myself in his shoes. Had he not already offered me one referral? And here I was, asking again.

"No, Heinrich," I muttered. "I haven't." *How much should I tell him?*, I asked myself. "Uh, Herr Braun had a bit of trouble with the floor in his apartment and it became apparent that it would not be safe for us to remain. So we left there after about six weeks."

Heinrich squinted his eyes and gave me a confused look. I suppose that did sound rather strange. But I didn't want to tell him that his friend was such a filthy alcoholic that he urinated on his floor until the ceiling below was weakened, causing the neighbors to call the police. I didn't think Heinrich would take too kindly to that description, true though it may be.

I decided it was best to just continue talking. "I found a place for my wife and her son, but I am not able to stay there myself. Therefore, I have come back to see if you have any ideas for me. I would be forever grateful if you could help me again. Do you know of anyone who would take me in temporarily? I'd be happy to pay them, just as I paid Herr Braun."

He looked at me and sighed. "You have no one else who can help you, Dagobert?"

"Unfortunately, no, Heinrich. I have already exhausted all of my other leads. I have no one else to turn to."

Hilde, who had walked into the room a few moments before, interjected. "Where have you been staying between the time you were with Herr Braun and now?"

"Well," I began, "I have stayed at a few apartments of people who have been kind to me. But for various reasons, those apartments are no longer safe. For much of the time I have been sleeping in the rubble of bombed-out buildings."

"What?" she asked, seeming horrified. "In bombed-out buildings?"

"Yes," I nodded. I looked over at both of them. They seemed appalled. I'm sure it was hard for them to fathom that a Berliner could be roaming the streets with nowhere to go. *Good*, I thought to myself. *Perhaps they'll take pity on me.*

Heinrich looked at me. "If I were to find someone for you, you would have money to pay them?" he asked.

"Yes, Heinrich. I would have money to pay them," I said.

"Have you been working for this money?" Heinrich inquired. This was sticky. I did not want to reveal anything about the source of my funds.

"It is money that I have," I told him and hoped that would suffice. Telling him more wouldn't be good for either one of us.

A few moments of nervous silence followed. I looked at both of them, my eyes pleading. Hilde could not deal with the situation. She was quite uncomfortable and I knew that the stress of having a U-boat in her home was just too great. Heinrich seemed a bit more at ease but kept looking over at his wife, as if seeking direction.

After a little while, Heinrich finally spoke. "There may be someone, Dagobert. There is a man I have recently met. You see, in spite of how nervous Hilde and I appear to be, we are actually quite against the Nazis. Especially me. Adolf Hitler and his crowd, as you know, do not hold disabled people like myself in high esteem. There is little respect for those who have physical problems," Heinrich began.

"Yes, I understand this," I muttered, trying to show the great sympathy I really did feel.

"I have endured this as long as I can. I have finally decided to do something about it. I have begun attending some secret Communist Party meetings."

"Heinrich!" Hilde whispered loudly, as though her husband had just publicly confessed to murder. I understood her. It was extremely dangerous to be a known Communist.

If the Gestapo got wind of Heinrich's activities, that would have been the end of him. It was especially daring of him to attend the meetings when the rest of the time he worked for the Nazis in the gun factory.

If he was discovered, the Nazis would probably accuse him of being a spy. The result would be torture and death.

"Well, Hilde, yes, I suppose it is dangerous for me to have mentioned that. But I can no longer hide my feelings. I am half the man I should be. Hilde, you and I should be hiding Dagobert ourselves. The Nazis are our enemies too."

"Heinrich! We have been over this!" Hilde yelled under her breath, turning very red in the face.

"Yes, I know we have, dear," he said gently, trying to calm her. He turned to me. "Dagobert, I know you will understand when I tell you that today must be the last time we see you. It is too dangerous and we are nervous about it. I will send you away, however, with the name of a man. A man who I think will help you as I wish I could, if I had the courage. His name is Paul Richter. I met him at party gatherings. He is like me in his personal hatred of the Nazis. Richter is blind and therefore also looked upon as being unworthy of life."

I was amazed by what I had just heard. The Nazis had an intense determination to perfect the "master race" through their odd theories of genetic control. The seriousness of this determination was demonstrated in a campaign that took place between 1939 and 1941. It involved gassing to death approximately fifty thousand German citizens whose crime was to be retarded or mentally ill. By eliminating these "defectives," eventually the German race would breed its way to perfection.

Although these "mercy killings" were initially limited to those with mental problems, it is likely that those with physical defects, such as Heinrich, would be added to the list. According to Heinrich's sources, elimination of the Jews had priority. But once Germany had dealt with the Jews, Germans who did not meet the physical requirements of the Nazis would likewise be eliminated.

Heinrich continued, "Now that I think of it, the fact he is blind will be even more helpful to you. His disability makes him unable to work. He is at home much of the time, so I imagine you would have more freedom to walk around during the day. I don't know his address, but I know he lives in the suburb of Steglitz. Hopefully, you will be able to look him up."

I sat there, amazed. Heinrich looked at his wife, pleading for for-giveness. She had tears in her eyes and seemed really very frightened. I knew I had to leave.

"Heinrich, my friend," I began, "may you be blessed for all that you have done for me. Never let yourself think that you have done nothing. You have saved my life, perhaps three times now. I will never be able to thank you enough for the great bravery you and Hilde have shown. I promise that I will never come back here again to bother you, and your secret is safe with me."

"Thank you, Dagobert," Heinrich said humbly. "Good luck to you."

Rising to get up, I said, "Thank you, thank you. Many, many thanks to both of you." And I left. I knew this would be the last I saw of them.

It took two S-Bahn trains to get from Neukölln to Steglitz. Getting off at the Steglitz stop, I walked to Steglitzer Damm, a main road, and went in search of a post office. Hopefully, Paul Richter would be listed in the phone book there. I walked a few blocks and finally came across a post office.

The place was crowded and it took a moment to get access to the phone book. As chance would have it, there were two Paul Richters in Steglitz. I took down the addresses for both of them and proceeded to the first listed address. It was on a street not too far from the Steglitz cemetery. Luckily, this was the building that Heinrich had recommended to me, the building where Paul Richter, the blind Communist, lived.

14

COMMUNISTS
AND BLIND MEN

My first impression of Paul Richter was of an ill-tempered, middle-aged man. Beyond that, he was not at all what I had expected. He had gray hair, brushed back, with a wide mustache all the way across his face, more like Stalin than Hitler. He was of solid build, very broad-shouldered, and about six feet tall. He had huge hands and large fingers and held himself ramrod straight. Although he appeared to be between forty-five and fifty years old, I felt sure he was physically very powerful. Not at all the little old blind man I expected.

I had found his apartment with no difficulty and was soon knocking on the door. He had answered immediately. After a series of questions to establish my identity and how I found him, he, reluctantly it seemed, invited me in. Preceded by a guide dog, he led me into the living room. A woman was standing there, looking toward us as we walked into the door. She was petite, about a head shorter than he, with black hair.

"Sit down," Richter ordered, interrupting my observation of the woman. I thought it quite probable that she was also blind. Most of the furniture was strategically placed around the room's perimeter to make it easy to find. Having no need for bright lights, Richter kept the room dark and gloomy. The sole exceptions were the two windows, one on each of the outer walls of the room. There was a sofa and two chairs on one side and a table up against another wall.

So I did as ordered and sat down, waiting for the inevitable series of questions and my equally inevitable series of answers, explaining that I was Jewish, homeless, and in desperate need of assistance. I had grown to hate this part of my conversations with potential benefactors, when I would beg for their help and then wait for the pronouncement of my fate. It was like going before a judge for sentencing. It wrought havoc on my nerves as I prayed, each time, that the other person would be kind to me.

I waited for him to take the lead. This was my first contact with a blind person and I felt awkward, unsure of how to act.

"Now who is this Heinrich Schultz supposed to be?" Richter demanded irritably.

"You know him from meetings you have both attended," I said worriedly.

It quickly became apparent that Richter and Heinrich were far from close friends. I had to explain who Heinrich was and how he had picked Richter as someone who might help me. I tried to remain vague about details, not wanting to give information that could be hazardous to Heinrich if I could possibly avoid it. Then came the dangerous part. I launched into the details of my circumstances and how I lived as a Jewish U-boat.

If I were to be arrested, it would happen soon. Heinrich had said that Richter was a committed Communist, and I therefore hoped that he would avoid doing anything that would aid the Nazi Party, such as turning me in. The Communists and the Nazis were bitter enemies. I remembered times when I would look out of my parents' apartment window and see Communists and Nazis engaged in violent street fights. Before Hitler became chancellor, such clashes were a regular occurrence. They would use knives, clubs, brass knuckles, guns, even their bare hands in an attempt to annihilate each other. Party members on both sides were injured and killed with astonishing regularity.

Once Hitler came to power, he unleashed his armed SA thugs on the Communists and a reign of terror followed in which thousands of

Communists were arrested, imprisoned, tortured, and killed. In July 1943, all other political parties were made illegal, but there were many individuals such as Richter who refused to submit. The Communist Party went underground, holding their meetings in secret. They continued to be a potent force working against the Reich and were therefore a target for the Gestapo and their informants. I had reason to believe that I would be safe from betrayal here. The next few minutes would tell the tale.

There was silence in the room now, as I waited to learn my fate. Finally Richter spoke, still standing there with his dog beside him. "Call me in two days. I will tell you then if I can help."

Call him in two days? "On the telephone?" I asked, wanting to clarify.

"Yes, on the telephone," he said. "Here's my phone number."

I did not know many people who had telephones then. Few people I knew could afford them. "All right, I will call you in two days," I said.

"And your name is, again?" he asked sternly.

"Dagobert," I said, not willing to give my last name. "My name is Dagobert."

"Yes. Very good," he said, and he walked me out the front door.

I spent the next two days much as I had the last few, simply trying to survive. I located another bombed-out building to sleep in. This one had no basement and I needed a hiding place that would conceal me from casual view, so I found an unobtrusive corner and set about making an area where I could sleep unobserved.

I piled bricks and stones on top of each other, forming a space big enough for me to lie in. This was not easy, as it had to be done before night fell, when the darkness would be absolute. The bricks proved to be easier to stack, so I concentrated on gathering them and cleaning the old mortar off their faces so that they would lie flat. Slowly, the walls grew until they reached a height of about two feet. I then placed a discarded door on top of the three brick walls, forming a "roof" for my compartment. I left one end open to serve as an entrance, and the shelter was complete.

I spent two nights in my little compartment, with the days spent wandering Berlin trying to avoid drawing attention to myself. On the morning of the third day, I returned to the post office and phoned Richter. It took a while before a connection was made.

"Hello?" he answered.

"Hello, Herr Richter," I said. "This is Dagobert. I hope my call does not come at an inconvenient time?"

"You can come to visit us," he said, ignoring my pleasantry. "Today or tomorrow. I prefer between one and two o'clock in the afternoon."

"Very good," I said. "I will be there this afternoon."

Although he was a Communist and therefore an enemy of the Reich, I still was unwilling to trust him completely. So I arrived at his house, not at one or two, but at eleven o'clock in the morning. I positioned myself so that I could not be seen but so that I could see anyone going in or out of the door. If his intention was to turn me into the Gestapo, they would certainly arrive before one o'clock. I was confident that I could spot them and thereby avoid the trap, if in fact it existed.

I stood there at my observation point, watching and waiting. No one entering the building aroused my suspicions. As I waited, I decided to trust this Paul Richter. He was a stern man, somewhat ill-tempered, but there was nothing in him that led me to suspect that he would betray me. His apartment would be a particularly good place for me to hide, since the neighbors were aware that two blind people occupied the apartment and would therefore be home most days. Noises coming from the apartment would not arouse suspicions. Just as important, the fact that they were blind would probably greatly decrease any notion that they would harbor a fugitive. People would believe them to be too limited by their handicaps to carry it off.

Close to two o'clock, I went in. I had seen no one suspicious in the two and a half hours I had watched the front door.

I went inside, up the stairs, and knocked on the door of Richter's apartment. My heart beat fast. I prayed I had not just made a stupid mistake.

Richter answered the door. He opened it without a greeting and waved me inside.

I walked inside. Back through the small foyer. Back into the living room. Back onto the chair where I had sat two days before.

Richter came in and sat down on a chair. The woman was also there, sitting on another chair. Richter began to speak.

"Regina and I have decided that we are willing to keep you in our apartment for a time. But we want you to tell us more about your background, your family, and in particular about your parents. We will do our best to help you by providing you with a place to stay and a limited amount of food."

A smile came across my face. I was extremely happy to hear this. But he continued speaking before I had a chance to say anything.

"In return," he went on, "we ask that you help us with anything and everything that we cannot do for ourselves. In the past, we had a woman come into our apartment two or three times per week. Now, she is unable to come, because her husband has fallen ill and she has to remain with him constantly. Being blind, there are things we cannot do, including some types of cleaning, attending to our laundry, certain amounts of food preparation, and other tasks of a similar nature.

"We have limited means available to us, but we are willing to share what we have with you. If this is agreeable, we will keep you and do our best to protect you. It should be understood that you must take certain precautions. You must be very careful in contacts with others, especially when it comes to shopping and traveling with us."

"Traveling? Where do you travel to?" I asked.

"We do only a modest amount of traveling and it is always to our little house in the country. We go there in the summer and stay approximately four weeks. We would expect you to travel with us, stay with us, and return with us. Is all this agreeable to you?"

I did not have to think about it. I gladly agreed to anything and everything he asked of me, beginning immediately. "Yes, all of your conditions will be fine. However, I think that it would be safer if I did not stay with you for more than a few days at a time. I know this would mean you would not be able to count on me for those periods when I was gone, but it would be safer for all of us if I did not stay with you continuously."

Paul Richter sat silently, thinking about this. Finally he spoke, "Yes. I suppose that will be fine. While it would be more convenient for us to have you here continuously, you are right that it might look suspicious. But when we travel to the country, you will need to stay with us the whole time. We will be away from Berlin, though, so the chances of anyone recognizing you will be greatly reduced."

Now it was my turn to think. Yes, that would be fine, I told him. I would stay with them for their entire month in the country. *But there was just one more catch*, I thought to myself. I had to tell them about Ilse.

"Herr Richter," I began, "there is one other matter I need to talk to you about regarding my staying with you. You see, and I am sorry I have not brought this up before, I am married."

"What?" Richter barked in surprise.

"Well, yes, I suppose I failed to mention it before. I hadn't said anything because I wasn't sure whether you were going to let me remain here. Your new terms about staying with you in the country for a lengthy period of time mandate that I bring this up."

"You think so?" he asked sarcastically. Perhaps it hadn't been a good idea not to come right out with this at the beginning.

"I'm really very sorry, Herr Richter, but as I was saying, I have a wife named Ilse. She is fine where she is for right now, but if I am to be with you for an extended period of time, it will be necessary for her to be with us."

He motioned as though he wanted to interject. I ignored him, thinking that if I got it all out, it would be better than arguing back and forth.

I continued, "My wife will be a wonderful addition for you. She is a nurse. She will be able to help you in more ways than I could, and she will be very helpful to Regina. I am sure that Regina would feel very comfortable with her. And Ilse will not be any trouble, I assure you. And she's a good cook too!"

Richter was silent and seemed to be thinking about what I'd said. I prayed my points would win him over. A nurse to care for them while they're in the country. A female companion for his blind girlfriend, Regina. And a cook, too! Wouldn't blind people need someone to cook for them? Otherwise, wouldn't they risk burning themselves?

Richter rose and went over to discuss this new information with Regina. He returned shortly and stood over me.

"Fine," he said. "All four of us will leave for the country in one week. Both of you should be here next Monday at 8:00 AM sharp."

And that was that. I rose and attempted to thank him. It did no good, though. Richter did not seem to be one for pleasantries and small talk. *Quite a reserved man*, I thought to myself as I left the apartment. I wondered if he would loosen up as I got to know him. A fascinating man. A blind Communist! Not the kind of person one meets very often. I smiled a bit to myself as I walked to the train. Things were looking up. Ilse and I were going to get out of Berlin. We were going to a place where I hoped we would feel safer.

I went back to the Kusitzkys and told Ilse all about the plans I had made. She seemed agreeable to the whole thing, though she wasn't happy to be leaving Klaus. But it was time for her to leave the Kusitzkys. They wanted Klaus, but hiding adults was more than they had bargained for. They would never push Ilse out the door, they would never say to her, "Leave." But the intent was clear. It was wise for us to lessen the burden.

For the next week, I stayed with Ilse and the Kusitzkys, leaving in the early morning before dawn and returning after nightfall. I spent two days in the middle of the week sleeping in the rubble in Berlin, in spite of Ilse's protests. She was afraid something would happen and I wouldn't be able to return to get her in time. But it was too dangerous to be in one place for so long.

During this time, Alex went to work at the meat processing plant every day. Anni tended her garden. Ilse concentrated on preparing Klaus for her absence. The idea of Ilse leaving was very hard for Klaus to accept. There was a lot of crying on both sides. "When are you coming back?" Klaus wailed. "Why are you leaving me, Mommy?" It was all very heartbreaking, but it could not be avoided. Ilse had to leave.

Klaus complained about everything he could think of, poor thing. Eating alone. Playing alone. Sleeping alone. Anni tried to counter all of his protests. "You'll eat with Uncle Alex and me." "You and I will play every day." And finally, "If you are scared you can always climb in with your Tante Anni and Uncle Alex."

Each night when I returned to the Kusitzkys, I spent much time talking with Ilse, trying to help her to understand how important it was that she not stay in one place for too long. "There are informers everywhere," I reminded her, even though she knew this. "The Nazis want to scare everyone, to keep everyone in line. That is why there are such great incentives for people to turn others in."

One thing that wasn't a problem was packing our goods. I had the clothes on my back, including a light jacket, and the shoes on my feet. Our luxury items were a comb, toothbrushes, a small rag that could be used as a towel, and a small piece of soap that I kept in my pocket. We definitely were not weighed down with possessions.

And so, with tearful good-byes to Klaus and the Kusitzkys, we headed for Richter's apartment. Paul Richter himself opened the door, and behind him I could see that their bags were packed and they were ready to leave. I introduced Ilse to them. We probably had said not more than three sentences to each other when Richter moved everyone out the door. We began to make our way to the train station.

Richter held the guide dog's leash with his right hand. Regina then hooked her arm into Richter's left arm. In this way, the guide dog led Richter and Richter led Regina. It was interesting that they were both blind and yet they only had one dog between them. *They must always be together when they are out in public*, I thought. That would be the only way to get around with only one dog.

We arrived at the train station and boarded the train. Ilse and I sat together across from Richter and Regina. None of us said much the entire trip. Ilse held my arm tightly and looked out the window, teary-eyed, thinking of Klaus. I kept looking around, watching for police and army patrols.

Traveling to their vacation home took about two hours. I had never been in that area of Germany before. It was flat country, mostly cultivated for growing common crops such as potatoes, wheat, and the like.

We stuffed ourselves—four adults and a dog—into a taxi. The driver, a man in his early sixties, recognized Richter from his past visits, which was not surprising. I was sure that there wouldn't be too many blind couples roaming around the train station in this small town.

"Who do you have with you, this young couple?" the taxi driver asked Richter. This nearly made me panic. I hoped that Richter could think on his feet, since we hadn't anticipated the need to explain my absence from the army quite this soon. If Richter gave the wrong answer, we could all end up in prison. Of course, there was no way to catch

Richter's attention. He was blind and unless he could sense us and our feelings, he had no way of knowing.

I squeezed Ilse's hand very tightly and prayed. "Oh," Richter began confidently, "he is home from the front, on leave for a little while. We have hired him and his wife to help us."

This explanation seemed to satisfy the taxi driver. I breathed a heavy sigh of relief. Richter was sharp. He'd obviously thought about this before.

After about ten minutes of being in the taxi, we pulled up to a little house. It stood by itself on a small lot, surrounded by fields. The nearest houses could be seen, but they were several hundred yards away.

I took a deep breath of relief, seeing this. When Richter had made me promise to come and stay with him for a month, I had worried about how risky it would be. Staying anywhere for more than a week was against my better judgement. But now, seeing that the neighbor's homes were so far away and that this was a rural area, I relaxed a bit. Perhaps this would be OK after all.

Richter paid the cab driver and, bidding him good-bye, we walked the short distance to the house.

The place was quite bright and cheery. There were a few windows with sunlight streaming through them. There was no foyer or front hall. Instead, we walked straight into what seemed to be the living room. It was simply furnished, equipped with comfortable upholstered chairs, a sofa, and a sturdy wooden table. The furniture and the walls were decorated in dark colors even though the room appeared bright from the sun.

All of a sudden Richter started talking in my direction. "There is a small room in the corner that you and your wife can use. You'll find everything that is necessary in there. There is a bed and a table and chair and an armoire where you can hang things up if you want. Unfortunately, we have only one bathroom in this house and we all have to share it. You'll find it between our room and your room. I'm sure we'll work that out to everybody's satisfaction," Richter said.

"That's all fine with us," I replied, looking at Ilse, who met my eyes with a worried smile. "I'm sure that will be just fine."

Richter and Regina also had a small kitchen in the house, accessible from the living room. It seemed very simply equipped: a sink and an electric stove with two burners. There was no refrigerator, but there was an icebox standing on four legs on the floor. This allowed access to it without having to stoop down.

A small water heater was mounted on the wall, above the sink. This was something one saw only in poorer areas. It was powered by electricity. Soon after we arrived, Richter went into the kitchen to turn it on. He then turned around to talk to me.

"Over there is our icebox. Please walk into town and order some ice delivered."

I hesitated. While I wanted to avoid seeming uncooperative, walking into town alone might attract attention that could prove unhealthy.

"Herr Richter, I am very sorry, but I do not think that would be a good idea. It would be risky for me to be so exposed. My presence in town would give rise to raised eyebrows and questions by anyone I see. They'll wonder why I'm not in the army."

"Oh yes," Richter said pleasantly. "I didn't think about that. You're absolutely right. That could cause problems for all of us. Just stay put now and I'll go into town to make the order. Then, when the man with the horse and buggy comes to deliver the ice, you and Ilse can hide in your room and keep quiet."

It was a relief to hear this. For a moment, it had seemed that my employment might be extremely short-lived. I was also glad that he did not seem upset about it. My previous impression of him had led me to believe that he might be too strong-willed and cantankerous to admit being wrong, at least without throwing a fit. I was glad to see that he could take things in stride.

Richter interrupted my thoughts. "I'll go into town and do it myself," he began. "It isn't that far—only a mile or so. The walk will do me good. In fact, I'll go right now."

He whistled for the dog. "Sascha!" he called. "Let's go!"

Richter left with the dog. Ilse was in our room. Regina and I remained in the living room. I looked over at Regina, who stood by the wall. She seemed shy, and I wondered to myself whether I should start up a conversation. Then I decided against it. There was always time for that later.

"I'm going to go into our room to help Ilse get settled," I announced and slowly made my way out of the living room.

The room designated for our use was very small. It had the table, chair, bed, and armoire that Richter had told me about. Absolutely the barest of necessities. I went over to the bed and lay down on top of the covers, staring at the ceiling. I took a deep breath. The next thing I knew, the dog was barking. I realized that I must have been dozing. I jumped up, pulled the curtain slightly open, and saw the iceman helping Paul down from the seat in the front of the wagon. Paul, led by the dog, walked toward the house while the iceman worked on getting the block of ice out of the rear of the wagon.

As Paul reached the door, I opened it to let him in. He said, "Dagobert, go to your room and stay there with Ilse until after the iceman leaves."

Retreating into our room, I watched the iceman as he made three trips with blocks of ice resting on his shoulder, which was protected by a wide leather strap. Ilse and I sat on the bed, trying hard to be as quiet as possible. It reminded me of our time at Herr Braun's apartment. At least we didn't have Klaus to worry about now.

It was a time of constant stress and strain. There was no way for me to really feel comfortable in any situation. *I wouldn't be able to relax*, I thought, *until Hitler was defeated*. Until I no longer feared for my life. Until I had a home again. Until I could find my parents, if they could be found.

There was also the fact that I was not just an "I" anymore. I was part of a "we." I looked over at Ilse as she occupied herself with cleaning the room. She said nothing, but I could tell that Klaus's absence bothered her deeply.

My life right now is so strange, I thought as I lay on the bed, staring fixedly at a white spot on the ceiling. For as much as I kept trying to maintain my sanity and some semblance of a sense of humor, every single minute of my life was full of anxiety. Anxiety about my safety, anxiety about my parents, anxiety about this strange role I was thrust into, husband and pseudo-father. *What am I doing? How am I going to survive?* So many questions I had no answers for. I could do nothing except rise the next morning and try to face each day as it came.

15

JEWISH SS

WE PASSED OUR DAYS at the summer house performing the mundane tasks for which we had been hired. I was servant, caretaker, gardener, handyman, and general jack-of-all-trades. Ilse was cook, cleaning woman, and companion to Regina. With four people plus a large dog, things were crowded. The dog turned out to be a very territorial creature and would constantly engage in campaigns to increase the area allotted to her, which would require us to do battle to reclaim the kitchen or living room or whatever place she had invaded.

When everyone was happy, all went well. When Paul's mood would darken, the atmosphere would grow tense and we would quickly become aware just how small the house really was. He would usually select Regina as the target for his anger. Regina seemed to have a harder time coping with her blindness than Paul did, and she would sometimes stumble and break things. This would be the signal for a full-blown tirade from Paul, which would inevitably leave Regina in tears. We tried to act as peacemakers, with varying degrees of success.

I don't mean to imply that Paul did not love Regina. As a rule, he was usually very nice to her. He took her into account whenever he was making plans. "How do you like this?" he'd ask her. "Do you think we should go here and there, or buy this or that?"

But it became painfully obvious that Richter's greatest love was Sascha, the dog. He was very protective of her, always making sure she had plenty of food and water. He would take her down the paths around the house to answer the call of nature and would walk her down the little country road that the house was situated on. Even being blind, the walks were no problem. Traffic was so light that Sascha easily kept him away from the occasional car or horse and buggy.

After four weeks had passed, we returned to Berlin. After a month's absence, Ilse was understandably anxious to see Klaus, so we immediately made our way to the Kusitzky house. The reunion between mother and son was a sight to gladden anyone's heart, and I was relieved when Anni invited Ilse to stay a while, for Klaus's sake. But as for me, I knew I had to keep moving. So after a few days, I left once again at dawn, returning to Berlin on my own.

My first stop was the post office, thinking perhaps I'd get a note from Dr. Finger. But there was nothing waiting for me. He hadn't written in a very long time, which I considered ominous. I hoped nothing had happened to him.

I walked toward the door but paused when something on the wall caught my eye. It was a notice about regulations regarding sending and receiving mail. Having nothing better to do, I started reading the notice when, out of the corner of my eye, I caught the profile of a man standing at one of the counters, talking to the clerk. He looked familiar, which meant he was either a threat or a possible ally.

Accordingly, I became simultaneously nervous and excited. If he was a *greifer*, or "catcher," I might have a problem. It was my firm intention to survive the war and that was best done by taking no chances. None. I turned to walk away, but as I moved, his face came into full view. It was a face of a young man, about my own age, with brown hair, brown eyes, and a straight nose. It was the face of Günther Gerson.

Günther was the son of one of my father's friends and customers. Herr Hermann Gerson owned a store on Kurfürstendamm, the most fashionable street in Berlin. My father had constructed and installed several display cases in front of his store.

Seeing Günther there, alive and in front of me, was something of a shock. For a moment, I couldn't move. It seemed to me that everyone else I loved or knew well had been sucked down into the black whirlpool of the Nazi death machine, never to be seen again. Somehow, I remained alive, but I was destined to be alone. The others were all dead and gone.

And now, a vision appeared in front of me of a familiar friend who looked to be not only alive but prosperous and healthy. I felt as if I were losing control, as if a flood of dammed-up emotions would break loose and overwhelm me. But although I was a Jew, I had been raised in the tradition of German stoicism and I would not allow myself to get out of control.

By the time I got a grip on myself, Günther had seen me and come close, a strange look on his face. "Dagobert?" he asked in a hopeful voice.

"Günther," I responded with a smile. "I can't believe it is you." I looked around at the crowd of people and decided it was best to leave. I didn't want anyone to hear us.

I motioned with my head that we should leave. We walked out of the post office and onto the street.

"How have you been?" Günther asked, "Are you all right? Your father and mother?"

I grimaced a bit and I saw by the look on his face that he understood. "Deported," I said, unable to meet his eyes.

There was silence as this news sunk in.

He looked at me. "You're a U-boat?"

"Yes," I mumbled.

Without saying anything further, I began moving slowly down the street and Günther followed along.

As we walked, Günther began speaking in a low voice, telling me how he had lost his own family. Günther's father, Hermann Gerson, was Jewish but his mother, Else, was not. When Günther was a boy, his family had been quite well off. However, after Günther's father died when Günther was nine, they experienced financial difficulties. They had to move out of their large apartment in Berlin-Templehof into a smaller apartment, and Else had to get a job. As anti-Jewish tensions rose in Germany, his mother's non-Jewish family withdrew from them, and his father's Jewish family moved away to the safety of other countries. His mother found herself bullied for having married a Jew and having half-Jewish children, and she committed suicide when Günther was fifteen, leaving Günther and his sister, Senta, orphans and unprotected.

Then one day Senta disappeared off the street, likely picked up by the Gestapo and deported, so Günther decided to go underground and live illegally. He became a U-boat, just like me.

We continued to walk and to talk, wandering the streets, going nowhere in particular. I told him about how my parents had been deported, how I had been made to work in the gun factory, and how I had narrowly escaped the factory action.

Then I told him about Ilse and Klaus. Günther was especially curious about Ilse. "Is she pretty?" he wanted to know. "Yes," I said. "Does she have a nice figure?" he asked. This seemed a bit absurd to me, given the context of the war and terror around us. But it was also nice to think even momentarily like a normal, red-blooded young male. "Yes," I winked at him. "A very nice figure."

Günther carried himself with such confidence, and he was quite a handsome young man, so different than the awful ugly caricatures of Jews in Nazi propaganda. Of course, this whole business of Jews always having large, crooked noses was absurd. Many Jews had straight noses or blond hair or blue eyes. The caricature of the ugly person with the hooked nose was simply one of the many ploys of the Nazi propaganda ministry. The chief disseminator of these falsehoods was a man named Julius Streicher.

Streicher was a Jew-hater of the first order. He published a newspaper called *Der Stürmer*, meaning "the one who storms or advances rapidly." This newspaper was strictly written to promote Nazi Party propaganda about Jews, Gypsies, homosexuals, and anyone else the Nazis disliked.

Jews were shown as vermin, being trampled by a mighty boot of a big Nazi storm trooper. This concept of reducing the image of Jews to vermin was used to justify destroying them.

Der Stürmer was made widely available to the populace by means of display boxes, which were placed near bus stops, train stations, and major intersections. The boxes were made out of wood and painted bright red, to attract attention. Each had a large glass window through which that day's issue was displayed.

As we strolled down the street, Günther continued to recount his experiences to me. He had interned for Friedrich Zwiebel, who was a prominent electrical engineer in Berlin who specialized in the movie industry. His next revelation left me awestruck. It seemed that the intrepid Günther Gerson had, as his girlfriend, the daughter of a man with strong official Nazi connections.

Apparently, he had met this young lady, Eleonore Stindt, well before the war had started. For five years, they had conducted an affair that would have horrified most Germans. Eleonore was half-Jewish. Her mom, Tilla Stindt, was Jewish, but her father, Bruno Stindt, was not. After Günther's parents had both died, Tilla Stindt became the foster mother to Günther's sister, Senta. That is how Günther came to know Eleonore, and that relationship had now blossomed into something more.

Eleonore's father, Bruno Stindt, was a cameraman and producer for the US entertainment company Paramount News/Paramount Pictures. He had fantastic Nazi connections and was considered to be Hitler's favorite cameraman. Stindt was very involved in the 1936 Olympic games coverage, and he was also involved with Leni Riefenstahl's film company, which among other things created propaganda films for Hitler and the Nazi Party.

Disseminating Nazi propaganda among SS officers and troops was considered a matter of great priority, as was the basic goal of influencing the public. Hitler himself was an avid viewer of movies and considered propaganda films to be the most important way of imprinting the Nazi philosophy on the populace. Herr Stindt's company supplied projection equipment to both private and military movie theatres in order to show the films to the target audiences.

Günther got a job with Herr Stindt and used Stindt's Nazi connections to his advantage. Günther apparently had a real gift for solving some of the more complicated problems occurring in the projection equipment. He also served as a troubleshooter for new and intricate projects in a field where the technology was rapidly changing. Günther was the only person Stindt could find who could make things work.

Both to make sure he remained in the business and to please his love-stricken daughter, Stindt paid Günther well for his services. Stindt even let Günther spend nights in his apartment, at his daughter's request.

I was absolutely flabbergasted by what I was hearing. My Jewish friend was not only dating the daughter of a man with strong Nazi Party connections, but he was also a cherished, well-paid employee of her father. And to top it off, her father allowed him to sleep with his daughter and stay at his house! It was so fantastic that I had to laugh. At that moment, I couldn't think of anything more incredible.

"Günther, are you certain that they know the Nazis consider you to be Jewish and that you are a Uboat? Perhaps Herr Stindt isn't aware of it?"

"No way," Günther said. "He definitely knows I am half Jewish."

"Do you feel safe? Don't you worry that he will have you arrested?" I asked, my mouth agape.

"Oh, I have no doubt that I am in great danger, in spite of my favored position with Stindt. I'm sure that I am on the Gestapo wanted list. But Stindt needs me, he truly does. And Eleonore loves me. So for now, I feel comfortable with the situation. If I sense the wind changing, I'll move on."

I was amazed at Günther's confidence. His tone of voice was so assured that one might have thought he was discussing what he would have for dinner that night, rather than matters that might mean life or death for him.

We continued walking and talking, hitting it off exceptionally well. We spoke about missing our parents and the rumors about the camps. We had heard stories about extermination camps in the East, especially in Poland. It was difficult to allow this to register in our brains. The ramifications were too hideous to consider.

I told him about my hide-and-seek lifestyle, staying only a few days in any one location, living with friends and in bombed-out buildings. After a few hours of catching up, we decided to meet again soon. We chose a day and time to meet and agreed that we favored a public place, preferably with large crowds milling about.

We continued to meet now and then. Our favorite rendezvous was the branch post office. At other times, we would meet at Aschingers Restaurant. Sometimes we met at the train station or the subway station.

Günther was full of surprises. On the day of our third meeting, he told me that Herr Stindt had supplied him with an SS uniform, identity papers, and a pistol. He required these items to perform an important installation in an SS facility near Frankfurt an der Oder, which was closed to anyone not a member of the SS. Günther was not enthusiastic about being sent on this job and mentioned it only in passing.

I was surprised by the effect this news had on me. I was growing envious of Günther. Though we were both U-boats, merely surviving was difficult for me. Hiding in carcasses of decrepit buildings, walking the streets scavenging for food, not being able to bathe, having no place in society—I had no rights, no identity, nothing. As far as the rest of the world was concerned, I didn't exist. Günther, on the other hand, though a U-boat, was being given all the privileges of one of Hitler's elite SS. He had not only clothes to wear, food to eat, and work that provided him with money—but now he had priceless, perfect identity papers. It seemed unbelievable, but I knew it was true.

Though he mentioned the assignment to me only casually and in passing, I could not resist. I turned to him and asked the question that had been haunting me since he first described his upcoming trip. "Günther, can I go with you?" I practically begged. "I am tired of dodging bombs every day, tired of freezing at night, tired of Berlin. I would be very grateful if you would allow me to come along."

Unbelievable, I thought to myself. After all these months of avoiding contact with the Nazis at any cost, here I was begging someone to take me straight into their arms. But at this point I didn't care. I trusted that if Günther were safe, I would be too. And I was desperate for a respite from the constant fear and worry. The idea of having a few days of guaranteed stress-free food and shelter seemed like heaven.

Günther looked at me and laughed, caught up in the absurdity of the moment.

"Günther, the only catch is that I don't have identity papers. I assume you are going by train, and there is no way I could go on that train with you without papers of my own. But if you could get papers for me, then I would do anything to come with you."

Günther laughed again. "OK, Dagobert. I'll do it. I will try my best to get you papers. Meet me at the Alexanderplatz one week from today at this same time."

I spent the next few days with Richter and Regina. Finally, on the day of the rendezvous, I bid good-bye to them at their Berlin apartment and made my way to Alexanderplatz. There I saw Günther, strutting around, looking as though he had nothing in all the world to fear. I made my way over to him and his face lit up with a friendly smile as soon as he saw me. I prayed he would have good news for me.

"Well, Dagobert, my friend, you're in luck. I was able to get papers for you as well as permission for you to come along to help. Come, follow me. I'm about to transform you into a vision that would make your poor mother faint with shock." He chuckled to himself at the insanity of what we were doing.

"Where are you taking me?" I asked.

"To Stindt's office," he replied.

The office turned out to be a storefront with large, extensive work spaces, a warehouse, and a shop in the rear. It was loaded with all kinds of equipment and movie theater gadgets. We walked farther inside. In the back of the warehouse there were two people working in a shop area.

I asked what they were doing and learned that they were reconditioning equipment that had been traded in, or were repairing equipment that would be returned and installed at the customer's theater. Günther himself sometimes assisted in making the repairs, especially if there was a problem that no one else could solve.

Günther spent a few moments engaged in small talk with some of the employees, then led me into another room, away from the other workers.

Hanging on a rod along the wall in front of us were uniforms. SS uniforms, I saw immediately. My heart pounded a bit as I looked at them. I glanced over at Günther to see if the uniforms were there for the purpose that I supposed. For us. For me.

Günther looked over at me and saw my face, probably looking like a worried child, wondering if I would get to play some risky game or not. He immediately started to laugh. He walked over to the rack and took down one of the hangers and handed the uniform to me.

"Time to put it on, Herr Lewin," he said, still laughing to himself.

I inspected the uniform's front and back, running my hand over the fabric of the shoulder. Excitement and revulsion coursed through me. To have my hands on the uniform of the enemy I despised sent a chill up my spine.

Günther was way ahead of me. I looked over to see that he had already put on his uniform, undergoing a metamorphosis that turned him into the perfect image of an SS officer before my eyes. He leaned down and tossed me a pair of boots, a belt, and a hat. I climbed into all of the garb, feeling strangely secure as I transformed myself from an outlaw Jew into one of Germany's elite military officers. I turned to look in the mirror. Unbelievable! A Jew turned SS man!

Günther threw out his hands as if he were onstage, ending a brilliant performance. He walked over to a nearby shelf and pulled out two holsters. He left the room for a couple of minutes, returning with two sidearms, which we put into the holsters and buckled on. We sat there in silence, side by side, gazing at ourselves in the full-length mirror. We were now fully accoutered SS.

Just then Günther broke the silence. "We probably should take all of this off. Stindt wants us to leave tomorrow. I need to get everything ready for the trip."

And so we stripped. I helped Günther pack some sensitive optical instruments into aluminum carrying cases. We packed the items in fabric to ensure that nothing would happen to them in transit, even when handled roughly. Still larger items, which would have not been practical or feasible to carry, had already been shipped.

Günther and I met the next day back at Stindt's office. Luckily, Stindt was not there. I was not eager to meet him, in spite of the fact that he was serving as my unknowing benefactor. Stindt had arranged for a driver to take us to the train station. Günther wasn't familiar with the driver, but the automobile we rode in definitely belonged to Stindt.

Even though we looked very convincing, fully outfitted in the SS uniforms, we were still apprehensive as we boarded the train. We weren't sure about the validity of our identification papers. There was no choice but to wait and see.

The suspense didn't last for long, though, as a police patrol soon walked through the train, asking for papers. When we presented ours, the policemen examined them, handed them back to us, and saluted smartly. We saluted back, "Heil Hitler." Günther and I exchanged glances. We had gotten away with it. This time, at least.

There wasn't much to do on the train. I was thrilled to be getting out of Berlin and into the countryside. I spent the whole trip with Günther with my eyes glued to the scenery outside the window. What a treat it was to be able to see all of that!

We were fortunate to have a compartment all to ourselves. Not many people could travel on trains at this point in time. Most of the men were in the military and many women were working in ammunition plants. Few people had time to travel.

Finally, we arrived in Frankfurt an der Oder. We did not have a lot of baggage with us, since most of the equipment required for the installation had been shipped ahead. With us we carried a number of the smaller items required: lenses, controls, special switches, tools, and the precision measuring instruments we had packed the day before. We also had a special paper issued by the authority of the SS to make certain we did not have any problems with overanxious police patrols, who would normally have insisted on inspecting the metal containers we carried.

Once we left the train station, it was only a short trip to the SS facility outside of Frankfurt an der Oder. An SS car picked us up at the train station. The car was an impressive sight, but Günther did not seem very excited. Günther was something of a cold fish. He did not get too excited about things, or if he did, he didn't show it.

We drove through the countryside for an hour until we arrived at the SS complex. I did not see any sign stating that we had arrived at such a place. The whole complex was enclosed by a barbed-wire fence. Guards with dogs were patrolling. I could see that there were also guard towers at the corners of the complex. Big lights were posted all around, in order to illuminate the area at night. Günther had told me that this was a training center for SS soldiers and officers and therefore required the security.

We arrived at a gate, which guards immediately opened. Our driver took us to a large building nearby. This was where we were scheduled to install the projection equipment. He let us off there and took us into the building to introduce us to the manager, who greeted us with the proper Nazi salute of "Heil Hitler." Like actors on a theater stage, Günther and I threw out our arms, shouted back "Heil Hitler," and clicked our heels.

The manager led us up a staircase where the projection room had been prepared for the installation. Günther was well pleased with the preparations that had been made, including the special heavy wiring and other provisions. Günther announced that everything seemed to be in order. "We're ready to begin."

We spent the next four days installing the equipment. The job went very well. I helped Günther with virtually everything. We both felt very comfortable, at ease among the enemy. With my uniform and identification papers, I felt secure. Günther and I even took off our restricting uniform jackets and walked around in our undershirts.

We were able to do most of the job by ourselves, though Günther did have to call on one of the SS electricians a few times to clear up some minor problems. Twice, some of the big SS bosses came around to check on our progress. Günther did all the talking, with me remaining quietly in the background. Some of the SS personnel offered to help us, but we turned them down. We wanted to do the job ourselves. It was safer that way. We didn't want to have to carry on a conversation about subjects we knew nothing about. One wrong word could have spelled disaster for us.

At night, we stayed in a hotel especially reserved for guests of various government officials. Günther had received money from Herr Stindt for the hotel and restaurants. To our surprise, the food and the accommodations were excellent. I had not had anything like this in a long time. I spent most of my time as a U-boat close to starving. Now, I abandoned any attempt at reserve and ate until I was bursting.

At the conclusion of the project, several of the supervisors and two equipment operators came by to inspect the installation and to get instructions. Here again, I kept quiet. Günther did all the talking, sticking to the project at hand. We then presented a paper for the SS chief to sign, acknowledging that the installation was complete and satisfactory. As soon as the paper was signed, we left for Berlin. When we arrived, there was a note waiting for Günther. After reading it, he turned to me and said, "Dago, we have to return our ID papers to the SS. They can't be used again."

"Oh," I said, disheartened. I had hoped I'd be able to use them for a while. The possession of the papers was a tremendous advantage for me.

"And we have to return our uniforms too," Günther continued.

"Will we be able to borrow them again?" I asked.

"No. Stindt says he could get them only one time. And that was it. He's out of political favors."

"I guess it's not the type of thing he could do every day," I mused.

"That's right. Giving us the uniforms violated SS regulations. Herr Stindt told me that he thought the higher authorities had actually made a mistake in providing the papers and the uniforms. He's certain they won't make that error again."

I sighed.

Günther continued, "The only reason Stindt went to all that trouble in the first place was because I told him neither of us had sufficient identification papers to travel on the trains. Since the installation was extremely important to Stindt's business and since he did not think anyone could do the job as well as I could, he decided to take the risk and obtain the documents for this job."

"I see," I replied. "Well, it was fun while it lasted."

What a joke. It was more than fun. It was security. It was a respite from the stress of being constantly hunted. To Günther and I, this was all very bad news, a considerable letdown. We both had felt so secure while we were in uniform and in possession of valid papers. Now they were gone.

After some time, Günther did manage to get himself another kind of paper, certifying his lack of fitness for military service. Unfortunately, he was unable to get any identification papers for me and we were both well aware that I had to have them. Without identification papers, I was not likely to survive very long on the streets.

"There's only one thing to do then," Günther then grinned. We decided to obtain papers for me using another tried and true method. We would steal them.

We met at a predetermined time at the S-Bahn ticket counter. Günther had come from Stindt's apartment, where he lived off and on with Ella and her family. I came from the Kusitzkys, where I had returned to stay for a few days. I winked at him and he at me. It was game day.

We approached the ticket counter. I bought tickets for riding the elevated S-Bahn train. "The S-Bahns are always extremely crowded," Günther said. "That fact will be in our favor."

We passed through the guarded entry and walked into the station, showing the purchased tickets. Then we got out of the swarm of the crowd and perched on the railing at the side.

We watched others passing through the gates. Good Germans, making their way to whatever destination they had in mind. Most of them had bought tickets like we had. But then there were others. Germans who, with the wave of a card, were allowed to pass through. These were Gestapo.

We could see that their cards were usually in leather pouches, with a photo was on one side and a name on the other. It was obvious that these special cards gave the bearer certain privileges. None of these people had to stop at the ticket window. None of them had to pay.

"Aha," Günther whispered to me. "The cards let them ride free."

"Yes, it seems so," I replied softly. "They probably get to use all sorts of transportation without charge. Probably buses, streetcars, perhaps the U-Bahn too."

And so we stood there, continuing to watch the procession of folks, both privileged and not, walking through the gate and past the guard.

After ten minutes or so, we chose our victim: a heavyset, middle-aged woman in a raincoat who moved slowly toward the guard. After a bit of fumbling, she took out her ID card and showed it to the guard, who quickly waved her through. Then she slipped the card into the pocket of her raincoat and began shuffling towards the S-Bahn trains.

Günther and I looked at each other, smiled, and nodded. This was it. We had our target. We followed her upstairs to the train platform. When the train pulled into the station, the doors opened and a large crowd exited. Many others who had been waiting started pushing to get in.

Günther and I positioned ourselves behind the woman with the ID card. I was behind her and made a quick but gentle grab for the card. Then I stepped back out of the car as the doors were closing.

Günther was to remain in the train and to get off at the next station. The purpose for this was twofold. First, he was to observe whether she noticed that her ID card had been taken, and secondly, if she attempted to chase me, he was to prevent her from doing so.

Günther and I met shortly afterward. "Perfect," he said, beaming. "She hasn't even noticed that it's gone."

We looked at the card. It identified the bearer as a Gestapo operative.

Günther took the card from me and left. He contacted a middle-man he knew who dealt with a passport forger. The Gestapo ID was passed to the forger for alteration, along with a picture of me and my payment of 300 marks.

After a few days, the ID was returned. The photo of the woman had been replaced with my photo. One half of the official stamp was still on the card. The other half of the stamp, which had been on the woman's photo, was now on my photo. It was a perfect match. What's more, the forger had changed the bearer's name from Gerda Schultz to that of Gerd Schultz, a man's name.

So Dagobert Lewin now became Gerd Schultz. I now had an air of authority. As a Gestapo employee, I had a new sense of security. Maybe too much of one.

"How did the forger do it?" I asked Günther.

"The middleman told me he used an egg. Hard boiled. He trans-ferred the stamp from the woman's photo to yours via the egg. The rest is up to your imagination."

I'd never look at eggs the same way again.

With our project completed and my identity transformed into that of Gerd Schultz, Gestapo operative, walking the streets and riding the trains was less hazardous. Günther and I parted ways for a while. But we would meet again soon. I bid him adieu and made my way by train and then by bus to Lübars, back to the Kusitzkys.

I didn't arrive until late afternoon. Ahead of me, I could see Anni's body in profile, on her knees and leaning over a vegetable bed. As I approached, she turned her head and saw me. She jumped up and walked quickly toward me.

"Dagobert! Oh my goodness! How wonderful to see you! We were worried! I'm just out here gathering some things for lunch tomorrow. How are you? Are you all right?"

"Everything is all right," I replied, wanting to be polite but impatient to make my way into the house. I was uncomfortable being outside while it was still light. One never knew who might be watching, and I was not interested in taking chances.

"Go inside and wash up," Anni began, excited about my arrival. "I just have a few more things to do out here and then I will come in and make you dinner."

That was music to my ears. Dinner. Washing up. I hadn't been able to take much of a bath since traveling with Günther. It was very nice to be here. I felt as though I was coming home, back to friends. And it would be nice to see little Klaus and Ilse.

Then I saw something which stopped me in my tracks. A man, an old man, stood near the front doorway, mumbling under his breath. My heart started racing. Who in the world could this be? I feared it was a neighbor, someone who could turn me in.

This was bad. I wanted to turn and run, but it was too late. By the time I noticed him, I was only a few feet away. I would just have to bluff my way through. Why couldn't I be a visitor? Surely a neighbor wouldn't suspect anything of a simple dinner guest. I kept walking to the front door and nodded at the man as he glanced in my direction.

"Hello. Lovely evening, isn't it?" I asked, then turned to the door as calmly as I could.

The man looked at me, perplexed, but said nothing.

As I entered the foyer by the stairs, my mind was racing. *I would have to leave*, I thought. Very, very shortly. I could never come back. I was anxious over my safety and bitterly disappointed at the same time. *Yet another option lost*, I moaned silently to myself.

As I stood there by the foot of the stairs, the door behind me flew open again. I turned to see Anni, carrying a basket of vegetables she had just harvested from her garden. She took one look at my face and knew something was wrong.

"What is it, Dagobert? You seem upset."

"I just met someone who I assume is a neighbor."

"Oh?" she asked, not seeming to understand what I thought was obvious.

"Wasn't there a man standing outside your front door as you walked in?" I asked.

"No," she replied.

This was strange. Had he left to call the Gestapo? Perhaps I needed to leave right now, before dinner.

"Tell me, Dagobert, what did this neighbor of ours look like?"

I described him. "He was a very old man, at least in his eighties. He was very hunched over and quite short because of it. His face was crumpled up, he had a long, straight nose, a lot of wrinkles on his forehead and around his jaws, and big ears."

"Hmm," Anni replied. "Did this man say anything to you?"

"Well he mumbled a bit, but to be honest, I didn't understand any of it," I said, telling the absolute truth. The sounds that came out of his mouth sounded like gibberish to me.

"Oh, Dago!" Anni exclaimed, "It seems you have met my father-in-law! That's all!"

My eyes opened wide. A father-in-law? Of everyone that Anni had mentioned to me those first few days I had stayed with her, she had never mentioned having a father-in-law.

"Is he visiting?" I asked.

"No, Dagobert. He lives here!" she said.

He lived here? Here in this house? How? Where?

Anni saw that I was confused and began explaining, "He lives in the basement. There is a separate entrance for him. He and Alex built this house themselves. All my father-in-law ever wanted was to have a small space to himself, separate from ours. So he lives in our very rudimentary cellar. The whole Kusitzky family came from a rural area of Germany, where they were very poor. They lived under what you might think of as a feudal system, where Alex's father worked for the local landowner. They came to Lübars seeking a better life, but Alex's father insists on living as he did before he came, with almost no sort of luxury whatsoever. They are simple folk, the Kusitzkys. All he wants is a space to live. That's it."

"How is it that I did not see him before? How could I not see someone who actually lives in this house?"

"Because he rarely leaves his cellar. I take his meals down to him every day, but he is generally content to stay put. Just him and his unfinished walls," Anni said.

That was a relief. I smiled at Anni, thinking she must know how much she had just calmed my nerves. Then I turned and went upstairs to wash and get ready for dinner. When I reached the top of the stairs, Klaus barreled over and threw himself in my arms.

"Hi, little man!" I exclaimed, glad to see him.

He hugged me and clung to me. "Where's Mommy?" he asked.

"Maybe she's in the attic. Let's go see."

Sure enough, Ilse was there, mending Klaus's sock as she sat on our bed. I ran up to her, gave her a kiss, and told her all about my adventures. Ilse was amazed. She warned me to be careful.

We spent the next few days relaxing, listening to Anni's continuous dialogue, helping her around the house, and catching up again. During those few days I felt exhilarated, though never totally at peace. All too soon, it was time to leave Lübars and meet Günther again.

We met at the post office, one of our favorite spots. Günther had a confident grin on his face. I was instantly intrigued.

"Yes?" I smiled. "What have you got up your sleeve now?"

"Oh, it's something I think you'll enjoy," Günther said. "I've got another job, another installation out of town. I want you to come with me. The only catch is that you will not be able to actually do the job. You'll have to stay in the hotel while I work. But the trip itself will still be a change of scenery."

Another trip! Another chance to get out of Berlin. "Will we go as SS again?" I asked.

"No. That is done. We'll probably never do that again. But I think it should still be safe. I'll have my identification from Herr Stindt. And you, of course, will be Gerd Schultz."

Ah yes, my alter ego, Gerd Schultz. Having that identification card, though stolen and subsequently forged, did make me feel much better. So much so that I thought I'd even risk another train trip. "Done. I'll come and stand guard in the hotel room while you are away!"

The next day we went to Oranienburg. It turned out that we didn't have to take a train, as we had on our last trip. Oranienburg was the last stop on the S-Bahn and the trip was not as dangerous. But the SS patrolled the S-Bahn too, so my Gerd Schultz ID card served me well.

Günther's installation job was another project for the SS. This time, it was at a facility attached to the Sachsenhausen concentration camp. The Sachsenhausen camp was quite large and had become infamous as time went on. Hitler began sending Jews to this camp very soon after he came to power. Some of these Jews were released during those early days and allowed to come back to Berlin. While we were there, though, I had no idea that Sachsenhausen had become a death camp. Jews there weren't gassed or burned. They were shot or starved or worked to death. All I knew was that Jews had been taken there. I didn't know the specifics, the extent, or the magnitude of the Nazis' actions.

Ignorant of what was occurring nearby, I took advantage of the time to recharge my batteries, to rest, eat, and avail myself of the bath and toilet. This was not something I had available all the time, especially during those periods when I had to walk the streets of Berlin with no place to go. So I relaxed in the room and waited for evening to come, when Günther would return and we would have a meal.

I couldn't help in the installation because I didn't have special ID papers Stindt had supplied to Günther. Stindt was not willing to do anything else for me, that was clear. If anything had gone wrong, he would have been in great jeopardy. He wasn't about to risk himself again for someone he had never met.

Günther's job went well and was over in three days, at the end of which we took the S-Bahn back to Berlin.

It was time again to part for a while. Günther had no jobs coming up, so he suggested that, instead of a predetermined rendezvous, we correspond through the post office. I went back to the Kusitzkys to see Ilse. Soon after I arrived, Anni came barreling through the house with news for Ilse and me.

"One of my friends needs a live-in housekeeper at her home not far from Lübars," Anni said to Ilse. "You would have some time off each week to visit Klaus."

It sounded like a good plan. We knew she needed to leave the Kusitzkys. So, the next day, she went to interview for the job. The woman hired her, and Ilse began work that very week.

I also had to leave. I had been at the Kusitzky house far too long. I left that night, heading back to Berlin, shivering all the way. Fall had arrived with a vengeance, and rubble was not a good form of insulation. I simply could not survive on the streets. I had to find a new place to stay.

16

DAMN YANKEE

I SPENT THE NEXT DAY, like many other days, wandering the streets of Berlin. I noticed my shoes were beginning to wear out, which didn't surprise me. My aim was to avoid the police and the Gestapo, which I could only do by moving around. I couldn't afford to become too familiar a face in any one spot, since attracting official attention could be deadly. I still had the Gestapo ID that we had stolen, but I presumed that by now the Gestapo must have discovered that it was missing and would be on the lookout for anyone attempting to use it.

As I walked, I constantly scanned the faces of people around me, ducking into doorways whenever I saw police or SS patrols. Sometimes, when I reached the point of absolute exhaustion, I would go to a park and sit on a bench. This was breaking yet another law. The benches read "No Jews Allowed" and Jews were forbidden to even enter the parks. I didn't care. I was a fugitive, no longer wearing a yellow Jewish star.

I thought a few times of keeping a diary, but each time I quickly abandoned the idea. If I were caught, the Gestapo could use the diary against me and those who had helped me.

My list of allies had been whittled down. In Berlin, I now had only Paul Richter's apartment for shelter, but the last time I had been there an incident occurred that dampened Richter's enthusiasm for helping me. A Wehrmacht patrol had come to his apartment house, looking for an army deserter. They'd been tipped off that this man was hiding in

Richter's apartment building. When they knocked on his door, they were advised that he and Regina were blind and obviously couldn't identify anyone. The army patrolmen accepted their explanation and left, but the experience had left Richter reluctant to have me around. They asked me to stay away for a while, until some time elapsed or the deserter was found.

So in Berlin, I was completely on my own. Life got especially difficult whenever it rained. I could go into the U-Bahn subway or the S-Bahn and spend the day riding around, but I had to be extremely careful to avoid attracting the attention of the Gestapo.

But today it was a clear day, so I stuck to the streets. I wandered up toward Humboldt University, the foremost university in Berlin. I loved this area of the city. I had always found it to be interesting. The main state opera house was right there, as was the national library.

I wandered into the Bebelplatz. This was a large outdoor plaza between the university, the state opera house, and the national library. These institutions were the foremost of their kind in Berlin and formed an area of academic resources the equal of any in Germany. Since I was a little boy, I had dreamed of attending the university; I had always found going to school to be exciting. But the Bebelplatz held another type of meaning, not only to me, but to all Germans, because of what occurred there some ten years ago.

One of the few families with whom my parents had socialized were the Switzers. They lived close to us. Hans, one of their sons, attended the university. He was always encouraging me to read and study, hoping I would follow him to university one day.

On May 10, 1933, I returned home from public school and found Hans waiting for me. He had time, he said, to take me to see the national library. Being too young to go by myself, I was thrilled at the prospect.

In those days, the Bebelplatz was called the Opernplatz. As Hans and I approached it, we could not help but notice a tremendous pile of books in the center of the square. Even as we watched, storm troopers and university students continued heaping more books on the pile, shouting and chanting their slogans.

Hans asked one of the bystanders what was going on. "There will be a book burning tonight," he said. "Dr. Goebbels has ordered that books by Jews and other undesirables be collected from libraries and bookshops."

"I cannot believe this," Hans whispered softly to me, in horror. "I have to see it."

Sometime after darkness set in, a large procession of thousands of people, many carrying torches, gathered in Opernplatz. As Hans and I watched in amazement, some of the students doused the books with cans of benzene or gasoline. Everyone was shouting, encouraging each other. Huge smiles plastered the faces of many of the people standing around as they screamed for the burning to begin.

Two of the students then put their torches to the huge pile of books. The whole thing exploded into a column of flames many feet high. More

The site of the 1933 book burning. Books by about six hundred Jewish authors and others who had been declared degenerate by the Nazi party were burned in a huge bonfire here.

books were then thrown onto the pile, with the names of the authors being shouted for the amusement of the crowd.

I was too scared to say a word. It was my first experience with the power of a mob, and even though I didn't completely understand what was going on, I did realize I was witnessing something monumental. As it turned out, it was indeed a historical event. Some twenty thousand books were burned that night in Berlin as Nazis tried to exorcise the spirit of Jewish scholarship from German culture.

After another few hours, I decided to walk toward Hirschfeld's apartment. I'd been to see him a week earlier to sell another stamp, and now was as good a time as any to collect the proceeds of the sale.

I walked up the steps of his apartment house and knocked on the door. Within a minute or two, the door opened.

"Dagobert. Come in," Hirschfeld said as he opened the door, waving me inside.

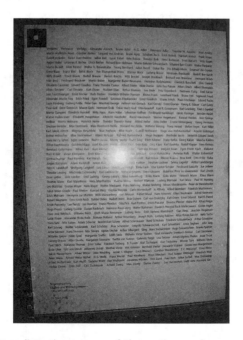

A plaque lists the names of the authors whose works were burned. It is attached to the post in the previous picture, where the bicycle is parked. The first line reads: Forbidden, Burned, Persecuted.

I went back to the living room and walked next to the couch near the stamp albums and reference books.

"Sit down. I will be right with you," he said, leaving me there to go into another room.

He returned in a few minutes and presented me with an envelope that contained almost a thousand marks. I silently thanked God for my father's ingenuity and foresight.

With little more in the way of conversation, Hirschfeld escorted me to the door. A cold man, I sometimes thought, but then again, this was wartime. I did, however, want to find out if he knew of anyone who might be willing to put me up. It didn't occur to me to ask him if I could stay with him. I knew what the answer would be. With as much civility as I could summon, I thanked him for his assistance with the sale of the stamps and inquired if he knew of anyone who might be willing to hide me for a time.

Hirschfeld looked at me and muttered "Hmm," and scratched his head. He looked up at a corner of the ceiling, then got up and very slowly walked around the room. I waited, watching him. There was a bemused look on his face that made me wonder what he was up to. Finally, he spoke:

"Dagobert, I may have something for you. I would have to contact them first myself, though. I would not feel comfortable sending you to them directly. Come back in two days."

Again, this come-back-in-a-few-days business. It was frustrating, but I had nothing else to do.

"Two days?"

"Yes, Dagobert. Two days," he said succinctly.

"All right. Two days then," I repeated.

"Yes. See you then," he said, never one to waste too much oxygen on conversation.

I gathered that this was my cue to show myself to the door. I thanked him again and walked toward the door. I turned around and gave a single wave, to which he absentmindedly nodded his head.

I roamed the streets of Berlin for the rest of the day, searching for a building to sleep in. I eventually found one that seemed suitable. Dreading the cold that my blanket could no longer protect me from, I chose a corner to sleep in and went out to find food. I went into a bakery and bought more sawdust bread, using up another of my bread ration cards, then on to the butcher's for more salami. This was a monotonous menu, but it was the best I could do at this point. I had no place to cook or store anything.

After two cold nights sleeping in that little corner, it was time to return to Hirschfeld's. I had not washed since I had left the Kusitzkys, so I stopped by one of the circular pissoirs. Washing in a public restroom was too conspicuous, but I did manage to splash my face with water from one of the troughs and smooth back my hair.

Arriving at the Hirschfeld residence, I knocked and waited. Hirschfeld soon answered, waving me in. As usual, there was little chitchat and no exchanges of niceties. I sat there and waited for him to speak.

"Dagobert, I know of a small auto repair shop, specializing in electrical systems. It is run by two people whom I have met a few times over the years, a husband and wife team.

"The owners are Jehovah's Witnesses. They believe in the Old Testament, as do we. However, they don't recognize national symbols like the Nazi flag. Recently, this couple sheltered someone who was living illegally in Berlin. I don't know if that person was Jewish or not, but I know that they did this. This person has left and they are in need of someone to help them in the shop. I approached them and asked them if they would be interested in having you. I told them I knew of a young man with a mechanical background and they were very interested. Here is their address. Go visit them and see if things will work out."

He then walked over to me and handed me a sheet of paper. I looked down and read it. "Stoltze," it said, and then gave me the address of a shop. I looked back up at Hirschfeld. "You are certain that they would be helpful? They would not betray me?" I asked.

"Yes, I believe it would be all right," he said. "Why don't you go now?"

As usual, Hirschfeld was not going to waste much breath with me. It would have made me feel better if he could somehow have been a bit more effusive in his enthusiasm for this couple. But again, I could not expect any more of him. He had already been kind enough to give me their name, I told myself. I had no reason to believe that Hirschfeld would wish me harm in any way. Still, it was difficult to push down my fear of betrayal.

Nevertheless, beggars cannot be choosers and I had certainly been demoted to a member of the begging class. I made my way out of the apartment and started off for Stoltze's shop. I would arrive near closing time, to avoid the presence of customers who might overhear our discussion.

Just before they were about to close, I went inside the shop. I walked into the small office where a woman was sitting behind a desk. It was a simple place with the basic equipment and materials required for the business, but nothing more. There were several types of testers, an armature lathe, arbor presses, and other miscellaneous tools.

After a minute, the woman, who looked to be in her mid-fifties, looked up at me and asked, "Yes? Can I help you?"

"I hope so," I said. "I was sent by Herr Hirschfeld. Are you Frau Stoltze?"

"Yes," she said, looking at me quizzically.

"Herr Hirschfeld suggested I come to see you and talk to you. He said that he had already told you about me," I said, praying that all that was true.

"Yes," she said again, without seeming to want to say more. So far, she was reminding me of Hirschfeld in her verbosity. Then she rose from her chair, "Please wait a moment, I have to call my husband," she said.

She turned and went out of a door behind her. I could see her walk over to a car and bend down to talk to someone underneath. After a few moments, she stepped back and a man emerged. He was a skinny fellow with brown hair and a long nose. He also looked to be close to sixty years old. He wiped his hands and headed back toward the office with her. I continued to stand there, in front of the desk, waiting for them and hoping.

When they came back into the office, the man was still wiping his hands. After he had cleaned them to his satisfaction, he said, "I presume you are Dagobert."

"Yes, I am," I said, stretching my hand out to meet his. In all the time I had been a U-boat, I could recall no one who had extended me this courtesy. This was a far cry from the treatment most Jews had received while we were living legally in Germany under Hitler. No German in the gun factory would have shaken my hand. I was clearly Jewish and thus lower-class to them.

"Herr Hirschfeld has told us about you," Herr Stoltze said. He went on, "Tell me more. What kind of work have you done? I want to know everything about your life, as much as you can tell us."

Herr Stoltze spent some time questioning me about my life and my mechanical knowledge. After several hours of this, he took me to see his shop. As we walked around the floor, Stoltze would point to the various machines and ask me about them. After another hour or so of this tour and questionnaire, Herr Stoltze asked me to come back into the office.

I obeyed him gladly. An hour ago, I had been glad to stretch my legs. Now after roaming around the shop for another hour, I was looking forward to sitting again. Sitting was a precious luxury, I had come to understand. U-boats on the run do not get to sit much. Most of their time is spent wandering the streets on foot. One never feels comfortable sitting for long in public.

"Sit down," he said. I took the chair across from Frau Stoltze's desk. "You seem to be an intelligent young man. I am convinced that you are who you claim to be, a refugee running from the Gestapo. That being the case, I will offer to help you on two conditions. The first is that you do whatever work we request of you, no matter when or what. We need help in our business, so you have come at a good time for both of us. Secondly, while you are here, you are not to talk to anyone other than ourselves and then only when we are alone. No matter who comes in and tries to talk to you, you must pretend to be mute."

I looked at him eagerly, quite happy with the offer he had made me.

"Is this all right with you, Dagobert?" Herr Stoltze asked.

"Yes, yes, it is fine. I am happy to do everything that you say and more than glad to not have to talk to anyone. I think it is a good strategy and I will be a very devoted mute," I said wholeheartedly.

I was happy that this would be a mutually beneficial situation. These people were taking personal risks by having me here. If they needed my help, they would be motivated to protect me. I was constantly nervous about the danger I was in. Good Samaritans or not, I knew that any individual under stress might accidentally slip and cause great harm to me. The more isolated I was, the safer I would be.

Frau Stoltze took me out of the office, through a stockroom, and down some steps into what appeared to be a cellar. "This is where I keep my fruit and vegetable preserves," she said, speaking for only the second time the entire evening. "It is a little cold here but I will bring you lots of blankets, and we will bring down a cot for you to sleep on. You won't be able to leave our shop much, but we will feed you and take care of you in exchange for all of the hard work that I know you will do."

I stood there, grateful and amazed. I would have a place to sleep, with enough blankets. I would have three meals a day! I did not care if I didn't see daylight for weeks on end. I was thrilled and I looked it. Anything above and beyond bare survival was a luxury for me.

I spent the next three months there, quite satisfied to be totally cut off from the outside world. I wrote a letter to the Kusitzkys, explaining that I wouldn't be back for a while and asking them to tell Ilse and Klaus. I missed them and was worried about them, but I was very happy to have a secure place to sleep and eat.

There was always the chance that someone would question me about why I wasn't in the army or ask for my identity papers. But I was totally isolated there, never leaving the shop for any reason.

The Stoltzes were pleasant people to work for. We talked from time to time, mostly about Hitler and the Nazis and about their experiences living as devout Jehovah's Witnesses in the Third Reich. They frequently condemned Hitler and the Nazi party. They thought that Hitler was the great Satan. Of course, they only said this type of thing to me, never in front of anyone else.

Most of our conversation was about the work we were doing. I worked very hard with Herr Stoltze, servicing the cars and trucks. Most of them were civilian, belonging to small businesses.

I spent most of my time doing maintenance work. Installing starters and generators for cars and trucks was a big part of the business.

No one was able to buy new cars, of course, so the starters, like other moving parts, would break from wear.

I saw the clients on a daily basis, but they always talked to Herr Stoltze and he would tell me what to do. Occasionally, I would play the role of a mute. Sometimes the customers would come over to try to talk to me and I would point to my ears and shrug my shoulders, then point to my mouth while I moved my lips. I would not make a sound. They would soon turn away from me to go find Herr Stoltze.

If Stoltze had any friends or family I didn't see them, and they didn't talk about them. If anyone did show up unexpectedly, I would retreat to the basement and hide until they left. They didn't want anyone to know I was there or to ask questions about me, which suited me perfectly. That would have opened the door to trouble for all of us.

The Stoltzes themselves seemed quite content. I never saw or heard them fighting or arguing. They had two or three bibles, one of which they displayed in their small office. I never saw them reading the bibles, but then I didn't socialize with them. They lived in an apartment attached to the store office, and I lived in the basement. I never once went into their private quarters. They never invited me and I never presumed to intrude.

This was strictly a business deal between them and myself, and yet it was more. They had to take a personal interest to risk their lives for me. They hired me and kept me partially because of their need for help, but also because of their convictions.

The end came unexpectedly. One morning, as we were working diligently on cars, I looked up from the inside of the hood of a car and saw a uniformed SS officer walking toward me.

My heart leapt into my throat. *Oh my God*, I said to myself. *This is it. I have been denounced!*

I tried to compose myself as he walked closer to me, his shiny black boots clicking against the bare concrete floor. As he got closer, I could tell from his uniform that he was a high-ranking officer.

He yelled at me, "Herr Stoltze?"

I looked up at him, not saying anything.

"Herr Stoltze!" he demanded.

I took my hand and outstretched it and then pointed to the office window. He immediately grunted something and headed over that way.

I tried to continue to work. My palms were sweating and I was breathing rapidly. *Calm yourself!* I screamed silently. I looked over at the office window every few seconds. I could see Herr Stoltze gesticulating wildly with his hands, moving his head from one side to the other. The SS officer had his hand out, pointing at him, shaking his finger at Herr Stoltze as if he were reprimanding him. Frau Stoltze was standing against a wall, watching what was going on. At one time, she held her hand in front of her mouth as if to gasp, "Oh my God!"

None of this helped me in my efforts to stay calm. I was convinced that this was the end, that I was about to be arrested. I looked around and debated whether to make a run for it. I was greasy and filthy. It would be easy to guess I had just come from working on cars.

To my great relief, the SS officer opened the shop door and strutted toward the street. Then he walked over to a car parked on the street. I could make out that the driver of the car was also in SS uniform. The officer got into the car and they drove off.

A sense of relaxation washed over me. I hadn't been arrested! I felt as if a miracle had occurred. A moment later, the door to the office opened again. It was Herr Stoltze, and he didn't look happy. He walked over to me and I stopped what I was doing—not that I had accomplished much since the SS officer had arrived.

"Dagobert," Stoltze began, "I want you to go and wash up. As soon as you have done that, come into the office. I want to talk to you."

This seemed perplexing. Go and wash up? Stop working early? In the three months I had been there, he had never suggested such a break to me. I had worked twelve hours a day, 7:00 AM to 7:00 PM, every day. Stoltze did too. Here it was, not even lunchtime, and he was telling me to quit. This did not bode well.

I did what I was told and went down to my basement area to wash. I decided not to change my clothes. That had been another nice thing about staying with the Stoltzes. They gave me a new mechanic's uniform to wear every two to three days.

I walked back up the stairs and back into the office. Both Herr and Frau Stoltze were sitting there waiting for me. Herr Stoltze asked me to sit down.

"Dagobert," he began, "it is with regret that I must tell you that your days with us have come to an immediate end. The SS and the Gestapo have requisitioned our business to work exclusively on their cars. Their own facilities were just struck by bombs and have been completely destroyed. Therefore, they are requisitioning several small businesses such as ours to work on their vehicles."

I looked over at Frau Stoltze. She sat there silently, looking straight at her husband and listening.

"In fact," Herr Stoltze continued, "they are going to send over several cars this afternoon. These are cars that have been damaged in the last bombing raid."

I tried to let this sink in.

"Obviously," he said, "it would be a grave mistake to allow you to continue to be here with the SS coming and going constantly. It would be no good for you and certainly no good for us. Therefore, as much as we regret having to do this, we must ask you to change your clothes and leave right away. We have been very pleased to have known you and happy with your work here. But I'm sure you can understand why we have to let you go."

This was terrible news for me. He was right. I knew he was. It would have been insane for me to stay there. I had practically had a heart attack just seeing one SS officer come into the store. It was one thing to play a deaf-mute in front of a normal civilian customer. It would be quite another to have to try to lie to someone in the Gestapo. There was no way I could stay. I started to try to speak but Herr Stoltze continued.

"In appreciation for your faithfulness and all of the work you have done, we want you to have this money," he said as he handed me fifty Reichsmarks.

Money had never been part of our deal. Instead, they had provided me with room and board. I was happy to get the money because it meant that they were satisfied with my work but, on the other hand, it was disappointing to have to leave. Still, it was the only thing that made sense.

He reached out to shake my hand and I returned his grip.

"Thank you," I said, looking at both him and Frau Stoltze. I then walked down to the basement, took off the mechanic's uniform, and put on my old jacket and pants. I also put on the shoes that the Stoltzes had given me. They had steel caps across the tip for safety, as well as steel across the heel for longer wear. My old shoes were worn out, and these made a welcome addition to my small bundle of possessions.

I went back up the stairs and back into the office.

"Dagobert," Herr Stoltze said to me, "I want to give you the name of someone who may also be able to help you. He is also a Jehovah's Witness. He manufactures parts for the armaments industry. His specialty is turning metal and making parts for tanks. I think that your metalworking background might prove useful to him. I have just called him and told him that you are coming to see him. I told him about you and your problem. You can trust him."

This was another unexpected bonus and I thanked both of them sincerely as I walked out the door.

I was outside on the street for the first time in three months. Though it was a bright, clear day, I felt no desire to linger. I immediately headed to the address Stoltze had given me. It was close by, and as I approached the multistory factory building where I had been directed to go, I hoped that, once again, I would find someone who would keep my existence secret.

My benefactor's business was four floors up. As I trudged up the steps, I wondered how he managed to make what must certainly be large, heavy tank parts so far off the ground. Breathing hard, I reached the correct floor and entered the office.

A dirty-looking man approached me.

"Yes? May I help you?" he asked.

"I'm looking for a Herr Klimt," I responded, trying to smile and appear as if I belonged there.

"I'll get him. Wait here," the man responded. He wandered off, presumably to find him.

I looked around. From what I could see, there were a lot of high-speed, precision lathes here, as well as some other metalworking machinery. And in front of me, a short man approached. I guessed him to be about sixty years old. As he drew nearer, I could see a face that was comical with loose wrinkles all over it. A *zerknautscht* face, as they would say in German. It was a face that looked like it had been pushed and squished together. Out of one side of his mouth hung a large, long cigar. It wasn't lit and he seemed to be chomping on it. He wore an old shopcoat with tools bulging from most of the pockets.

"I'm Oskar Klimt," he said in a very low, guttural voice. Between the cigar and the voice, he reminded me of the American gangster movies I had seen when I was younger. If I hadn't been so scared, I probably would have started laughing. *This is quite a character*, I thought to myself.

"Hello," I said, shaking his hand. I was hesitant. I knew that Stoltze had already told him about me, but my habitual tendency to keep my mouth shut made conversation difficult. "Herr Stoltze sent me," I said, trying to be polite.

"Well, don't you have a name?" he scowled, his voice vibrating.

"Uh, yes, well, of course," I began. "Dagobert is my name."

"Didn't you have a father?" Klimt asked, his voice dripping with sarcasm as he smoothed his hair back with dirt-encrusted fingers. "Didn't he give you a last name?"

"Oh, ha ha, yes, of course," I stuttered. "Lewin is my last name."

"Hmm. You Jewish?" he asked.

Apparently, Herr Klimt did not believe in the subtle approach. I reminded myself that this was Stoltze's friend, as I struggled to speak openly. "Yes, um, Herr Klimt. Yes I am."

"*Gut,*" He muttered. Then he bellowed, "I don't care what you are. I want to know what you can do!"

I looked around the shop, evaluating the machinery and types of equipment. "In all modesty, Herr Klimt, I am quite familiar with every machine you have here. I can operate them. I can produce whatever you require."

"Really?" he said, cigar bobbing up and down with every syllable. "But you're just a young *pisher*! Where would you have learned all this?"

"I spent three and a half years in an apprenticeship as a machine builder," I responded. I looked over at him. I now had his complete attention.

"And where might this have taken place?"

"Here in Berlin," I told him. "In Werner Werke."

"OK," he said, seeming satisfied. Without further questioning, he said, "I am a man of few words. Can you start tomorrow?"

"Absolutely yes."

"I pay sixty marks for nine hours of work to start. Depending on how you perform, I may increase your pay after the first month."

"Very well," I answered.

"I have twelve machines, but only one worker other than yourself. I haven't been able to find anyone else. They're all in the army, a population of fools. It is impossible for Germany to win any war against America. I lived there for a while and I know this firsthand. There is no way Germany is going to win against the damn Yankees!"

I nodded, not knowing what else to do. I spoke no English and was totally unfamiliar with some of the phrases he was using. So I just nodded and tried to look as if I understood.

"To hell with them, the German fools," he continued. "I loved living in America. I came back only because my mother was sick. But now she's better—old as a fossil, but healthy. As soon as I'm ready to go back to America, the damn German government decides to start a war. They screwed up all my plans, those sons of bitches!"

I nodded again. I resisted the impulse to ask what "sons of bitches" were or what "screwed up" meant. Although I didn't understand the words, I gathered, by his tone of voice and the furious waving of his arms, that he wasn't being complimentary. But now didn't seem like the time to ask for translations.

He continued, "So I'm just in this to make money. If I'm going to be stuck here with the fools, I might as well get something out of it, something I can take back to America with me when the war is over."

I just nodded, not knowing what else to do.

He babbled on in his low, guttural voice, his cigar bobbing in time to his speech. "I just wish I could hire more people. I'd hire five or six more workers if I could."

I decided I couldn't go wrong by nodding my head and did so enthusiastically.

He changed subjects. "We make semifinished parts for the German armaments industry. Generally, we supply them to other companies who then sell them to the big guys."

I nodded as though it sounded quite interesting. And, in fact, it did.

"The parts are for tanks. German Panthers and Tigers. There is a never-ending demand for them. You're going to work hard," he said, cigar flapping. "And you'd better be efficient. I hate to waste time. 'Time is money.'"

I smiled in agreement, wondering what "time is money" meant.

"That's why I carry all these tools with me. Hate to have to walk to the storeroom to get something I need."

"Great idea," I said, continuing to nod.

He coughed, but didn't take the cigar out of his mouth. "See you tomorrow. See yourself out," he said and then turned around and left.

"See you tomorrow," I called after him. "And thank you!"

I left, puzzled by Klimt's behavior but delighted that I had been hired. Klimt was obviously a risk taker. He could easily be thrown in prison for his remarks about the Third Reich. But I supposed he felt comfortable saying these things to me, a Jew. I could hardly denounce him, even if I had the slightest inclination to do so.

I spent the next few months working for the cigar-chomping, tool-carrying Klimt. The raw materials came to him in long rods of special steel, with metallurgical characteristics specified by his customer, the big weapons producer who built the tanks. Klimt had an automatic sawing machine that would cut the long rods to a rough length. Just cutting the rods was nearly a full-time job. The loading had to be done manually. Once a piece had been cut off, the machine would feed the rod forward, beginning the cutting cycle all over again. After the rods were cut into the short pieces, they had to be stacked on a pallet.

When pieces had been cut, I would put them, one at a time, into the automatic lathe, which would cut the rods along their length, producing different diameters. Klimt needed my expertise because I was able to prepare the cutting tools on each of the machines. I would grind them and then insert them in the tool holders and position them so they'd produce what we needed.

Klimt knew how to do all this. He did the most difficult setting up himself, handling the most critical machines that required superaccuracy and uniformity. He didn't trust anyone else to do it. I never knew what his training was, but he seemed to know all the tricks of the trade.

The other man who worked with us was more of a helper than a trained machinist. He did simple things. He was the one who did most of the initial work, cutting the rods to the correct length. He received the material when it came into the factory and took care of getting the finished parts shipped.

Everything we did had to follow the drawings and fixed measuring gauges Klimt's customer supplied to us. Klimt was always looking over my shoulder, though he knew he didn't have to. I knew what was expected. I wasn't about to mess it up. Not only because I desperately needed this job, but because I was trained in Germany. I was a German. Germans didn't make many mistakes. If they did, they were made to suffer.

The great thing about this job was that it gave me a way to get off the streets. We worked seven days a week, twelve hours a day, which was fine with me. At night, I rotated between Richter's place, bombed buildings, and occasionally, the Kusitzkys'. It was hard to commute from Lübars and I rarely went back.

One day, Klimt announced that he would be going home to visit his mother. I decided, since I had this break, that I would go visit Ilse. From what I heard from Anni Kusitzky, she seemed to be doing well at her housekeeping job. It gave her food and a roof over her head. An added benefit was that she could be close to Klaus, close enough to visit him.

Two days later, I returned to Klimt's factory. The Allied bombing raids were getting especially fierce. There were many days when we arrived at the factory, all of us tired to the bone from lack of sleep. The noise and destructive power of the bombs were horrendous and it was impossible not to be affected by them.

One day, after an especially horrible air raid, I arrived at Klimt's factory as usual. He was there, for the first time minus the cigar. He was as white as a sheet. "Dagobert," he began, "I'm done."

I looked at him perplexed. "What?" I asked.

"Done. Done, I say. Damn war. Damn raids. I can't take it anymore. I've made a ton of money already. I don't need anymore. What's it worth if they're going to kill you with bombs before you can enjoy it?"

"I'm sorry?" I asked, not understanding him.

"I'm finished, Dagobert. Sorry, buddy. Damn fools are going to get me killed. So much bombing. Just isn't worth it. I'll just have to live with what I've got."

I just continued to stare at him, perplexed. What was his point?

"So, here's a bit of extra cash, young Herr Lewin. Good luck to you."

He held out an envelope to me. I took it, dumbfounded. "Herr Klimt, you mean you're firing me?"

Klimt begins to howl, his belly shaking with laughter. "That's good. I am firing myself too!"

It didn't seem funny at all to me. "You mean you're closing your business?"

He continued to laugh, sticking the half-chewed cigar back in his mouth. "I'm going home to Mama," he said.

I probably didn't want to hear what he was saying, because it didn't sink into my anguished, shell-shocked brain very quickly. "You're leaving Berlin?" I asked him.

"Yup," he grinned. "Going to become a country boy. Get away from this hellhole. Commune with Mama and the birds and the bees. Then hopefully I'll survive this war and move back to America."

He rose and stretched out his hand in my direction. I looked at it and did what I thought he expected. I shook it.

He grinned and laughed and then pounded me on the back in what he must have thought was a friendly gesture. "Look me up in Philly after this thing blows over," he said, and then led me out the door.

He closed it, and I turned around and stared at the spot on the floor where he had been. "Philly?" I mumbled to myself. What was he talking about?

My job and more importantly, my cover, had vanished in the blink of an eye. I turned around and climbed down the four flights of stairs, utterly downcast. Once again, the vagaries of war had cast me out into the streets, to seek shelter yet again in a city filled with enemies.

17

D-DAY

Feeling the need for counsel, I returned to Paul Richter's apartment. I went over everything that had happened with Herr Klimt and asked for his advice. Richter was not shy in giving it. I sometimes forgot that he was a hard-core Communist ideologue. He could be ferocious when the mood struck him.

"Money!" Richter screamed. "That's what this war is about for Klimt. Money! Damn the workers! Damn the Jews!"

Richter had been a member of the Communist Party even before Hitler's rise to power. Had he not been blind there is no doubt that he would have been in a leadership position. After Hitler became chancellor, the Communist Party was outlawed and had no choice but to go underground, all their activities continuing clandestinely. In our discussions, Richter would seldom talk about the innermost workings of the party or his contacts in it. When he did, I was fascinated.

He told me about a young Jewish man named Wolfgang Pander who, along with several other Communist activists, produced and distributed leaflets calling on the German people to commit acts of sabotage and to overthrow Hitler's regime. This appeal was particularly directed at workers in the armament factories. The leaflets stressed the hopelessness of continuing the war. Pander and his friends were eventually discovered by the Gestapo. They were arrested, sentenced to death, and executed in December 1942 at the Plötzensee prison in Berlin (where thousands of so-called enemies of the Reich were executed by guillotine and hanging, often six at a time).

Richter was a furious foe of Hitler and the Nazis. He looked forward to the day when they would be conquered by the Allies. "Without the Soviet Union," he was fond of saying, "even mighty America can't defeat Germany. The Soviet Union is going to be the defining factor in this war. With Russia on their side, the Allies will win. And then, at the conclusion of the war, the Soviet Union will dominate. They will lead the world."

Richter constantly preached against the corruption and greed of the system. I asked him once if he wanted to go to the Soviet Union to be with his comrades, as he called them.

"Bah!" he'd yelled as he rose to leave the room. "I'm blind, haven't you noticed? Too hard to move around! We'll just have to have a revolution here."

Plötzensee execution room. Shown here are five hooks, used for the summary killing of prisoners. A guillotine (not shown) was also used. As many as eight prisoners could be executed simultaneously.

An hour or so later, Richter reappeared in the living room and made an announcement. "We're going to the summer house the day after tomorrow. Get ready."

I looked up at him and smiled, though he couldn't see it. "Great," I said. Somewhere far away from the Wehrmacht.

I left that evening to go to the Kusitzkys, arriving after dark and leaving before dawn. I told them all that I was going to be gone for a few weeks and not to worry. I asked them to please let Ilse know. She was still at her housekeeping job, happy to at least be near Klaus. And so Richter, Regina, the dog, and I set out for the country house.

I was looking forward to being out of Berlin, away from the bombings and the chaos. On the train, I found myself thinking of Klimt. Regardless of what Richter said, I understood what he was talking about, why he had simply had enough. It was 1944. City life had become progressively more and more terrifying. The city was bombed nearly every day or night and sometimes both. Fear, fires, and sleeplessness dominated our lives.

During the times when I was roaming Berlin and the air raid sirens sounded, I would try to hide in the air raid shelter of the nearest building. But this was a dangerous strategy. Though it would get me out of harm's way, it also exposed me to questioning. At that time, every building had its own air raid warden whose job it was to organize the residents. The warden made sure that everyone in the building went into the basement. He kept the peace during raids, preventing fistfights that would break out because of accumulated tensions.

The air warden also had to make sure there were adequate supplies: food, first aid, cots, chairs, shovels for emergency evacuation. There had to be rope, flashlights, candles, matches, sand to put out fires that might start, blankets, water, gas masks, and innumerable other items vital for survival during a raid.

The air warden was usually familiar with the residents of a building. When one would notice me and fail to recognize me, he would become inquisitive. "Who are you?" he'd want to know. "Where do you live? Why aren't you in uniform?"

These situations put me on the spot and I would have to come up with a plausible story. Usually, I would tell them that I was visiting in the area and had not had a chance to reach my own designated shelter.

Sometimes this worked, and sometimes not. If I was unlucky, the warden would threaten to talk to the police about me at the first opportunity. As soon as the raid was over, I'd be the first one out, running. There was at least one time when I had to make a run for it while the bombs were still falling.

The warden was by no means the only danger during bombing raids. Even though the shelter might protect one from flak fragments, if a bomb hit your building, everyone in the shelter was usually killed or badly injured. The bombs always fell at an angle, which meant that they could hit any part of a building. Depending on how the rubble fell and which part of a building was hit, people could die from being crushed by falling debris or from asphyxiation.

More than once, I was in a building that was hit. On one occasion, the top part of the building was sheared off by a bomb. Most of the building disintegrated, but the basement where the air raid shelter was located did not suffer any serious damage. We walked out of the basement unharmed. Once out, we saw that the top of the building was completely gone. No one realized the severity of the damage until we were outside. On another occasion, a bomb hit only one side of the building I was in. That side was almost completely destroyed, but again, I walked away unharmed.

Because of the ever-present possibility of being questioned by the warden or by others in the shelter, I eventually decided to seek shelter elsewhere during the raids. When the sirens went off, I would try to find an unoccupied building. Otherwise, I would look for a building already in ruins that had nooks and crannies where I could hide.

There were also times when I was unable to find shelter in time. On those occasions, the biggest danger was the antiaircraft flak. The bombs themselves caused massive amounts of destruction, but each bomb fell in only one place. The flak munitions, shot from antiaircraft cannons all around the city, would explode in midair into many fragments, some a foot long. These would rain down on anyone and anything below, often injuring large numbers. I saw many people who were severely cut up by these fragments. Death from a bomb would at least be quick. If I were injured by flak, death could be a long time in coming. Even worse, I could be knocked out and taken to a hospital, where the Gestapo would almost certainly discover who I was.

If a Berliner happened to be away from home when the air raid sirens went off, they would seek what shelter they could find. Many sought refuge in U-Bahn (subway) stations, because they were underground. I had once been present near an entrance to a U-Bahn when the sirens went off. Hundreds of people, panic-stricken, rushed to the entrances and to the steps leading down to the underground track level, myself among them. There were older men, women, and children. Many fell and were trampled by others on the way down. It was a horrible sight. I managed to get down the steps into the subway station without falling.

Once the bombers had left the area, an even-toned "all clear" siren would sound, allowing us to leave our shelters. On rare occasions, though, the "all clear" would sound prematurely, as bombs were still falling.

Now, as I sat on the train next to Richter, I realized it was a miracle I hadn't already been killed by flak fragments or bombs. Eventually, the train reached at our destination and Richter, Regina, and I made our way to his country house. I was relieved to be there. I recognized early on that traveling in this party was not exactly a way to stay inconspicuous. Two blind adults, led by a huge dog, could hardly fail to attract attention wherever they went. It was good to be done with the trip and to hole up for a while in the country.

These occasional breaks helped keep me sane. I knew that I was not the same person I had been on that day my parents had been taken from me. I had become hardened to the war's tragedies. I was filled with rage at the injustice done me and my fellow Jews and this anger protected me. I never thought that I just couldn't take it anymore, that I should turn myself in or commit suicide. Some U-boats did. Many became depressed and gave up the willingness to fight. Once that was lost, it was all over. Some turned themselves in, to the Gestapo. Others took their own lives.

We spent our days at the summer house much as we had done the year before. Richter and Regina read their Braille books much of the time. I read others, sometimes out loud to them, and made repairs around the house. We stayed for a few weeks and then returned to Berlin and their apartment.

During the day, my life in the city continued much as it had in the country. I cleaned. I fixed things. I read to them. The only difference was that in the city I didn't stay with them for more than a few nights at a time.

In the evening, Richter would take out a small radio he kept hidden and we would listen to the German language broadcast of the BBC or to Radio Moscow. This was a strictly illegal activity but one that thrilled me to no end. I loved listening to the British account of the war. Many times they would talk in riddles. We supposed that this was a method of passing signals to undercover agents or resistance fighters.

Most of the time, we listened to the BBC's German service. The BBC broadcast in several languages. The announcers would talk about the defeats the Germans had suffered. They would tell us how the Americans had landed in North Africa. They would talk about the fighting there, about how Montgomery had defeated Rommel.

On June 6, 1944, Richter, Regina, and I ate dinner. We had dark sawdust bread, pieces of salami, and some margarine, all from Richter and Regina's ration cards. They were allowed a bit more than normal Germans because they were blind and they generously shared their food with me, even though rations were being reduced as the war dragged on.

All of a sudden Richter, Regina, and I heard the clock strike nine. It rang out every hour and every half hour. "Oh!" Richter announced excitedly. "Time for the BBC News!"

We all jumped up. Richter ran to turn on the radio. Regina started to pick up the dishes and clear the table. "Don't worry about it, Regina. I will do it," I said. I proceeded to take them to the kitchen and placed them in the sink. *I'd get to them later*, I thought to myself. I could hear the jingle signaling that the BBC radio was about to come on! I ran into the living room and sat down on the sofa next to Paul and the radio.

"This is the BBC Radio Network," the voice crackled in German. "Early this morning, at first daybreak, Allied troops began the greatest and most massive invasion. . . ."

I jumped to my feet. Paul and I cheered together. "Finally, the time has come!" he yelled.

The announcer told of the beginning of the invasion at Normandy. We listened raptly for the next hour of continuing news and comments from the BBC. Paul and I sat on the edge of our seats. Regina, as usual, sat quietly. She never seemed to get excited about anything. When it was finished, Paul announced, "This is the news we've been waiting for. We can lie down to sleep, with the certainty of knowing that the days of the Nazi regime are numbered!" I did the dishes with a grin on my face, feeling like my ancestors must have felt when they learned that Pharaoh was setting them free. I went to my little room in the apartment. It had a tiny bed and virtually nothing else, but I was too excited to sleep much. The news had given me a great boost in morale. Perhaps our suffering would soon be at an end.

The bombings of Berlin continued. The Allies obviously had enough soldiers and equipment to both invade by ground and to bomb Germany by air. Berlin changed to meet the threat of the bombings. The street curbs were painted with fluorescent paint (phosphorous). Car and bus headlights were painted black except for a small slit that would allow just enough light for the driver to see where he was going.

Bombardment of Berlin continued virtually every day, carried out by flights of several hundred bombers at a time. Most of the night missions were carried out by the British, with day raids assigned to the Americans. Whole city blocks were destroyed by heavy bombs containing large amounts of high explosives. Fires were started by small, hexagon-shaped phosphorous bombs, which rained down by the thousands. What the heavy bombs did not destroy, the phosphorous bombs burned. Untold numbers of people died from the resulting flames or under collapsing buildings. Smoke and confusion were everywhere and fire departments were helpless, overwhelmed by the sheer volume of damage. Within a matter of minutes, thousands could be and were made homeless.

The British and Americans kept the air raids over Berlin purposely erratic, some days skipping raids altogether, some days bombing both day and night, and some days with anything in between. This served to keep the Berlin population in a very high state of anxiety. These raids were not only conducted to cause the maximum damage; the Allies also wanted to demoralize the German people. And it worked. People would cry out that they were going crazy, that they didn't know how much more they could stand. It was also difficult for me, but with every bombing attack, the Allies were one step closer to defeating my enemy.

On occasion, the Allied bombers dropped other types of payloads. Sometimes they dropped large quantities of aluminum foil strips called chaff, to confuse the German antiaircraft artillery. Sometimes the bombers dropped propaganda leaflets. Germans were strictly forbidden to read enemy literature. The penalty could be imprisonment, or even execution, if you were found in possession of these leaflets.

On March 6, 1944, during the biggest daylight air raid ever by US bombers and fighter planes, propaganda leaflets were dropped and I picked one up. It was written in German and titled "Stalingrad No. 2." It said,

> You can thank the Führer
> for the defeat of the German army
> at Stalingrad a year ago.
> 100,000 German soldiers were killed or captured.

It also went on to mention other military disasters and stressed that the war was a lost cause for Germany.

Ignoring the risks, I immediately took the leaflet to Paul Richter. When I read it to him, he said, "See, I told you the Soviet Union is the most important of the Allies. Even the Americans think so. Why else would they tell the Germans about the Russian successes on their front?"

Sometimes the Americans paid dearly for their bombing raids. Planes were shot down by German fighter planes or damaged by flak shrapnel. One day after an attack, I emerged from an underground subway station and walked onto the street. There I saw an American in a pilot's uniform lying in the middle of the road. Several women were standing next to him, kicking him every so often and spitting on him, shouting insults and curses. As I came still closer, I saw that the corpse had been beheaded. Whether this happened as a result of the pilot ejecting, or whether it was done by Nazis, I never learned.

Another time, after the all clear had sounded, I ventured out into the street. A few blocks away, I saw an American plane, obviously shot down by flak or a German fighter plane. Parts of the plane were scattered all around. Smoke was rising from the smashed wreckage. Three crew members had been thrown from the plane and were lying in the dirt, their bodies twisted into bizarre positions. All three were obviously dead. Several people were standing around the plane, staring at the bodies as if the crew members were aliens from another world. The onlookers were yelling, "We hope there will be many more dead American bastards, just like them!" "They deserved to die!" "Death to them all!" and other derogatory outcries. A feeling of disgust and revulsion came over me. I had to turn away from the Germans. I couldn't stand their outpourings of hate.

It was soon after this that the irrepressible Günther Gerson made an appearance.

His relationship with the Stindts was now drawing unwanted attention. The Gestapo had become more suspicious than ever, even of their own people. There had been a failed attempt on Hitler's life by a consortium of generals and other highly placed officials. The would-be assassin was Colonel von Stauffenberg, a highly decorated veteran of the war. He was greatly respected throughout the Wehrmacht, but unfortunately, this did not help him when his assassination attempt failed.

As a result of this assassination attempt, Günther thought it wise to limit his time with the Stindt family. He would wait a number of weeks before contacting them again. These were the times when he would usually seek me out, setting up a meeting through the post office. We used the system I had been taught by Dr. Finger. One person would write the other via general delivery at the post office. On the postcard, a meeting would be requested for a certain day and a certain time, always in code.

I received the card from him and met him as he had proposed, at the Alexanderplatz. Because he was staying away from the Stindt family, Günther had been reduced to the same status as most other Germans, meaning he had to get by on the less than adequate rations allowed by the government. While bemoaning the sad state of our stomachs, Günther, as usual, came up with a plan.

Because such a large number of Berlin citizens were being bombed out of their residences, the government was offering assistance in the form of ration cards. They also gave out temporary IDs, ration cards for clothing, and sometimes a small amount of cash. Günther proposed that we join the ranks of the newly homeless, standing in line to apply for these benefits.

The plan sounded good to me. Risky, but doable. And so we put it into action. We would find a location where people were standing in lines to apply for government relief, pretend we lived in the area, and request benefits.

The plan worked flawlessly, or so it seemed. It worked so well that we began repeating it on a regular basis, moving around town, pretending to be refugees and standing in line for government handouts. Each success made us bolder, more confident. And I have to admit that I enjoyed putting one over on the Nazis.

It was also very risky. In order to get anything from the officials, you had to make a statement of where you lived. You had to give the street name, the house number, which apartment, what your name was, and various other information. Naturally, all the information we gave was fictitious.

The saving grace in all of this was that when bombs hit an area, more than one apartment building was usually destroyed. Most of the relief lines were made up of residents of different buildings, and the chances of being picked out as a fraud were small.

Unfortunately, this numbers game eventually caught up with us. One day we were in a relief line talking to the official about our misfortune. The people behind us heard us claim that we lived in a certain building and immediately protested that we were lying, that we were strangers who in no case lived in their building.

We tried our best to wiggle our way out of the situation, but we were well and truly caught. We were arrested and taken to the police district office. Günther tried to bluff it out, saying that we were undercover agents for the Waffen SS and that we were not allowed to reveal any details of our identity, but the captain wasn't buying it. Luckily for us, there was a bureaucratic mix-up having to do with who was in authority in that particular region, which made it difficult for the captain to act. Then there was another bombing raid and the captain told us that he didn't have time to deal with us and to get out.

Good fortune had saved us from disaster. My days as an impersonator had come to an end.

18

CAR THIEVES

As THE WAR CONTINUED, life in Berlin became ever more difficult to endure. By 1944, it had become clear that the Luftwaffe was not going to be able to effectively protect Berlin, especially since the Allies had added fighter escorts to protect their bombers. The Allied strategy of making the war unendurable for the ordinary citizen was working well.

In fact, it worked so well that some people became desperate to leave, and Günther was one of them. In our next meeting after the public relief fiasco, Günther told me that he wanted to escape to Switzerland.

After the initial surprise wore off, I listened to what he had to say. His plan dictated that we steal a car, buy appropriate IDs on the black market, and simply drive to Switzerland. I was also finding Berlin to be an increasingly difficult place to survive and after a little thought, I agreed with his plan.

A few days later, we positioned ourselves near the entrance to the Anhalter Bahnhof station, where we had a commanding view of the parking lot. There were crowds of people entering and leaving the station, most of them SA (brown shirts), SS, and a sprinkling of civilians. All arrived in their automobiles and parked in the lot.

As we watched, we saw one man, clad in a black leather coat and a soft brimmed hat, rush into the station, leaving his car unlocked. By his dress, the man was almost certainly Gestapo and probably assumed that no one would dare steal his car. It was an assumption that he would be forced to reevaluate when he returned to the parking lot and found his space empty. Günther hot-wired the car and we drove off.

We now had a car but little in the way of fuel. Gasoline was very difficult to get because it was an absolute top priority for the military. Much of Hitler's success was based on the ability of his tanks to move quickly. The Reich was having a great deal of difficulty supplying the tanks with enough gas to keep going, and without ration cards, gasoline was next to impossible to obtain.

After a few minutes of driving, Günther pulled into another parking lot, driving up next to another car that was parked behind some trees. From his jacket pocket, Günther removed a hose. He quickly got out of the car, looked around to make sure no one could see him, and stuck the hose into the gas tank of the parked car. He bent down and started sucking the end of the hose as if it were a straw. After siphoning off some gas, he jumped back in and we rapidly departed the area. We planned on repeating this performance all the way to Switzerland.

We headed for Lübars, to show the car to Anni and explain our plan to Ilse. We also had discovered a case of pistols in the trunk of the car and we wanted to hide them there. Ilse was less than pleased with our plan, thinking that we would certainly be caught. She became extremely upset, but as it turned out, she had nothing to worry about.

Günther and I returned to Berlin and went our separate ways. We were to meet in several days to leave for Switzerland. By that time, Günther would have the appropriate IDs for us as well as tags for the car, road maps, etc.

As fate would have it, the British chose one of the next few nights to conduct the largest air raid ever made on Berlin. They chained several of their largest bombs together, which exploded with devastating impact. Many of these chained bombs were dropped on Berlin and in nearly every case, they destroyed an entire city block.

While waiting for our day of departure, I had been spending as much time as possible riding back and forth on the subway. This not only helped me to avoid Gestapo, it also afforded some measure of protection from the bombing raids. It was much safer than walking around aboveground, and I was joined on my rides by other Berliners who felt the same way.

The problem with being underground was that when the bombs dropped anywhere near the subway line, sound and pressure waves traveled along the underground tunnels, dimming the lights and causing the ground to shake and the cars to sway violently. We worried that the bombs would penetrate the ground above the tunnels and cause the subway cars to crash. From among quite a few dangerous situations, this was the most terrifying experience I had yet endured.

During this bombing raid, the electric power in large sections of Berlin was interrupted and the car I was riding in must have been in one of these sections, because power failed and the lights went out. After more than two hours of sitting in total darkness, the conductor informed us that there would be no power for an indefinite period, perhaps days. He offered to walk us along the tracks to the nearest subway station. Most of the passengers, including myself, took him up on his offer. Sitting in the dark was demoralizing, and because power had been cut to the ventilation system, the air was becoming stale and foul-smelling.

We finally arrived at the next station and walked up the stairs to the street. As we went through the exit, we were greeted by a scene out of Dante's *Inferno*. As far as the eye could see there was nothing but chaos and ruin. Fires engulfed the wreckage of entire city blocks. Six- and seven-story buildings had been pounded until there was nothing left but huge piles of debris.

People ran about, some carrying the wounded, some simply overwhelmed by confusion. Many of the victims were buried alive in the cellars of collapsed buildings. Ambulances and fire engines, lights flashing and horns blaring, mixed with the screams of the wounded, adding to the turmoil. Unexploded phosphorous bombs had penetrated the asphalt in the streets and stood upright, looking like plants in some horrid garden of desolation. Thousands of these had been dropped from Allied planes.

It seemed that, once again, chance had favored me when it really mattered. My life had been preserved where others had died.

Another piece of good fortune was the raid itself. Although the raid and the resulting chaos was a disaster for most, it was, in a certain sense, a godsend for me. The large number of bombed-out buildings gave me a huge new selection of hiding places. I much preferred to sleep in a warm bed like everyone else, but if need be, I was now skilled at surviving in the ruins of former apartments.

All this is not to imply that I should have changed my name to Lucky Lewin. I got my own share of bad news the next day. Günther and I had chosen this day to meet, with the intention of wrapping up our affairs and departing for Switzerland. By the time I reached our meeting place at the Alexanderplatz, I was almost dancing in excitement. At last, an end to the fear, the hiding, and the never-ending struggle to survive!

I saw Günther at the other end of the square and rushed to meet him. As I approached, I noticed that he looked depressed and before I could even open my mouth, he fairly screamed at me, "Dagobert, you're not going to like this! I hid our car between two tall buildings downtown, where I thought it most likely to be hidden from sight. This morning, I went to retrieve it. Both of the buildings were hit in the raid, and they collapsed on our car!"

My heart sunk as I worked out the ramifications. Just to make sure, I asked him, "Was it badly damaged?"

"Damaged? Dagobert, it was completely demolished! There is no more car!"

We briefly discussed stealing another one but abandoned the idea. Security, in the aftermath of the air raid, was bound to be much tighter. There would be too much concern with spies and saboteurs. My dream of a new life in Switzerland had vanished like smoke in the wind.

The disappointment of not being able to leave Berlin hit me hard. I was on the edge of giving up, of wanting to bury myself in a hole somewhere and never come out. I had come so close to leaving the nightmare that Nazi Germany had become behind me forever, only to find success snatched from my grasp at the last instant. All of the pain and horror that I had experienced in the last couple of years came rushing back, as if something had battered down a door I had constructed in my mind, a door that had been locked and double-bolted to protect me from experiences too painful to bear.

Trying desperately to pull myself together, I walked slowly up the garden path to the Kusitzky house. Ilse was there. She looked at my face and knew immediately that something was very wrong. I told her what had happened to our plans for Switzerland and then collapsed on the bed.

The next morning, I arose and greeted Anni, as usual. I said nothing of the day before. Anni put me to work repairing a cabinet door. Around noon, the air raid sirens went off, warning us of the imminent arrival of American warplanes.

"Dago! Come on! We have to get into the cellar!" Anni yelled. I called Ilse and Klaus to come and climbed down the rickety ladder. The cellar had been prepared for this situation in advance. Alex had stocked it with candles, matches, a water tank, and a quantity of canned goods. There were cots, chairs, and a table.

Ilse and Klaus finally arrived and we sat on the chairs and listened to the bombs exploding in the distance. Without warning, there was a sudden whistling sound, followed by a tremendous concussion that literally shook the walls of the house. Ilse screamed. I was sure that the end had come. The explosion knocked us off our chairs and onto the floor.

"Oh my God!" Anni screamed, over and over again. Klaus was screaming in fright as the lights went out. I sat there quietly, trying to brace myself.

After a moment or two, all was still. We managed to get up and crawl out of the cellar, into the open air. There was a tremendous cloud of dust hanging over the garden, accompanied by a disgusting odor.

"Have you ever smelled anything like this before?" Anni asked.

"No, never."

Once the sirens sounded, we walked around in the garden. There, in the front yard, the source of the dust cloud and the foul odor was revealed. A tremendous crater had been blasted into the soil of the garden. It was about ten feet deep and forty feet in diameter.

"My God! We've been hit!" Anni cried. "I can't believe it!"

"We are lucky to be alive," Ilse said, trying to calm Anni down. She was despondent over the destruction of her property.

"Anni, look at how lucky we are," I interjected. "I think that the house, though damaged, was saved from more destruction by slope of the ground in your garden. "

Anni didn't seem to be listening to me. She dropped to her knees and said, "Thank God, *Danke Gott*, I thank you for preserving our lives."

When Alex came home a few hours later, he said to both Anni and myself, "Just think if the bombs had fallen a few feet more to one side or the other, you could have been dead and the house would have been utterly destroyed. That is something we can all be thankful for." He then clasped his hands together in prayer.

As was so typical of Alex, he got up and immediately went to work repairing the damage that had been done to the house, starting with the roof shingles that had been blown off. The front windows had all been shattered and I began cleaning up the broken glass, boarding up the windows with heavy cardboard.

The next day, Alex began to inquire where he could find glass and shingles to make the necessary repairs. He also enlisted some of his coworkers from the meat plant to help him. It would take weeks to fill in most of the bomb crater with soil Alex would eventually obtain from a nearby property.

I spent the next few days at the Kusitzkys, helping with the repairs. Alex told me how he had built the house himself, brick by brick. The only help he had was from his father, who was a partial invalid and rather old.

That night, whether by coincidence or because he had heard about the bomb damage, Heinz showed up. Heinz was Alex and Anni's son. He had classic Aryan looks, with blond hair, a stocky build, and even less to say than his father. He wore a regular Wehrmacht uniform, seemingly with pride, though his father didn't appear to share in it.

Heinz was a constant disappointment to his parents. While Alex and Anni were extremely hard workers and as independent as possible, Heinz tended to be lazy, satisfied with the most menial positions. He was enlisted in the Wehrmacht but worked at an inconsequential job in the kitchen or served as a barracks cleaner. The Kusitzkys would complain about him frequently, and I was sure that Heinz's behavior had been a lifelong problem. They would occasionally make comments like, "Why can't Heinz be more like you? Why can't he have your initiative?" While this was flattering, it created an uncomfortable situation and potentially a dangerous one. All it would take to have me arrested would be for Heinz to say the wrong thing to the wrong person.

The next morning, I decided it was time I left. Without his specifically saying anything, I got the feeling that Alex was uncomfortable with me being around at the same time as Heinz. Before dawn, I left my customary good-bye note and departed for Berlin.

19

PIGEON FOOD

BERLIN WAS BECOMING MORE DESOLATE EVERY DAY. The city was a decaying carcass, like a child's model that was disintegrating from lack of care. Rubble from destroyed buildings was everywhere. The army patrols, called Feldgendarmerie, increased in frequency as the number of deserters from the Wehrmacht increased. They always traveled in pairs, patrolling the streets, trains, subways, and other public places. I was too obvious a target to feel comfortable roaming around in public places. Aside from the fact that I was Jewish, I was a young, apparently healthy man who, had I been an Aryan, should definitely have been in the Wehrmacht.

For a while, I simply avoided the Feldgendarmerie. They were easy to spot: always in uniform, with metal breastplates on a chain around their neck. I would dart away whenever I saw them. For a time, this strategy kept the dogs at bay. But the first time I was almost caught by a patrol, my enthusiasm for this aimless wandering diminished rapidly.

I had just turned the corner on a busy intersection when I noticed a pair of Feldgendarmerie. One of them was looking directly at me. He turned to his partner and said something, then pointed straight at me. I knew that I had only seconds until they approached me and demanded my papers. At the same moment, a streetcar pulled up in front of me, hiding me from view. I stepped into the car just as it departed, leaving the patrol behind. I took a deep breath and let the air escape slowly.

I needed a basic change in tactics. After mulling over the possibilities, I decided that I would leave Berlin for good. I knew that the end was fast approaching for Hitler, but the long chase was wearing badly on my nerves. I read discarded newspapers left on the S-Bahn and kept my ears open for hints of how the war was really progressing. Goebbels was a master of propaganda, but even he could not completely quash the truth of Nazi military disasters. Soldiers would come back from the front, badly cut up and complaining bitterly about needless defeats. Rations of basic staples were being decreased, which meant that the ability of the Reich to produce war material was also decreasing. The public knew that things did not look good.

Even though the tide of the war was turning, I knew that it was just a matter of time until I was captured. With the number of patrols increasing, one mistake was all it would take, and it was inevitable that I would make it. I could not continue this way. The price of failure would be my life, a price I considered to be exorbitantly expensive and one I did not care to pay. I had to get out of Berlin.

Without money or proper papers, moving to another city would have been almost impossible. I decided to try my luck at living in the forest surrounding Berlin. I knew it would be hard, as I was woefully underequipped for any type of outdoor living. I had a blanket, a pocket-knife, a hat, the same jacket I had worn throughout the war, and a few other basic necessities.

In addition, I had a small supply of food in my rucksack, courtesy of the Kusitzkys, just enough to sustain me for one day. After that, I hoped to walk into the nearby town and buy more food, but it developed that the small stores refused to sell to me, saying that they did not have enough for their own local customers. I was told the same thing by other stores in town. It was now apparent that obtaining food was going to be a major problem. But since the alternative seemed to be inevitable capture, the choice was not hard to make. At least I wouldn't have to worry about the Gestapo or the bombs.

I wanted to find a little meadow where there wasn't a lot of under-brush or sticks and stones but that was still hidden from casual view. I found a spot where the grass wasn't too high yet. It seemed suitable, so

I laid down the blanket and wrapped myself up in it and tried to sleep. The next day, I walked to the edge of the woods to explore some more. I knew my biggest problem would be food. I had no experience with hunting, and even if I had the requisite knowledge, I had no equipment.

As the days wore on, I became hungrier and hungrier. I had existed on reduced rations for much of the war, but this was something completely different. I was slowly starving to death. I was amazed at how overwhelming the desire to eat had become, as if every cell in my body was literally screaming to be fed. It had now been days since I had last eaten. I found myself experiencing an excruciating need to chew. Desperate and with a vast sense of disgust, I took my leather belt and gnawed on it, swallowing the saliva. I chewed on the leather tongue of my shoe in a pathetic attempt to ease the hunger pangs.

I found some berries growing wild, but I had no idea whether they were poisonous. I couldn't take the chance, so I limited myself to chewing the leaves. I had been able to drink a bit from little brooks, cupping the brackish water in my hands. In the early morning, I'd lick leaves from the surrounding bushes, lapping off the dew. But that was far from being enough. I had to do whatever it took to get something to eat.

As I searched the area, I looked for unoccupied houses. There were all kinds of situations that prompted people to leave their dwellings. Some left because they were afraid of the bombs and wanted to move away from the city and its environs. Others left because they thought they would have access to more food in the country. Still others left their houses because their men were in the army and the family preferred to stay with relatives elsewhere.

Although the thought of sleeping in a warm bed was inviting, my goal in finding an abandoned house was the hope that someone had left some food behind. The prospect of finding canned goods, abandoned because of their weight, or some fall or winter vegetables abandoned in a garden was tantalizing.

I succeeded in locating a house that was obviously unoccupied. My hunger easily overcame any sense of propriety I had left. I broke in by smashing one of the glass panes in the back door. To my vast disappointment, the house was utterly barren. It had been completely stripped of food, furniture, blankets, candles; in short, anything that I might have found useful. Not wanting to risk the sudden return of the rightful owners, I left to sleep in the woods again.

The next morning, I got up, willing myself to continue my search for food. My legs worked, but my equilibrium was off. I was fast losing strength and was becoming slightly delirious. I came across another house that seemed to be empty. Along the back of the house, an outdoor verandah was attached to the upper floor. Stairs ran from the verandah to the backyard below. Most important, I could see pigeons flying onto the verandah and staying there for a while, apparently to feed.

I decided that if there was something there that the birds could eat, seeds or nuts perhaps, then I could eat it too. After watching for a bit to make sure no one was at home, I walked to the back of the building and climbed the outside stairs to the verandah.

Once up there, I saw that the pigeons were eating something that had blown off of the trees and onto the verandah. Whatever it was, it was too small to be a viable source of food for me. Even the pigeons looked as if they were working hard to find anything edible. Though my plan to share a food source with the pigeons had failed, I had another thought. If I couldn't eat what the pigeons were eating, why not just eat the pigeons themselves?

It struck me that it might be possible to catch a pigeon or two. I tried to run after them and catch a few with my hands, but they were much too fast. They would allow me to approach only so close, then they would fly away. I racked my brains for some method of capturing or killing them. I briefly considered trying to make a bow, or fashion some sort of spear with my knife as a spearhead, but quickly abandoned both ideas as impractical.

Then I had another idea. One of my few possessions was a blanket. It was made out of a rough gray wool and looked like a horse blanket, but it kept me from freezing during the night. It was possible that I could throw it on top of the birds, trapping them as if with a net.

I searched the grounds for something that could be used as bait. After looking around for some time, I came across a patch of ground that had some type of seeds lying on top of it. Hoping that they would attract the pigeons, I gathered as many as I could and put them in my pocket.

If I could get the pigeons accustomed to coming close to me, I could catch them. I tossed a few of the seeds out among the pigeons, which they immediately consumed. Then I withdrew a few steps, throwing a few more seeds in a trail leading straight to me.

I sat waiting for them. They dutifully ate the seeds, then advanced forward for the next bite, coming ever closer. I threw my blanket, catching two of them underneath. I twisted the blanket into a bag and threw it over my shoulder with the pigeons still trapped inside. Exultant, I walked down the steps with the bag in tow and headed back into the woods.

Once I was far enough away to be hidden from view, I killed one of the birds and built a fire. Using a sharpened branch as a spit, I held it over the fire until it seemed roasted enough to be edible. Unable to wait one second longer, I took the bird out of the fire and started to eat. I tried to eat slowly, but after starving for so long it was almost impossible. I had never tasted anything even vaguely as satisfying. I ate virtually every last morsel of the first bird, burned parts and all.

I held on to the second pigeon. I didn't pluck the feathers but instead dug a little hole in the ground and buried it. I hoped this would prevent some other animal from eating it. It would be cool there. I could come back the next day and cook it.

I soon repeated my hunting expedition, overjoyed at having found a source of food. I used the same method and soon returned to the woods with my second round of birds. I had a few branches for firewood but some of the larger ones would need to be split to be small enough to burn.

Using my knife as a wedge, I pressed it into one end of the branch. I tapped the other end against a rock, which forced the blade to split the branch lengthwise. Some branches required a lot of force to make them split, but this piece must have been softer wood than I had used before. After just two or three taps on the rock, the knife suddenly shot down the branch, splitting the wood and penetrating deep into the inside surface of my palm.

"*Verflucht*! Damn it!" I yelled. Blood spurted out of the wound, shooting out a good six inches. I knew immediately that I had hit an artery and that I had to do something or risk bleeding to death. I yanked my belt out of my pants and formed a tourniquet, which slowed the flow of blood to a drip. But I knew that I would have to get to a doctor quickly.

I left my blanket and other things and started walking. There was a small village a few minutes away, and I wasted no time in getting there. I knocked on the door of the first house I came to. A woman in her sixties answered the door.

"My God! You're white as a sheet! What happened to you?"

I turned around so she could see my hand and the tourniquet. I was barely able to talk. "I must see a doctor . . ." I uttered very softly.

"There's one just down this block," she said pointing her finger. "I'll walk you there."

I nodded my head in thanks and walked beside her as quickly as I could. She tried to ask me a few questions but I was so weak it was nearly impossible to answer and walk at the same time. We arrived at the doctor's office. It was also his residence, she told me, so there was a very good chance he'd be there.

The doctor, an old fellow, took one look at me and immediately led me into his office. He walked over to a metal doctor's cabinet and rummaged around. After a moment or two I heard him say "aha." He pulled out a circular-shaped needle and some cat gut. Neither of them were in any sort of packaging and through the fog that seemed to have enclosed my brain, I wondered if they shouldn't have been sterile. But I was in no position to engage the doctor in conversation.

He threaded the needle with the cat gut and inserted it into my hand without any attempt at anesthesia. It hurt so badly I almost jumped out of my skin. He then tied a knot around the artery with the cat gut. It stopped the bleeding, but the pain was excruciating. After he finished stitching the wound, he gave me an injection.

"This is pain medication. It is very strong. Now you must go to the hospital. You need blood tests and additional treatment."

I kept my eyes shut tight, squinting from the pain, but I understood what he was saying. I nodded my acquiescence but thought to myself that there was no way I'd be able to walk to a hospital. Then things began to get sticky.

"I want to see your identification papers," he said.

I hesitated, considering what to say. "My papers are with my clothes in the woods where I cut myself. My knife is there too."

"I need to see the papers. I need to establish a record as to what happened and how I treated you. I want to see the knife as well."

"All right, it is not very far. I'll bring it to you."

"No, you are too sick to go anywhere. You lie here and rest. I'll get you a glass of water. Then I'm going to get someone to take you to the hospital in an automobile."

And then he left the room. In a few minutes, a woman came in. I assumed she was his wife. She brought me something like chicken soup and some bread.

"Eat it all," she said.

I obeyed.

"The doctor will be back in a little while. He wants you to continue to lie here on the examining table." And with that, she left the room.

My mind worked furiously. I did not want anybody to take me to the hospital. I would certainly be found out if I went there. All doctors were required to report to the police any unusual circumstances or suspicious people.

After a few minutes, the pain medicine began to take effect. I rose from the examining table. The doctor's wife had already gone back to her part of the house. I stood and tried a few steps. I seemed steady enough.

I could not risk going to the hospital. I walked out of the doctor's office and back into the woods. As quickly as possible, I returned to the place where I had left my belongings. I put them in my knapsack and continued to walk away from the doctor's town, toward another little village. The woods seemed larger than I remembered, stretching forward as far I could see.

From there, I took a bus to an S-Bahn station. From the station I took a train to Waidmanslust. From Waidmannslust I took a bus to Lübars. And from there I walked to Anni's door.

The door flew open and Anni stood there, the blood draining from her face.

"Oh my God! What has happened to you?"

She pulled me inside and I sat down in her kitchen. Alex came in the room to join us. I explained to them what had happened. All about the wood, the knife, the woman in the village, the doctor, the dirty needle and cat gut, and the threat of the hospital.

They immediately understood. "Of course you can't go to the hospital," Anni repeated. "It would be entirely too risky."

Alex went to his bureau and found some pain pills. "They're all we have. Take them only when you cannot stand the pain any longer." They took me up to our room, pulled Klaus out of the way, and put me to bed.

"We need to get Ilse; she's a nurse," Anni began. "She's all we've got to help you. You need help!"

And so Alex went to get her from her housekeeping job in the nearby town.

As I lay there, the pain pills wore off and I felt like screaming. I tried to sleep, but it was no use.

Morning came and as the sun shone through the curtains, I looked down at my hand. I instantly saw what had made it so painful. Both the palm and the fingers were swollen to almost twice their original size. They looked more like a balloon than parts of a human body.

Anni came in to check on me and gasped in horror. She got a grip on herself and prepared a herbal remedy handed down from her grandmother, which she insisted I drink. Then she got a tub of warm water and some soap and bathed my hand several times a day.

Finally, Ilse arrived. She fixed a rod onto the head end of the bed and tied my hand to the rod so that my hand would always be higher than my heart. She took the rod down only for bathing the hand in a tub of warm water, so my hand was always up in the air. This position was very uncomfortable. I wondered whether this was really what a doctor would have prescribed.

Thankfully, my right hand was still operative. I could feed myself; I could use the portable chamber pot Anni brought up the stairs for me to use.

The wound had become infected. Pus oozed out of the cut and the flesh around it turned green and yellow. For short periods of time, I got up from the bed and sat down on a chair. I continued doing this, alternating between the chair and then getting back into bed to elevate my hand. After about ten days, I started feeling better. The swelling was going down.

20

ARRESTED
BY THE GESTAPO

WITH ILSE CARING FOR ME, my injury was healing well. The swelling was subsiding and I was gradually regaining my strength. There would be a large scar on the palm of my left hand, but that was inconsequential compared to what might have happened.

On this day, I lay in bed with my hand elevated, tied to a rod to keep it above my heart. Ilse sat on a chair near me, reading. I was resting comfortably, looking forward to being on my feet again soon. My eyes were closed as I dreamed of the end of the war and of finding my parents again.

At that moment, my ears were assaulted by a tremendous roar, as the door exploded inward. I lifted my one good hand to shield my eyes from the wood splinters that were now flying everywhere. After a second or two, I started to regain my equilibrium and lowered my hand to see what had happened.

I may have been better off if I had left it over my eyes. Standing just inside the entrance to my room were two large men in black leather coats and soft hats. Each had a weapon drawn and pointed at my heart. It was all too easy for me to recognize them as the Gestapo agents they were.

Ilse was screaming at the top of her lungs while I thought about the pistol hidden under my pillow. I had long ago decided that I would not be taken without a fight, but like all such situations, I had not expected it to happen while I was at my most vulnerable. Both of the Gestapo agents had their pistols aimed at me from almost point-blank range. Any attempt to reach my gun would have been suicide. After all the running and hiding, all the worrying and struggling and fighting to survive, it was all over in a couple of seconds. I was going to be arrested and there was not a thing I could do about it.

"Get out of bed and get dressed," the older of the two ordered. He was completely businesslike, as if he were collecting milk bottles instead of human beings. His partner walked over and untied the small scarf that held my hand to the rod, allowing my hand to fall to the bed.

Ilse stood there, quivering with terror. Unable to offer her any comfort, I threw off the blanket and started to get up.

"Where are your clothes?" the older one asked.

"There on the hook," I pointed.

The younger one left my side and walked over to the hook. He pulled my clothes off and threw them at me. As they flew through the air, a postcard fell out of my jacket. It was the last card I had received from Günther. I had forgotten to destroy it. The older Gestapo agent bent down and picked it up, read it, and then yelled, "Get dressed!"

I used my one good hand to put my clothes on. Being impatient and seeing my handicap, the older one pointed to Ilse and told her to help me.

They searched the room and in short order they found the pistol I had put under my pillow and a crate of weapons I had hidden. Without comment and without bothering to even look at me, one of the agents put my gun in his pocket and ordered me to accompany him. He led the way, walking in front of me down the steps. Ilse was next, followed by the younger agent carrying the gun cases. I was resigned. There was nothing I could do to prevent this.

Anni stood at the kitchen door, her face disfigured by a look of horrible sadness. She reached over and put her hand on my cheek as if to say, "Oh my God, what will happen?"

The Gestapo men pushed me out the door and down the path through Anni's garden. Behind me, they prodded Ilse, now holding Klaus, to follow. They led us to the street where two other Gestapo agents waited in another unmarked car. They put me in one car and Ilse and Klaus in another. With a sling on my arm, they did not even bother to handcuff me, supposing I posed no threat. They were, unfortunately, correct.

There was no conversation as they drove us to the Grosse Hamburger Strasse prison, the one where Ilse, Klaus, and I had been taken just after we were married.

The moment we arrived, Ilse and Klaus were led away. I was taken to a sparsely furnished interrogation room where another Gestapo agent waited. I sat there, wondering what would happen. Yet another agent entered and both of them sat opposite me at a wide table. They asked me a few questions about my background and, to my surprise, told me that there was nothing else for the time being. They would question me again later.

I was taken to a large room where Ilse and Klaus were waiting. She had spent her time being interrogated and filling out forms. I was taken to use the bathroom, and when I returned, Ilse and Klaus were gone. Another prisoner told me that they had been taken for interrogation.

I was now in a general detention area. Two Gestapo agents came to the room and called out my name. "Come with us," they ordered. They now outfitted me with a pair of handcuffs and escorted me to a waiting automobile, which drove us to the Jewish Hospital at the corner of Iranische Strasse and Schulstrasse. This is where Ilse had worked before we went underground. Instead of going to the main building, they led me around to the side of the pathology building. One of the Gestapo put his hand on my back and pushed me inside a small, dimly lit room, bare except for a table and a few chairs.

Another Gestapo agent sat behind the table, sneering at me as I walked in. Under the light of a bare bulb, hanging from the ceiling by a wire, they started questioning me.

"What is your true name?" the one behind the table asked.

I turned to face him. "Dagobert Lewin."

"The names of your parents?"

"Leopold and Johanna Lewin."

"Have you ever been to England?"

Startled, I looked back at them. "England?" I asked in puzzlement

"Yes, England. Have you ever been there, Dagobert Lewin?"

I looked at them in confusion. Where the hell had that come from? "No," I answered. "I have never been to England."

The Gestapo man continued, "We have reason to believe that you've had contacts with British intelligence."

My eyes widened at the thought of it. If they believed I was an intelligence agent, I was in for some rough times.

He continued, "You must be honest with us. We will eventually discover the truth, whether you tell us or not."

I was perplexed by the apparent courtesy this man was displaying. I had expected furious threats and violent displays. Later, I would learn that these would come in their turn. "I am telling you the truth. I have not been to England."

I thought back over the past few years, trying to understand why they suspected I had been in contact with British intelligence. I had had absolutely no contact with anyone British. The only time I had ever been out of Germany was during childhood trips to Lithuania, to visit my grandparents. Other than listening to BBC broadcasts with Paul Richter, I had hardly ever heard the sound of a British voice.

Could it be Richter, I wondered? Could they have arrested Richter and tortured him until he admitted harboring me? Certainly, he was in a vulnerable position. He was blind, of course. Anyone who came into his apartment would have the free run of it. He listened to the BBC every day and had the wavelengths and program notes to tune in, especially to get news of the British Communist Party. Perhaps it was he. But who knew about my staying at the Kusitzkys?

And then I realized that it could also have been Günther Gerson. Günther knew about the Kusitzkys. He had even driven there with me in our stolen car. He would never have given information of his own free will, but if he had been tortured, who knows what he might have revealed?

I could not totally rule out the Kusitzkys' neighbors. I knew that at least one of them had seen me during one of my longer visits. They might have informed the authorities, or I could have been seen through a window.

But all these ideas were purely speculative. The Gestapo excelled in obtaining information by arresting one individual and getting other names from him, then arresting the people on their new list and repeating the process. This is how they managed to catch many of the Jewish U-boats. The Gestapo could have done the same with the Communists, and Paul Richter would have definitely been one of them.

"We know you were on the run," the Gestapo man told me. "You have been on our list of open files since your escape from the factory action. It has taken us nearly two years to find you. Now we want to know about your British contacts."

Once again, I denied knowing any British agents. Hours went by as they continued their vain attempts to pump me for information I did not have. I told them nothing about the British because I knew nothing. Then they started asking questions about the postcard they had found at the time of my arrest. They believed that the card was to set up a meeting with a British agent. They said that if I told them everything, they would protect me and make sure I stayed safe. I did not believe any of this for a second.

Disappointed with my failure to provide them with the desired information, they ended the interrogation and escorted me to a bunker, where they kept their prisoners. It was a large, windowless room, quite dim because there was only one light bulb for the entire area. Prisoners were sleeping all over the tile floor. Some of them had mattresses, others only straw.

The guard led me to one of the mattresses on the floor. All the mattresses were immediately adjacent to each other, with no space in between. I sat down between two other prisoners, who wasted no time in asking me why I had been arrested. Then they introduced themselves. One was Benjamin Goldschmidt, a young man of thirty-six. Goldschmidt was a talented music composer who was also a U-boat. Christian friends had hidden him until a few days ago. The other prisoner was Aron

Wasser. He was also from Berlin and was married to a Christian woman, though this did not prevent his arrest.

The three of us hit it off immediately. We spent a lot of time talking, since there wasn't anything else to do in our dark, dank, basement of a prison. We talked about our families, about how we were caught, about the Gestapo, and, most important, about our hopes for the war's end.

I gradually became used to the routine of the prison. A major part of this routine was the ongoing interrogations. Each prisoner would be called by the guards and escorted upstairs. The building had been divided into a large number of individual offices, but only a few were used for questioning. These special rooms were soundproofed, to avoid others overhearing any details of confessions and, more important, to muffle the screams and groans of the prisoners as they were tortured.

The interrogations themselves had something of a set pattern. At the beginning of the session, the agent doing the questioning would act politely, almost kind, as they tried to convince you that they were concerned for your welfare. You had a chance to answer the questions without duress. If you failed to talk freely or if they suspected that you were lying, things got rough.

I soon got a chance to experience their methods myself. When I did not give the answers that they wanted to hear, they would begin by using their fists. As in most things, the Gestapo was methodical in administering their beatings. Most of the blows were to my face, but occasionally they would choose another target.

It was not uncommon to see prisoners walking around with black eyes or their faces cut up. Some prisoners had problems with their vision as a result of the beatings, while others sustained different types of permanent damage. The Gestapo always seemed to delight in inflicting pain—I think that this tendency was a prerequisite for employment. I never saw any indications of remorse or guilt from any of the torturers.

When I continued to resist, they brought out wooden rods, much like a baseball bat. They used the rods as clubs, mostly striking me on the back. This allowed them to inflict the maximum amount of pain without damaging me in a way that would make me unable to answer their questions.

Their main concern always seemed to be with my nonexistent connection with British intelligence. When I was arrested, I had a number of gun cases in my possession, some of which had labels indicating they were made in England. Other than this and the postcard they found, I could not come up with anything that would make them think I was a spy.

The only other possibility was that someone had told them I was a British agent. It was a fact that there were some Jews who informed on other Jews for some type of reward. It was also possible that Paul Richter had been arrested and had given me away.

I never was able to pin down exactly how it had happened, but one thing was certain—someone had denounced me. Of this, I was completely sure. If this had not been the case, the Gestapo would never have known where to find me.

The postcard that they had found was a source of great concern for the Gestapo. They spent a lot of time questioning me about the card. They wanted to know who had sent the card, where he lived, if he was Jewish, how long I had known him, and so forth. I would usually lie when answering them. I had no desire to assist them in any way. I was far too outraged with what they had done to my parents to even consider helping them.

One day, they brought a blank postcard and a pen to the interrogation. They ordered me to write a message to Günther, setting up another meeting. They leaned over me as I wrote exactly what they told me to.

"Meet me at 1:00 PM in the Gesundbrunnen U-Bahn station on Wednesday of next week. I will be sitting on one of the benches." And then I signed my name, exactly as they told me to do.

A week later, at 1:00 PM, four Gestapo in civilian clothes took me to the Gesundbrunnen U-Bahn station. I sat on one of the benches in the middle of the station. Two Gestapo agents sat at either end of the bench, pretending to read newspapers. The other two guarded the station's entrance and exit. They hoped that my "contact" would get out of one of the cars and walk up to me. At that point, the Gestapo planned to overpower him and put him in handcuffs. If he tried to flee, the Gestapo at the entry or exit points would catch him.

Subway station Gesundbrunnen. Gestapo agents were sitting on my right and left waiting for Günther Gerson to meet me there.

The appointed time came and went and, of course, Günther did not show. Without knowing about the code we used, the Gestapo were doomed to disappointment. We waited for another hour, but there was still no sign of him. The two agents on either side of me became furious.

"Liar! You have tricked us! You have deceived us!"

"No, I haven't! How should I know what happened?" I said. "Maybe he is sick. Maybe he was killed in a bombing raid. Perhaps he fled to another city. Anything could have happened."

They did not find this amusing. After waiting a little while longer, they took me back to the prison and threw me into an interrogation room. There, they gave me the worst beating I have ever endured. With every ounce of strength at their command, they beat me with their clubs until their arms grew weak. I fell to the floor, which somehow seemed to enrage them further. They struck me with renewed energy, wielding the clubs in great swinging arcs. I kept repeating that I did not know what happened and that it wasn't my fault. By this time, I was covered with blood and bruises. When they showed no signs of stopping, I began to think that they intended to beat me to death.

Between blows, they would scream at me, demanding that I stop lying to them. I continued to tell them that I knew nothing. Finally, when it became obvious that I could not or would not tell them anything else, they dropped their clubs, dragged me back downstairs, and threw me on the floor. Covered with sweat, still shaking with rage, they shouted at me, "We're not finished with you yet! Think about it!"

Everyone else in the bunker crowded around me, wanting to know what had happened to make the Gestapo so angry. But I had no interest in talking about it. I was certain that at least one of the inmates was spying on the rest of us and reporting to the Gestapo in hopes of winning special privileges.

I lay down on the straw and closed my swollen eyes. They would never learn about the code we used, at least not from me. Had they known about it, Günther would now be a prisoner and others may have eventually been captured. I could only hope that no one else ever told them.

21

ESCAPE

ONE MISERABLE DAY AFTER ANOTHER passed in the prison. Our routine was excruciatingly simple. We sat around, talking and speculating. Three times a day, we lined up to receive a bowl of watery soup and a piece of bread, which we ate sitting on the ground. Twice a day, the Jewish supervisors, or *kapos* (also called *ordners*), took us upstairs into the prison courtyard and walked us around in a circle. Two *kapos* would walk in front and two in the back of the group, in an apparent attempt to prevent escapes or sabotage.

The *kapos* were universally despised. It mattered not at all that they were Jews. They were Jews in privileged situations. Some were only half Jewish, others had Christian wives. They functioned as trustees, able to come and go from their homes. The Gestapo used them to watch the prisoners and to try to get information. They kept watch for escape attempts and revolts. The *kapos* played the tough guys, and everyone hated them.

The conditions were depressing. We spent the majority of our time lying on the cold tiled floor. Our prison was originally designed to be a morgue, and corpses did not care if their habitat was cold, dark, and wet. We, on the other hand, felt like we were living in a hole in the ground. The monotony was demoralizing in the extreme, broken only by the interrogation sessions and our daily "exercise." Not seeing the sun rise or set, not being allowed much in the way of personal possessions, slowly starving on our bread and soup diet, all this was enough to drive one insane. Life had not been easy as a U-boat, but at least I had my freedom. Here, we did not live, we existed.

Like the other prisoners, I worried about what fate had in store for me. Would I die under torture the next time I was interrogated? Would the prison be hit by Allied bombs, killing us all? There were rumors that the Gestapo would kill all the prisoners before the Russians captured Berlin, to prevent us from acting as witnesses and in obedience to Hitler's orders.

The prison was divided into two sections. Those who were deemed unable to supply information useful to the Gestapo were kept in areas above ground. Those who were security risks, or those judged likely to try to escape, were kept locked up in the morgue. It was now called "the bunker" by prisoners and guards. I was kept downstairs.

The number of prisoners varied. Downstairs, the usual count was from between ten and twenty. The upstairs area generally held many more. The makeup of the population changed when some were shipped out to the concentration camps and newly captured Jews would take their places. These transports became fewer and fewer as the number of Jews in Berlin decreased.

It was the certainty that I would not survive long as a prisoner that drove my obsession with escape. This was the favorite topic of conversation between myself and my two friends. We constantly discussed ideas on how this could be accomplished. The fact that we were locked up in an underground basement limited our options severely. There were no windows or doors to the outside. And there was a locked steel gate guarding the only way in or out of the prison.

Still, we tried to be creative. We considered digging tunnels, or attempting to get to the roof and climb down with ropes, or overpowering the guards during our walks. We discussed all types of possibilities, but none of them seemed feasible for one reason or another.

One day, around noon, as we were sitting around in our underground cells, the air raid sirens began to wail. We were lucky in one respect. Since we were well below the surface, we were protected from the threat of explosives, fire bombs and shrapnel fragments. The prisoners aboveground had to remain in their cells during the raids, which meant that, should a bomb hit the building, their chances of survival were slim. They would be blown apart or set on fire by the phosphorus.

I had seen people turned into screaming human torches after being doused by the phosphorus canisters the Allies dropped. The guards would not risk their own safety to move prisoners. Whether they lived or died was a matter of no importance to them.

This is not to say we weren't worried. Though we might not be harmed by the bombs themselves, if one hit the building and it collapsed, we could all be buried alive. We sat there quietly, listening to the all too familiar sounds of a raid in progress. Suddenly, a tremendous explosion shook the building, almost deafening us. Some thought the end had come and waited for the walls to begin falling.

To our relief, the walls remained where they were. Other than a cloud of dust, there was nothing to make us think that the building had been hit. For several minutes, there was almost complete silence. Then we began to hear voices outside, some shouting commands, some wailing in terror. In the distance, we could hear the sirens of fire and rescue units heading in our direction.

Two guards came into the basement, looking to see if anything had been damaged or destroyed. It was unusual to see them enter the cells. Normally they kept their distance from us. They told us that a bomb had fallen into the courtyard next to the building, causing substantial wreckage and leaving a huge crater in the courtyard. Finishing their inspection, they departed in an expeditious manner.

They were gone only a few minutes when they reappeared and told us that all prisoners would be required to help clean up the debris and repair the damage to the building, starting immediately. They led us outside to the courtyard, where we found a tremendous crater at the point of impact. Parts of the building had fallen into the courtyard, littering it with glass, bricks, stones, and wood. Giant dust clouds hung in the air, and in some places the fences and walls that surrounded the property had been demolished. For the first time, we could see the street.

A contingent of heavily armed German Wehrmacht troops were on the premises, organizing the cleanup. Their first priority was rebuilding the surrounding fences so as to prevent outsiders from coming in, or prisoners getting out. They made announcements as to how the debris would be removed.

I listened but continued to look around at the sight before me. Seeing how huge the crater was convinced me that it was a miracle that there hadn't been even greater damage to the building. Then I noticed something far more interesting. Running between the prison and the main building of the Jewish Hospital was a tunnel, which the blast had exposed. This must have originally been used to move dead bodies from the hospital to the morgue, which had now been converted into our prison.

I shivered as I pondered the implications of this. This could well provide the means of our escape! My daydreaming ended abruptly as a spade was shoved roughly into my hands. One of the soldiers had noticed me loafing. "Start working!" he shouted, "Fill the wheelbarrows with the debris!"

I nodded my head in acquiescence and ran over to where my friends had already started digging. I said nothing, but the expression on my face must have been enough to alert them that something was going on. To forestall any chance of being overheard, I whispered that I would talk to them later, after the work detail was dismissed. I let my mind wander while my body did the work of clearing rubble, loading wheelbarrow after wheelbarrow. Malnourished as we all were, I was so excited that I hardly felt the strain of working. I had to get a look at that tunnel!

We worked for days, using shovels, picks, and hammers to reduce the big chunks of concrete debris into smaller, more manageable pieces that could be hauled away by trucks.

By the third day, I was close enough to see that the tunnel continued onward beyond the limits of my vision. It was imperative that I find out what was in that tunnel. I knew it was risky, but I put fear behind me and walked down into the tunnel.

After just a few steps, I came upon an iron gate. I half saw and half felt a lock on the gate that blocked me from proceeding any farther. I turned around and walked back to join the others in the courtyard. It was getting late and the guards shouted, "Quitting time!" I was anxious to discuss this new development with my friends. As soon as we were locked up, I got Benjamin and Aron and we retreated into a corner, where I told them about the gate.

"Well, that's all very interesting," Benjamin began. "But how does that affect us? "

Aron said, "You say there is a locked iron gate. That doesn't sound too promising to me."

"Yes," I told them, "that is a problem. But on the other hand, if we should manage to get through the gate, we would have a good shot at fleeing into the hospital. The gate might be an advantage, since the guards wouldn't expect anyone to run in that direction, knowing that they would be trapped."

Aron's opinion was that it was a beautiful plan, except for the small problem of the locked gate. Benjamin asked if anyone had an idea on how the gate could be opened.

"It would be difficult," I said. We suspected that there were informers among the prisoners, so any efforts we made would have to be protected from prying eyes. I told them that, given a few basic materials and tools, I thought I could make a key for the lock.

"A key? You can make a key?" Aron asked, disbelieving, his expressive blue eyes focused intently on me.

"I am reasonably sure I could make a key," I said.

"But how?" Benjamin interjected. "How in the world could you do it?"

"You haven't even seen the key that fits into that lock!" Aron whispered hotly. "How can you make a key when you don't know what it's supposed to look like? When you've only seen the lock in bad light?"

"I may have told you," I said, "that I served a long and exacting apprenticeship in metalworking, as my father did before me. Part of my training was in the making of locks.

"More important," I continued, "to complete my apprenticeship, I had to design and make a wing-type lock with two keys."

"Yes and so?" Benjamin asked.

"So the lock on the tunnel gate is a wing-type lock," I told them.

There was silence, almost a sense of disbelief that fortune could now smile on us this way. They laughed with excitement. "You know how to make a key for that lock that would allow us to escape?" Benjamin asked excitedly.

"Yes, I hope so. But I need some basic tools to do it. I need one or two files and at least one sawblade. I would also need either a flashlight or candles and some way of working in secret, so that we would not be betrayed."

"This is amazing. Unbelievable!" Benjamin whispered under his breath. "What are the chances of not only having a bomb fall to expose a gate, but now to have someone with us who knows how to make a key to fit the lock? What are the chances of that? It is unbelievable!"

"It is God himself helping," Aron swore.

"That may be, but if God really wants to help, He is going to have to get us some tools. I also need something I can use as a key blank."

"What do you mean, a key blank?"

"A key blank is a piece of metal that the actual key would be fashioned from."

My heart beat fast. I didn't know where or how to get any such material. This could all be an unattainable dream, but at least it was a plan.

We heard someone approaching and quickly put an end to our conversation. We couldn't allow any attention to be drawn to ourselves or the game would be over before it began.

The next day, we started planning how to obtain the tools and materials I needed. Our best bet would be to use one of the *kapos* to help us. Though they were generally despised, Aron had struck up a mild friendship of sorts with one of them. This *kapo*, like Aron, had a Christian wife. By chance, Aron had known him and his wife before he had been imprisoned.

There were several hundred of these Jewish-Christian couples in Berlin. At one point, the Gestapo had rounded up a large number of Jewish husbands. In late February and early March 1943, the Christian wives organized themselves and appeared before the Gestapo building on Rosenstrasse. They started a virulent demonstration—screaming, "We want our husbands! We want our husbands!" When the police tried to disperse them, the Christian wives fought back and refused to move.

The SS threatened the women with machine guns if they did not disperse. They held their fire only because the Gestapo didn't want to further demoralize the population and perhaps provoke a riot by carrying out a massacre in the middle of Berlin. Finally, Goebbels himself ordered most of the men released. Others, for whatever reason, were not released. Aron was one of those unfortunates.

The Gestapo did, however, give one privilege to the wives whose husbands remained in prison: twice a month they allowed them to bring their husbands small packages of food, toothbrushes, combs, soap, and the like. As we discussed how we should go about getting the tools we needed, I remembered that Aron received these packages from his wife.

"Wait! I've got it!" I exclaimed, looking over at Aron. "You can ask your wife to include the files and candles in the package she sends you next month!"

"That's fine, but how is she going to know what to send?" Benjamin interjected.

"Why don't you send a message to her?" I told Aron.

"Yes, but how?" Benjamin asked.

We kicked the idea around all afternoon. Finally, it was decided that Aron would try to get the *kapo* to deliver the message. Benjamin thought that we were insane to risk our lives in this way. He felt certain that we would be turned in the moment Aron laid our request before the *kapo*.

"No," Aron said softly, still mulling the plan over in his head. "I've known him for a long time. The tables could well be turned and he knows it. I could have been the one chosen for *kapo* and he for prisoner. Besides, he's told me that he and the other *kapos* are very afraid of what will happen when the war ends. They know the Germans will eventually lose, and he's terrified of what will happen to him. The *kapos* have been doing much of the Gestapo's dirty work and they fear the Allies' revenge."

"As they should," Benjamin said. "They have much to answer for."

"Well," Aron said, "I think I can use this to our advantage. I'll tell him that if he will pass the message to my wife, I will stand up for him after the war. I think he'll help us."

We finalized our plan and, the next morning, Aron approached the *kapo*. But the *kapo* refused to do anything and threatened to report Aron to the Gestapo. The next few days were hard, not knowing if we would be hauled off by the Gestapo at any moment. Deportation was the usual penalty for anyone caught trying to bribe a guard. But Aron persisted, talking to the *kapo* every day. "What is there to lose by continuing to try?" he said. "If we don't escape, we are most likely doomed anyway."

The next morning, the *kapo* pulled Aron aside. He would agree to pass the message if Aron promised to protect him from the Allies. Aron assured him that this would not be a problem and ten days later he received a package from his wife. All such packages were carefully inspected by the Gestapo, so we could only hope that his wife had been clever in how she concealed the items. We waited anxiously as Aron opened the box. He pulled out a pair of men's shoes, some candy, cigarettes, a comb, and a toothbrush.

Later that night, we got up from our mattresses and went into a corner with the shoes. Aron and Benjamin stood in front of me, shielding me from view.

When the bomb exploded near the prison, it created mountains of debris. During the cleanup, I had picked out a nail, a piece of wire, and a piece of glass. I hid these on my person and smuggled them into the prison. I now took the sharp edge of the glass and cut some of the threads that fastened the soles to the shoes. I pried the soles away, exposing a cavity in each shoe. In one cavity, I found half of a metal cutting saw blade. In the other, there was a miniature file about four inches long.

"Will they work?" Benjamin whispered excitedly.

"They will have to," I said. "Nothing larger would have fit into the shoes. I'll try my best."

I looked over at my friends as they celebrated silently. "There is something else," I continued. "I am going to need a flashlight or a candle so I can light the tunnel well enough to see the gate lock. There's not much hope we can get either of those. And I still haven't found any material to make the key."

We had been continuing to dig out the collapsed section of the tunnel. Even though the tunnel was ten feet wide, there was only room for two people to work at a time. Two of us shoveled debris into a wheelbarrow. Once it was full, another prisoner would replace it with an empty one. This continued all day. We would take turns shoveling or emptying the trash.

During one of my turns to empty the wheelbarrow, I saw a piece of lead pipe sticking out among the debris. Lead was suitable as a material, because it was relatively soft metal, easy to cut and shape. The pipe could be cut lengthwise, pounded flat with a stone, then filed into a key. I reached down into the wheelbarrow, grabbed the lead pipe, and hid it beneath some bags of cement.

The next day fortune smiled on me again. I found two short pieces of candle among the debris. These obviously had been used by someone working in the tunnel before the bomb blast. I palmed both pieces and stuffed them into my pockets. Now I had everything I needed to attempt the manufacture of the key.

That night I began. The only place I could work in privacy was in the toilet. Aron and Benjamin had the task of standing in front of the toilet, blocking the view while I worked. When some poor soul came to use the facilities, they would say, "Wait a minute, we were here first. You have to go to the end of the line." They would stall them while I concealed my tools and came out of the stall.

I began by sawing the pipe in half, down the long axis. It was a tedious job, because the tiny saw blade cut very slowly. When my labor was finally complete, I had two curved pieces of lead, each about four-inches long. Next, I needed to flatten the pieces out. The best I could do was to strike the lead with a piece of brick. The impact of the brick striking the lead created too much noise to be done in the toilet, so I used my time in the tunnel to work on it. Acting as if I was breaking pieces of rubble into smaller chunks, I put the pieces on the concrete floor and struck them until they flattened out.

Now I had a fairly flat piece of lead, my raw material. From past experience, I was already familiar with the basic shape of the key. I stole as much time from working as possible to inspect the lock, trying to figure out the rough dimensions for my key.

Taking Aron with me to the gate, I held my piece of now-flat metal up to the keyhole. With a discarded nail, I scratched the metal, marking the rough size the key should be. That little piece of lead pipe was now becoming a key blank.

Every evening for the next few days, Benjamin and Aron would stand guard in front of the toilet while I whittled the lead to the dimensions I had marked. I used the saw to cut away pieces of metal to form a handle and the outline of a key. Matching the key to the lock was a little more difficult, but a few days later, I inserted the key and it slid in perfectly.

Now came the critical part. The key blank would slide into the lock, but I needed to cut the grooves that would allow it to turn. Under normal circumstances, I would have disassembled the lock and cut grooves in the key to match. But that would have been impossible here.

I knew that locks such as this one had several spring-loaded lifting plates inside. The key had to have grooves or notches that would correspond to each of the lock's lifting plates. When a key was inserted into such a lock, each of the grooves would meet their corresponding plate. Rotating the key caused the grooves to lift the plates, making the bolt to slide into the lock and away from whatever it was holding shut. This would allow the gate or the door to be opened.

Any chance of making the key actually function would require some way to mark the grooves so that they could be filed into the proper shape. After pondering the problem for many hours, I finally came up with something. I would blacken the key with soot.

I took the lit candle, held it up to the blank and let the flame coat the end of it with soot. Then I inserted it into the lock and turned it hard, as if trying to open the lock. When I withdrew the key blank, I could see where the first lifting plate had marked it. I would file a small amount of lead off in this spot and repeat the entire process, removing a tiny amount at each attempt.

Little by little, the lead blank grew to resemble a real key. Blacken the end, insert it into the lock, turn the key, withdraw it, and file where the plates had marked it. I repeated the procedure many times, carefully filing a little more on each attempt. Eventually, the soot would no longer rub off, which would mark the end of that groove.

But most keys had several grooves and this was the case here. Finishing one groove, I would use my marking procedure to start filing

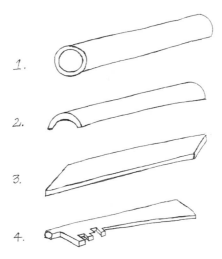

Primitive key that I fashioned from a piece of
lead pipe. This key opened a gate in an
underground tunnel between the Jewish Hospital
and the pathology building that served as a Gestapo
prison.

out the next one. All of this took a few weeks of running back and
forth between the gate and the toilet when the opportunity presented
itself. The necessity of keeping all of this secret meant that I could
only work when I wasn't being closely watched.

I realized during this process how fortunate we had been to find a
piece of lead, rather than steel. Lead is a much softer metal. Using steel
would have taken far longer and may not have been possible.

When I wasn't working on the key, I hid it, the file, and the sawblade
behind a loose brick in the wall. Had I been discovered, the punishment would have been severe. The Gestapo had the power of life and
death over all prisoners. I had been told that while the Gestapo interrogated and beat two prisoners, one of them resisted and struck back. The
Gestapo shot him dead on the spot. Another prisoner had tried to escape
by climbing over the fence that surrounded the courtyard. An army soldier standing watch gave him one warning, then shot him. He fell eight
feet down onto the ground, in front of me and the other prisoners.

None of this deterred me; in fact, it made me even more determined
to attempt an escape.

It was now early April 1945 and change was in the air. The guards began lugging large boxes of Gestapo documents and files into the prison yard. When the pile they made was sufficiently large, they set it on fire. They burned so many documents that the resulting smoke made it difficult to see.

It was obvious that the Gestapo were desperate that these files not fall into the hands of the Russians. There was talk of plans to murder all the inmates before the Russians arrived, to hide evidence of their barbaric treatment. All this made us extremely determined to escape as soon as possible.

I had been filing for weeks and now had something whose front portion resembled a normal key. It had a rough handle, a squared-off tip and a number of notches of varying shapes and lengths. I had done all I could using the soot-marking method, but still, when I inserted the key, the lock would not open. It began to look as if I would not be able to get the key to work. It should have worked before now, but something was not exactly right.

My friends were becoming despondent and my own spirits were flagging, although I would not allow myself to give up. That evening, I sat for hours, trying to examine every possible reason why the key did not work. Finally, I decided that I needed some type of lubricant. I knew from my training that a lubricant applied at a critical spot made mechanical devices of any kind work better. Sometimes a lubricant made it possible for them to work at all.

The only problem was that none of us had the slightest idea how we could obtain any grease or oil. It seemed that my plan was doomed to fail, until I remembered the candle stubs. Wax could also act to reduce friction between moving parts.

"Let's melt one candle with the other," I said. "We'll let the wax run onto the key."

They just looked at me blankly, but they went along with it. We went into the toilet and dripped candle wax onto the key.

I wiped the key with a rag and removed all the visible wax. I then rubbed the key again, trying to make sure there was no wax buildup. If there was buildup, the wax might interfere with the mechanism of the lock. A very thin coating of wax remained on the key, but that was what I wanted, an absolute minimal amount.

I then slightly chamfered the squared edges of the key's grooves with the file, hoping this would make it easier for the grooves to move the plates in the lock. Perhaps this would make up for slight inaccuracies in the key that were preventing the grooves from matching the plates. I thought that perhaps the original squared edges were getting caught and preventing the key from turning in the lock.

Finally, it was time to go try the newly chamfered and waxed key. We were still spending our days cleaning the bombed courtyard. All three of us managed to situate ourselves in the tunnel. Aron and Benjamin were working in the exposed part of the tunnel. I maneuvered myself until I was hidden from view and made my way over to the gate. I took a deep breath, inserted the key and very slowly turned it in the lock. Lo and behold, it turned all the way. The bolt moved, and I pushed the gate open.

Elated, I looked behind me to make sure no one was watching. I closed and relocked the gate. Now wasn't the time to escape. We needed to formulate a plan that would give us the maximum chance for success. I returned to my post cleaning out the tunnel. After I pushed my wheelbarrow past Aron, I put it down and walked over to him.

"By the way," I said. "Start getting your things together. The key works." I chuckled to myself and moved on. After a few seconds, I looked back over my shoulder and saw him standing with his mouth open, staring at me in shock.

That evening, we made our plans. There was a unanimous feeling that we should leave at night, using the darkness as cover for our movements. We needed to get to the outside, into the courtyard, and then into the tunnel.

The hard part would be getting through the courtyard. To get there, we would have to climb the steps that led from the prison to the toilet, then walk down a hall, through a door, then down the rest of the hallway. The hallway, thanks to the bombing, ended abruptly under the stars. What originally had been a locked door to the outside now was simply an open hole.

An armed guard sat in the courtyard twenty-four hours a day to ensure that prisoners did not escape. The guards worked in six-hour shifts. They had their own room, which, before the bombing, had a clear view of the courtyard. When the courtyard was hit, the same bomb also partially destroyed their room. While it was being rebuilt, the guards had to use our toilet facilities.

It was cold outside in the courtyard, and the guards generally had a fire going. They stayed there all the time, with the exception of bathroom breaks. It was this fact that we focused on. We knew we had to get past the guard in order to escape, and we decided that our best chance would be to overpower him on his way to the toilet.

"We could get him when he walks inside," Aron said. "I've noticed that he doesn't usually take his rifle with him when he goes to the toilet."

And so we had our plan.

Every minute would count once we had bolted into the courtyard. We knew that the underground tunnel would lead us to the hospital. But beyond that, we knew nothing. We would have to feel our way through the tunnel and into the hospital. Then we had to make it through the hospital without being recaptured.

We bided our time, waiting for darkness to fall. As the hours passed, we kept a close eye on the guard, waiting for him to either start toward the toilet or to drowse off. We had observed him dozing in weeks past.

Nights were difficult in the prison. With nothing to do, time seemed to pass slowly. Many of the prisoners would talk in their sleep. Others, in the throes of nightmares, would scream hysterically. Some prisoners, including myself and my two friends, didn't seem to sleep much at all.

Finally, close to dawn but while it was still dark, we decided to make our attempt. As quietly as possible, we made our way up the steps. We crept into the hall and then to the outside. About sixty feet in front of us sat the guard, dozing on a chair before a small fire he had built to keep himself warm. He had not attempted to use the toilet that evening, so overpowering him while he used the toilet was out.

We moved carefully along the side of the building, down the temporary wooden steps to the tunnel. It was tempting to break into a run, but we knew this would increase the noise we were making, so we kept our movements as slow and controlled as possible.

We entered the tunnel and approached the gate. I reached into the pocket of the pants I had been wearing for the last year and pulled out the key. I could hear the nervous, rapid breathing of both of my friends, but I ignored it, trying to remain completely focused on the task at hand.

I inserted the key and turned it. Nothing happened. The key wouldn't turn in the lock.

I tried again. I turned the key in the lock. There seemed to be some type of interference, preventing it from rotating. I carefully worked the key, not forcing it but twisting firmly.

The bolt moved. The lock opened.

Jubilation!

"*Wunderbar!*" Benjamin whispered.

Removing the key, I clasped one of the bars of the gate and pushed it open.

"Let's go," I whispered. After we had all passed through the gate, I turned around and closed it. I put the key in the other side of the lock and turned it. The bolt shot home. If our escape was discovered, this would delay our pursuers for a few more seconds.

The tunnel was pitch black. We all trailed one hand along the tunnel wall to help guide us. We moved slowly, so as to avoid tripping.

We continued hugging the wall, advancing. Ahead, under the dim glow of an electric light, we saw several hospital beds standing along one side of the tunnel. It was too dark to make out whether anyone was in the beds and we didn't want to stop to look. We just kept going. Within the next few feet, the tunnel came to an end. We found ourselves at the foot of a set of stairs. Mounting them quickly, we passed through a door located at their head and found ourselves in a hall leading to a room in which a number of hospital beds stood. This room was also dimly lit. We located the exit and rushed through it, but in the process we stumbled, crashing into some furniture.

The resulting noise was considerable, and we soon heard screams coming from some of the beds.

"*Was ist los?*" "What's going on?" "What are you doing here?" someone yelled.

We didn't stop to offer any explanations. Our only chance for safety now lay in speed. We rushed through a door, to find more steps leading downward. We had no idea where we were or where we were going, but we raced all the way.

We went down the steps, then down a hall leading to another door. When we opened the door, we found ourselves outside! We were in a courtyard that was lit up with floodlights. Encircling the courtyard was a wire fence, about ten feet high. Without stopping to think about it, we rushed to the fence, climbed to the top and over and then down the other side. Considering our physical condition, weak from months of malnutrition and mistreatment, this was an amazing feat. It would not have been possible had we not all been supercharged with adrenaline and made desperate by fear. Failure meant death and none of us wanted to die. We did not even feel the cuts inflicted by the barbed wire at the top of the fence until some time later.

We were now on the street—Schulstrasse. Initially, we all ran in the same direction, toward some apartment houses. We stopped at the first apartment house we came to and went inside a wooden gate, into the driveway. We closed the gate behind us and discussed our situation.

"What should we do?" Benjamin asked excitedly.

"We must split up," I said. "It makes no sense for all of us to go in the same direction. That way, even if they find one of us, perhaps the other two can still escape."

Aron asked me where I was going, but I refused to tell him. The knowledge would have been of no use to him but could have been extremely harmful to me. For the same reason, I didn't want to know Benjamin's or Aron's destination. We took a moment to wish each other good luck, and then we split up, each of us running in his chosen direction. There was no time for lengthy good-byes.

As soon as the others departed, I heard sirens begin to wail. The guards at the prison must have discovered that we were missing. Each of us wore our own civilian clothing, so we wouldn't be easy to spot. In prison, we always slept in our clothes and shoes. Otherwise, there was a good chance that they would be missing when we woke up.

Although I wanted desperately to get out of the area, I was too exhausted to run. I had decided to go to the Lebrechts' apartment. It was a very long walk, but I had to get there.

The date was April 15, 1945, and Berlin was in total chaos. As I walked along, I was amazed at the change in the city's appearance. I had been imprisoned for approximately four months, and in that time there had been more bombing and destruction rained upon Berlin than I had seen in the previous three years combined. As I walked, almost every building I saw had been completely or partially destroyed.

I saw lampposts where uniformed Wehrmacht soldiers were hanging from ropes around their necks, their feet dangling in the wind and signs around their necks with various inscriptions. One said, "I could not wait." Another said, "I am a traitor." The SS doubtless meant this to be a deterrence to any soldier thinking about abandoning his post.

After about a half hour, I felt confident that the Gestapo were not going to find me. They had other worries just then. The streets were one big mass of confusion, and I was now far away from the prison. I was much more worried about the SS stopping me, thinking I was an army deserter. I saw SS in military vehicles cruising the streets. I knew there was a real possibility that they would stop me, and I had no papers of any sort. I just kept walking. When I saw an SS vehicle approach, I would avoid them by ducking into a house or the ruins of a building.

Everywhere I looked, there was turmoil and chaos. I could hear the artillery from the distance—the Russians. Russian planes marked with red stars flew overhead, dropping bombs.

I walked and walked and walked. I was completely exhausted and my feet burned with pain. More than once, I wondered whether I would make it to the Lebrechts. I wanted nothing more than to collapse where I was. Only willpower and desperation allowed me to continue. This was my only chance to survive. If I stopped now, it was all over. After an entire day of walking, I finally neared the Lebrechts. Out of breath and nearly out of my mind, I arrived at 3 Lorenzstrasse—the Lebrecht residence.

The Lebrechts lived in the basement of the Nazi district headquarters building. I approached the building, standing at a distance to see what was going on. But I saw nothing to prevent me from going inside. I climbed the outside steps, trying not to weave as I walked. I went inside the building and downstairs to their apartment.

Terribly dizzy and barely able to stand, I managed to knock on the door.

Please let them be here! I prayed. If they had been arrested, or if they were too fearful to answer the door, I was finished. I didn't have the strength to look for another hiding place.

I put my hand against the wall to hold myself up. The door opened and I fell, instantly unconscious, into the arms of Jenny Lebrecht.

22

RUSSIANS

As I wrote earlier, the Lebrecht family cared for me until I had regained my strength. With the end of the war in sight, they invited me to remain with them, for better or for worse.

Some days, it appeared that it would be for worse. We didn't even consider leaving the apartment. Berlin was in absolute shambles. The Wehrmacht was falling apart, and much of the defense of the city had been assigned to the Hitler Youth. Between the fantastic losses Germany had suffered fighting and dying on two fronts and the large number of desertions, there weren't many adults left able to fight.

As it was, the racket of small arms fire increased daily. Rumor had it that the Russians would invade the city with tanks as well as infantry. All of this made the idea of being outside much too dangerous for the ordinary civilian. It was now May 1, 1945, and to anyone with eyes to see, the invasion was imminent. The Russians could literally arrive at any minute.

That night, most of us were unable to sleep. The din created by rifle shots and artillery rounds grew louder and more frequent. Near dawn, we began hearing sounds that seemed to be glass shattering. People were screaming in the background, but we dared not open the door to find out what it was all about.

I was sitting on the couch with Heinz and Horst beside me. Jenny and Leo were sitting on chairs at a small table against the wall. All of us were tired, but we were also afraid, worried about what would happen when the end finally came.

Even though we knew it was inevitable, it was still a shock when it finally happened. With a tremendous roar, the door to the apartment crashed to the ground. Through a cloud of dust, two Russian soldiers charged into the apartment, their machine pistols drawn and leveled at us. Two more entered immediately behind them.

For a moment, we all froze. Then we rose to our feet, our hands above our heads. My greatest fear was that they would shoot us before we had a chance to say anything. I'd had more than my share of weapons pointed at me in the last few years, but there was always someone who spoke German on the other end. I was deathly afraid that we would be killed before we had a chance to reveal ourselves as refugees.

One look at the soldiers told me instantly that if anyone made a wrong move, it would be their last one. The Russians had suffered terribly over the last few years. Their homeland had been invaded, raped, and looted by Germans, and they were wild for revenge. Now, they were fighting house to house with their hated foe, and it was obvious that these four were as hyped on adrenaline as it was possible to be. It was a miracle that they had not already started shooting.

They were dressed in olive-brown, high-collared blouses and had rope belts around their waists. Their pants were stuffed into their boots. I had never seen anything like them. If they hadn't been so terrifying, they might have been funny.

They glared at us with battle-hardened eyes, obviously eager to destroy something. They started yelling and cursing in Russian, which none of us understood.

"*Wir sind Juden!*" we shouted. "We are Jews!"

One of them yelled back, "You are liars!" he screamed. "Hitler killed all the Jews. You are Nazi scum living in a Nazi headquarters and we are going to enjoy killing you."

To my surprise, I realized that I could understand him. He was speaking what seemed to be a bizarre, broken German. Something about it made me recall the Yiddish language that my relatives spoke in Kovno. If I concentrated, I could just barely make him out.

"No, it is true! We are Jews!" we screamed over and over again, at the top of our lungs.

My heart was racing. If we could not convince them that we were Jews, we were doomed. They would kill us all! Jenny was crying. We kept repeating, "We are Jews!" over and over again.

It occurred to me that just repeating "We are Jewish" wasn't convincing them. I had relatives in both Kovno and Moscow. I had to try something different.

"I can prove it!" I asserted. "I have an uncle in Moscow who is also Jewish!"

The Russian soldier was not impressed. Was he ignoring me or did he not understand me?

I repeated it, "I have an uncle in Moscow who is Jewish!"

Now he listened. "Yes?" he asked. "What is your uncle's name?"

I had a problem. I had only met my uncle twice, the first time when he was on his way to a university in Toulouse, France, and then again when he was traveling to a university in Prague. I was nine during his first visit and ten during the second. I remembered very little about either occasion, not even his name.

What was his name? I ordered my brain to remember. And then, from some dark recess of my overstressed mind, it floated to the surface.

"Boris!" I yelled. "My uncle's name is Boris Levin!"

That produced an immediate response. The Russian's brow wrinkled in puzzlement.

"I don't believe it," he announced. "What does this Boris Levin do? What is his profession?"

What does he do? A good question and one I was at a total loss to answer. I had been lucky to remember his name. Now I had to come up with the profession of a man I hadn't seen in more than a decade and had only met as a small boy. When he had visited us, he had talked about things that a ten-year-old would be interested in. Unfortunately, that didn't include what he did for a living.

I wracked my brain, knowing I had only seconds before their patience was exhausted.

Once again, a memory surfaced that I did not even realize I possessed. In my mind, a picture formed of my uncle talking to my father about electrical motors. My father had been having problems with some of his motors, and Uncle Boris was giving him advice.

"He's an electrical engineer!"

More than ever, surprise distorted the soldier's face. "What did you say?" he asked.

"He's an electrical engineer," I announced. "Boris Levin is an electrical engineer."

The soldier paused and scratched his chin. "Maybe you're telling the truth," he said. "When I was in school, I recall studying something written by a Boris Levin. I read it when studying to become an electrician."

The Lebrechts, who still stood with their hands above their heads, gave a collective sigh of relief, as if granted a stay of execution, which is exactly what had happened.

The soldier put down his gun and said something to his comrades. They looked at him, perplexed, but also lowered their weapons. We slowly put down our hands.

The soldier who had been talking to me turned and addressed his fellows. They were speaking Russian so I couldn't understand them, but from the tone of their voices, it seemed that they were confused as to why they were being told not to kill us. Perhaps they were disappointed that they weren't going to have a chance to loot the place. Impatient to continue their mission, the three of them turned, walked over the door that still lay on the ground, and left.

The Yiddish-speaking soldier now turned to me, a friendly smile on his face, his initial hostility having evaporated.

"I am also Jewish," he said to me, "and I am from Moscow. When we saw the swastika on the door, we assumed that this was a government building and we were prepared to deal very harshly with whomever we found here. That is why I called you liars when you claimed to be Jewish. We assumed that anyone we found here would be a Nazi."

He lingered for a few minutes, talking of his life before the war, explaining that he was an electrician. I couldn't understand exactly what type of work he did, but I got the gist of it. He spoke about the German invasion and how Nazis had brutalized the Russian people,

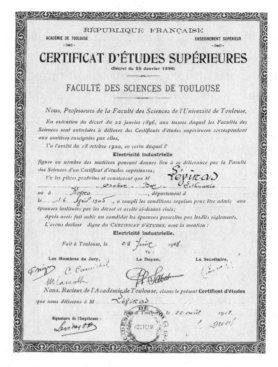

Diploma from Toulouse University in industrial electrics, earned by Uncle Boris. He also earned a degree in electrical engineering and authored several books dealing with these subjects.

raping Russian women and killing hundreds of thousands of men. Now all the Russian soldiers thought about was revenge.

He gave us some chocolate that he had taken from another house. Then he took out a piece of paper and a pen.

"What is your name?" he asked me.

"Dagobert Lewin," I replied.

"I am going to give you a pass that you must present to any other Russian soldiers you encounter. It will say that you are a victim of the Nazis and a friend of the Russian people. Without this pass, you might be arrested, so be sure to show it to any Russian soldiers who might stop you."

"When will the fighting stop?" Leo asked, unable to restrain himself any longer.

The soldier gave him a smile and said, "Nazis *aus*, Hitler *kaput*."

And with that, he bid us adieu and trotted after his fellows. After he left, we fell into each other's arms, shaking with relief. Jenny was crying. Once again, fortune had favored us to an almost miraculous degree. By all rights, we should have been lying on the floor, our bodies riddled with machine gun bullets. Instead, we sat, as warm and safe as anyone in Berlin, waiting for the conclusion of a nightmare that had haunted the dreams of an entire world.

23

BEGINNINGS
AND ENDINGS

BY THE NEXT MORNING, the aftershock of our encounter with the Russian soldiers had worn off. We decided to turn our attention toward practicalities. Our first concern was to replace the door that they had kicked down. We didn't want another band of soldiers, Russian or German, wandering in. So we took a door from a vacant apartment and used it to replace ours.

We also decided we needed to take down the sign that designated our building as an office of the NSDAP (the Nazi Party.) The swastika-laden sign would attract Russians like bees to honey. We removed the sign and threw it into an office upstairs.

We were comforted by the fact that now that the Russians had arrived, the tables had turned on the Nazis. It was they who were now hunted outlaws, and people like ourselves who were "legal."

As the day progressed, the sounds of battle diminished. Everyone was in a high state of excitement that had been building for the last several days, anticipating the changes that would arrive with the Allies.

The Lebrechts had a radio that we now played constantly. The announcer on the radio was saying, "People of Germany; resist to the last man! Believe in the Führer! We will defeat the demons of the Jewish Bolshevik conspiracy. They shall not succeed! The Führer has seen to it. Relief is on its way. Have faith in the Führer, he will bring about victory."

We got a good laugh out of that. We were hearing the last gasp of Nazism. No one on the radio talked about where the great Führer was, though. Apparently, he wasn't going to appear to save the Fatherland in its most desperate hour.

That task was left to the new draftees. In these last days of the war, the Nazis took to conscripting children and the elderly to fight the Russians in the streets. Every available male, from sixteen to sixty, was conscripted into the Volkssturm, the People's Storm. The younger boys were supplied with Panzerfäust shoulder-fired weapons, designed to pierce the armor of tanks. Elderly men, barely able to walk, were given rifles and whatever other types of weaponry could be found.

Boys as young as twelve were used to operate artillery units. As the Russians approached Berlin, entire battalions made up exclusively of Hitler Youth were outfitted in man-sized uniforms and ordered to defend bridges leading into Berlin. More than 90 percent of these boys were killed or wounded during the ensuing battles, many committing suicide rather than allow themselves to be captured.

Meanwhile, SS troops roamed the streets, looking for deserters. Anyone refusing to fight was shot or hung on the spot. Of course, all this was useless. In his insanity, Hitler would not allow surrender. If the Reich could not defeat the Russians and the Allies, it would go down in a blaze of glory, fighting to the last man—or so Hitler hoped. So strong was Hitler's control of the German people that Germany did not surrender until May 7, 1945, a week after Hitler finally committed suicide.

We eventually decided it was safe enough to really venture out. All around us, Berlin lay in ruins. The bombings had ceased by mutual agreement of the Allies, to prevent Russian soldiers from being killed. Everywhere we looked, people were wandering the streets, some just curious as we were, others homeless with nowhere to go.

Now most Berliners were in the same position we had been in during most of the war. They became obsessed with doing anything they could to secure food and other articles necessary for survival. The infrastructure that brought supplies to Berlin had been destroyed. In many cases, there was no drinking water, gas, or electricity. Few knew where tomorrow's meal would come from.

One day, we noticed that many Russian trucks and a few large cranes had arrived and were parked near factory buildings. The Russians literally ripped open factory walls, using the cranes to remove machinery from within the factories and to load them onto trucks. The trucks then took the equipment to railroad cars, in which they were shipped to Russia.

It was brilliant, really. The much-maligned Russians—thought by the Germans to be inept—were dismantling the guts of German industrial might and sending it home for their own use. In doing so, they were giving a boost to their own industrial efforts while simultaneously squashing Germany's ability to lift itself back up. Without machine tools, Germany's industries couldn't function.

The only trouble was that the Russians didn't have enough railroad cars to move all of the machines, so many were left to sit beside the railroad tracks, rusting. Eventually, many of the machines deteriorated to such an extent that they became unusable, at which point the Russians abandoned them.

A few days after the war ended, the Lebrechts somehow found a larger apartment for the five of us to live in. It was an empty apartment on Ringstrasse 95. The former occupant had been killed by the Russians when they were fighting house to house. He was a fanatical Nazi official who tried to resist the Russian soldiers. The Russians fired on and killed him with their Kalashnikov machine guns. The neighbors of Ringstrasse 95 gave us a detailed account of this when we moved in.

As I ventured out from Ringstrasse 95 each day, I was sure to carry with me the little pass given to me by the Russian soldier that miraculous day at the Lebrechts'. I showed it whenever I was stopped by the Russian soldiers cruising the streets.

In spite of the fact that the war was now over, I still looked over my shoulder constantly for Gestapo. More than two years of constant danger had ingrained in me the need to be on guard wherever I was, day and night. It was now a habit. I felt myself virtually incapable of taking a leisurely public stroll. Fear was still present, even if it needn't have been.

There were well over one hundred bridges in Berlin. To reach many destinations, one had no choice but to cross water and therefore, to cross a bridge. The Russian soldiers quickly grew fond of standing at the bridge's exit. They would greet those who had just crossed the bridge by asking them for identification. Generally, the conversation would end when they confiscated the person's valuables.

I had the pass given me by the Russian soldier and so I had little fear. Each time I was stopped, I would present it and be allowed to move on. One day, after crossing a bridge, the Russian soldier looked at my pass and then looked me up and down. After a moment, he turned around and grabbed a bicycle he had taken from some poor German soul.

He handed it to me, saying, "Get going! Get going!" in Russian, with a smile on his face. I didn't argue with him. I just jumped on the bike

Travel pass given to me by the Russian Commandant and the mayor of Berlin.

Translation:

CERTIFICATE

For the route to the workplace on the line between Lichterfelde-Ost and Berlin, the bearer of this Certificate, Mr. Dagobert Lewin, Berlin Lichterfelde-Ost, Luisenstr. 1, has to use a bicycle. Because of this, it is requested that he be permitted to pass freely.

Berlin-Lichterfelde, May 25, 1945
By order of the Commandant and the Mayor

and took off. Two or three days later, another Russian patrol stopped me. The officer spoke German, and once again I gave him my pass.

"You need to go and exchange this pass for a more official one," he said. "Go to the police precinct and get one with the proper stamp."

And so I rode to the command headquarters. It appeared that the Russians had taken over the German civil bureaucracy. The Germans still ran it, but now the Russians supervised. Everything had to be approved by the Russian commandant.

I handed over my pass and told them my address. After a few minutes, they gave me a new pass, with Russian on one side and German on the other. Both confirmed my identity and authorized me to travel in the area by bicycle.

Eventually I decided it was time to leave Berlin. I stayed with the Lebrechts for another week, and then it was time to go.

"But why, Dagobert?" Jenny had asked me, perplexed. "Where are you going? There is no transportation. Berlin is a mess!"

"I need to go see the Kusitzkys in Lübars. I owe it to them. I need to make sure that they are unharmed, and they need to know that I am well. I also needed to tell them about Ilse and Klaus." I had since learned that after we were captured by the Gestapo, Ilse and Klaus had been deported to Bergen-Belsen.

The Lebrechts understood and wished me well. We made plans to meet at a later date and all promised to stay in touch.

I mounted my bicycle and started making my way to Lübars. The ride was an all-day affair.

I was quite concerned about the Kusitzkys. Would I find them there when I arrived in Lübars? My great fear was that the Gestapo had deported them or otherwise harmed them when it was discovered that they had hidden me. It was well known that anyone who harbored Jews would be imprisoned, sent to the concentration camps, or worse.

I couldn't forget the look on Anni's face when the Gestapo arrested us at her house, so serious and sad. I would have a hard time forgiving myself if anything had happened to them.

There was a tremendous amount of destruction along the way to Lübars. Whole neighborhoods had been completely bombed out, and several of the roads I tried to use were impassable. As I made detour after detour, I began to wonder whether I'd be able to get there at all that day. Finally, I reached Lübars. I walked the bike up the steep path and through the garden, leaning it against the house. I knocked at the door, praying that the Kusitzkys were unharmed. After a moment's wait, the door creaked open.

"Dagobert!" Anni screamed. "Oh my God! It is Dago! Dago!" She hugged me, jumping up and down for joy. Alex came up behind her, staring at me as if he could not believe the evidence of his own eyes. He was a very cool customer, not given to overt displays of emotion. But I could tell from the look on his face that he was genuinely pleased to see me. Maybe even a little more than pleased, but he wouldn't or couldn't show it.

In between kisses and hugs, Anni pulled me inside the house and led me to the kitchen table, tears of joy streaming down her cheeks.

"I want to hear about what has happened to you, but first, are you hungry?" she asked.

"Yes," I said, "Like a horse."

Anni laid out a small feast, which I soon demolished. Then I leaned back, got comfortable, and told them everything that had happened since I had last seen them. It turned out to be a very long story and soon it was past midnight and I could talk no more. Anni took me to a bed, not in the attic but in the second-floor bedroom, the best room in the house. Now I was here as a legitimate guest instead of as a fugitive.

I slept nonstop for twelve hours, awakening only to eat once more. After breakfast, we all sat around the kitchen table and talked. Alex had been told not to go to work that day because of the tremendous food shortages in and around Berlin. Even if there had been meat, there was no transportation to get it from the slaughterhouse to the processing plant. And if there was no meat to be processed, there was no point in Alex going to work.

It was now my turn to ask questions. There was one matter in particular that I had worried over since the day I was arrested at the Kusitzkys' house. Fearing to know the truth, it took me a second to work up the nerve to ask.

"Anni, what did the Gestapo do to you after I was arrested?"

My palms grew clammy in anticipation of their answer. What if they had been tortured? I couldn't stand the thought.

Anni looked over at Alex and then back at me.

"Nothing, Dagobert. The Gestapo did nothing to us," she said.

"Nothing?" I asked in amazement. This was unheard of. The Kusitz-kys had committed a grievous crime in the eyes of the Nazi government. They had succored enemies of the state—Jews.

"Nothing," Anni continued. "They did ask us a few questions, but we just kept repeating that we were amazed to find out that you were Jewish. We said we had no idea. We only thought you were refugees who had been bombed out of your homes. We thought we were help-ing fellow Germans."

"And they believed you?" I asked in disbelief.

"Who knows whether they believed us?" Alex said. "It doesn't matter. What does matter is that they left us alone."

"It was as though the Lord himself was watching over us," Anni said. "God protected us."

I nodded, smiling. But tears began to well up in my eyes. For some reason, Anni's words had stirred something within me, a flood of memo-ries, thoughts, and feelings that the day-to-day demands of survival had driven from my mind.

For the first time in quite a while, I thought about my parents.

My poor parents! What had happened to them? Was there a chance that they were still alive, attempting to return and find me? I desperately, desperately wanted to believe it. All of my happiness at seeing Jenny, Leo, Horst, and Heinz alive; my joy that Anni and Alex were unharmed; the euphoria brought on by the war's imminent ending—all of this was tempered by my fear for my parents.

I fell asleep that night with my mind vacillating between jubilation at the fact that this hideous war had finally ended and despair at the probable fate of my mother and father. I had no way of knowing what had happened to my parents. From their postcard, I believed that they had been sent to a concentration camp in Trawniki, Poland. It would be a miracle if they had survived the war.

But then, I was no stranger to miracles. In my own case, the odds of surviving had been overwhelmingly against me. On three separate occasions, I should have died.

What were the odds that a Russian soldier would have read a text-book written by an uncle I could barely recall? And that this same soldier would happen to be the one to lead an assault on the building I was living in? That this soldier, poised on the verge of spraying the room with machine-gun fire, trembling with the tension of battle, would hesitate to shoot, deciding to question us instead? And that this soldier would, by chance, be Jewish and speak the Yiddish language, thereby allowing us to communicate?

It was beyond my ability to calculate, but I knew the odds must be astronomical.

What were the odds that I would encounter my friend Heinrich on my way to work at the gun factory? That Heinrich would risk severe punishment to tell me that all Jewish workers were being deported? That he would give me a lead that would help me find a place to hide? Had I missed him, I would have been deported along with all the other workers to a concentration camp where I almost certainly would have died.

And what were the odds that, once I was finally arrested, I would find myself in a situation that allowed me to make a key to a locked gate, enabling me to escape? What were the odds that I would meet the people and obtain the materials that resulted in my current freedom?

In each of these instances, something that could certainly be called a miracle had saved me.

Three miracles for three death sentences.

It would take a man far wiser than I to understand why I lived when so many others died. Was it fate, destiny, mere chance, or the Hand of God? Whatever the reason, if there was any reason at all, these three miracles saved me from the fate of millions of my fellow Jews. And for that, at least, I will be eternally grateful.

PART II

AFTER
THE FALL

24

ALONE NO MORE

For several weeks now, the war had been over. I had spent years hiding underground, concerned with little more than my own survival. Now I was faced with the task of learning to live in the aftermath of war, with no threats to my life or liberty. I was staying with Alex and Anni, resting and recovering and looking to the future. Gradually, I became used to feeling secure, having enough food, and sleeping in a regular bed.

As I grew stronger and my body filled out under the influence of Anni's cooking, my patience with life in the quiet Lübars countryside grew thin. Although I had never stopped thinking about my parents, their whereabouts now became an obsession. I was also very concerned about Ilse. I had heard nothing from her since her arrest by the Gestapo and felt compelled to search out word of her fate.

So one day, I left for Berlin, heading to Oranienburger Strasse synagogue, the largest and most beautiful synagogue in the city. It seemed to me that the most likely place to begin my search would be there, where Jews would likely congregate.

When I arrived there, I was stunned by what I saw. Almost all of what had been one of the most beautiful buildings in Berlin had been destroyed. I later learned that the damage was caused by a combination of Allied bombing raids and the events of Kristallnacht.

There was a small building near the ruins of the synagogue that served as a temporary office for the Jewish community center (Jüdische

Gemeinde). Holocaust survivors filled the building, busy filling out registration forms. The Gemeinde used these forms to record names and addresses that relatives could use to help locate lost friends and family members. The office was like a beehive, with swarms of people talking, yelling, shaking hands, hugging, and crying.

Almost everyone had been marked by the war. Clothing hung loosely on frames that were gaunt and haggard, having been reduced almost to shadows by privation and fear. But the atmosphere was warm and reassuring. It had been a long time since I been in the presence of a group of people containing not a single Nazi agent and even longer since I had been around a large number of my fellow Jews. It was almost overwhelming to be free, not starving, not hunted; gathered in peace with others of my religion.

There were refugees from every corner of Europe: Jews from Poland, Lithuania, Latvia, Estonia, and, of course, Germany. Most spoke Yiddish, a language I understood only imperfectly. For whatever reason, they had all wound up in Berlin, seeking families that had been scattered to the winds.

I talked to as many of them as possible, always seeking information about Trawniki, the concentration camp in Poland to which my parents had been deported in 1942. Up until this point, everything I had heard about the camps had been rumors. They were said to be places of death, execution camps for Jews. To my utter horror, eyewitnesses told me that Jews had been killed by the thousands and, as I later learned, the death toll eventually reached into the millions. They were starved to death, worked to death, gassed, beaten, and burned to death.

Among all the refugees crowding into the community center, I found not one person who knew anything about the Trawniki camp. For a time, I carried a sign saying LOOKING FOR THE LEWINS. I still held tightly to the hope that my parents would return, that they would show up in Berlin looking for me. The day wore on and I continued asking everyone I met if they had any information about the Trawniki camp, with no success.

As I left the community center office to go back to Lübars, I mulled over what I had learned. It now appeared that finding my parents would

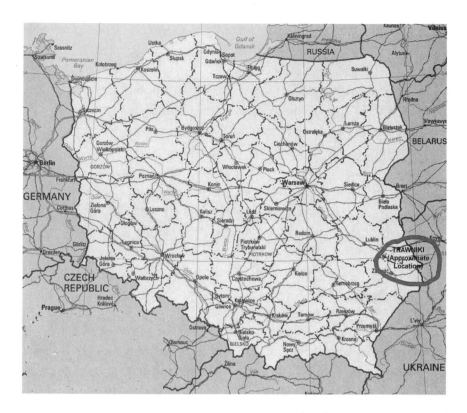

be neither quick nor easy. There was too much chaos, too many people, and too few resources. To my extreme disappointment, no one I met had been interned at Trawniki. Not a soul. The world was now learning the true nature of the Nazi "relocation" camps, and the odds that my parents had survived their internment were poor.

Every few days, I went back to the community center to check for word of my parents. Although the center continued to be filled with people searching for information about their relatives, I saw no one I knew. I didn't recognize a soul. Little by little, I began to lose hope. I sank into a depression so deep that I soon lost the desire to talk to anyone. Alex and Anni were aware of my mounting despair, but there was little they could do to help. At the community center, I talked to refugees who were in the same situation as myself, searching for lost relatives. There were quite a few people, but their efforts to find their missing family members rarely amounted to anything. There was an odd reunion or two, mostly of people who had been in the same concentration camps together. Very few found any relatives. Hitler's death machine had been too efficient.

Many of these people arrived in Berlin with nothing, their clothing ragged and torn. Just trying to obtain new clothing for them was quite a feat; there was a scarcity of practically everything in Berlin, including garments. International Jewish aid organizations such as HIAS and the American Joint Distribution Committee gave funding to the community center. They told us that Americans had joined together to give money to help us. Volunteers from America made themselves available to help the Jews who had survived the concentration camps.

I would return home to the Kusitzkys after each visit to the community center. As we ate dinner, they would always ask: "Have you found anything? Have you heard anything?"

But the answer was always no.

The people I met at the community center, for the most part, were of a stoic bent. Displays of emotion were minimal and there was little in the way of crying or weeping. The events that most of us had lived through had hardened us, forming a tough outer shell that seemed to isolate us and deny us the ability to grieve in a normal fashion. For many, there were no tears left to shed. Some were too overwhelmed by the magnitude of their losses and by the horrors they had witnessed to be able to weep freely. It seemed as if there were something in the human spirit that allowed most of them to endure only so much of the Nazi cruelties before, like an overloaded circuit, they shut down and became unable to feel.

But in spite of the numbness that seemed to have overcome me, some of the tales told by these concentration camp survivors still had the power to amaze. Their stories were so appalling, so beyond belief, that it was almost impossible for an ordinary person to grasp. These people assured me, time and time again, that they were not inventing their descriptions of the camps, as if they doubted their own memories. They named the camps death factories, whose purpose was to kill the maximum number of Jews as fast as possible.

One man I met had been a laborer at Auschwitz. His name was Paul Lewinsky, and he was deported with his parents in 1942, eventually winding up there, where he was forcibly separated from his parents. His parents were killed, but Paul, being tall and muscular, was assigned to work details.

Paul outlined for us how Jews were treated at Auschwitz. Those who were condemned to die were transported by railway car to the vicinity of the doors of the gas chambers. After leaving the cars, they were led through doors marked SHOWER, directly into a large, underground undressing area. They were told to undress for a bath and decontamination. To maintain the illusion, there were dummy showerheads and numbered pegs on which clothes could be hung, to be reclaimed after the showers.

Completely naked, the Jews were urged into the actual gas chambers. Any who resisted were beaten with rifle butts until they moved forward. The doors were closed and locked and the gas called Zyklon B was piped into the chambers. The screams and wails of the prisoners could be heard outside until, in a matter of minutes, all sign of human activity ceased. The work detail assigned to the showers would then open the doors and corpses would spill out, falling like broken dolls onto the ground outside. A team of dentists searched the mouths of the victims to remove any gold fillings, and the bodies of the women were examined to see if any valuables were concealed in their private parts. The heads of the women would also be shaved and their hair placed into bags for industrial uses.

Paul was one of the prisoners assigned to load the bodies onto wagons. Other prisoners would take the wagons to the camp ovens, where the bodies would be burned. Paul told me that they would periodically replace the prisoners who did this, killing the original laborers as they became unable to face the work and substituting new ones. He had been given his job toward the end of the operation of Auschwitz and was lucky enough to survive until the camp was liberated by the Russian Red Army.

There were three camps that, taken together, made up the Auschwitz-Birkenau complex. These camps were operated with factory-like efficiency. "Production" records were kept, documenting the number of Jews killed per day. The average was around two thousand gassed and burned in twenty-four hours, but a figure of almost nine thousand had been reached during periods of overcrowding or under other special circumstances. Estimates based on records left behind by the SS indicate around 1,100,000 Jews were killed this way.

Nothing was wasted by the Nazis, other than the lives of the prisoners themselves. Before his job loading the bodies, Paul had worked disposing of the clothing of the people who arrived there. Any valuables were confiscated. Paul had another skill that helped him survive. He was a silversmith. When the Nazis dug gold fillings out of the teeth of executed prisoners, he would use them to fashion jewelry and trinkets for the camp commandant and his cronies. The sheer volume of gold fillings, along with the prisoners' jewelry and religious articles, made the profession of silversmith one much needed by the commandant.

Paul was also ordered to melt down gold articles, taken from the Jews, into gold bullion. Ingots of gold were shipped to Berlin, presumably to be turned over to the Reichsbank, the German state bank.

Rings plundered from Jewish prisoners by the Nazis. *Courtesy of USHMM Photo Archives*

So great was the quantity of pilfered gold that Paul eventually required four assistants to keep up with the demand for recasting.

The frantic rate at which prisoners were killed did not lessen until Russian armies approached Germany. In late November 1944, the destruction of the Auschwitz facilities was ordered by Himmler, commander of all German SS and police forces. The SS did attempt to destroy the Auschwitz-Birkenau complex, but because of the rapid approach of the Russian Red Army, they only partially succeeded. When it became obvious that the Russians would overrun the camps before the job could be completed, the SS forced the remaining Jews to walk, in the dead of winter, toward and into Germany.

This herding of prisoners into Germany became known as the death march. People died from starvation and malnutrition. Many perished because they had no shoes. Lack of shoes was a death sentence; bare feet were cut and torn by rocks and debris until they became so badly mangled that walking was impossible.

If a prisoner couldn't walk, he was useless to the SS and death was certain. When Jews died during a march, the SS unceremoniously dumped their bodies on the side of the road. In some camps, such as Auschwitz, Russian soldiers arrived to find the SS already fled, leaving the prisoners to themselves. Battle-hardened though they were, they were shocked to find about seven thousand skeletal, emaciated Jews, many dead and the rest not far from it.

Hardened though I was, when Paul told me all this, I was almost overcome. The thought of this legion of madmen murdering my friends and family, desecrating their bodies while claiming to be civilized members of a "Master Race," was too much. In my mind, I pictured them digging the gold fillings out from the corpses of my kin, and then going home to dinner. Waves of nausea washed over me and I felt as if I might go insane when I thought that my parents might have suffered just such a fate.

But for an ordinary man to ponder too closely the workings of fate is a dangerous business, as was demonstrated to me the next day when I returned to the Kusitzkys. A stranger sat at the kitchen table. She was small of frame, with long black hair that fell over her shoulders. She looked to be in her fifties with a wrinkled forehead and creases that lined a smiling face. Despite the smiles, marks of long experience and deep pain could be readily seen.

Before I could say anything, Anni called out, "Dago! This is your aunt!"

Nothing Anni could have said would have surprised me more. I had not had the slightest expectation of anyone, least of all a relative, coming to find me. I just stood there, completely flabbergasted. Before I could gather my wits, she rose from her chair and came over to embrace me. She hugged and kissed me, muttering endearments.

From that moment on, I was no longer alone. We started talking and did not stop until the next morning. She was my aunt Riva Gutman, my father's little sister from Kovno, in Lithuania.

She told me that she had met me as a little boy in Kovno when my mother and I visited there. The night wore on, as we talked about the family, nieces and nephews, aunts and uncles, parents and grandparents. I still couldn't get over the fact that she had somehow managed to find me.

Riva had gone to the community center in hopes of locating my parents and discovered that I had registered there. After persuading the staff to give her my address, she walked all the way to Lübars. She had not expected me to survive the war and was surprised to discover that I still lived.

She had come to Berlin by train from the city of Lodz in Poland. Riva was aware that foodstuffs were in very short supply and commanded high prices in Berlin. In Poland, food was available in abundance and was relatively cheap. So she loaded up a large knapsack with items such as butter and salami and took the train to Berlin. The demand for food was so great in postwar Berlin that she sold everything she had within a few steps of the railroad station.

Riva wanted to accumulate enough money to pay her way to Palestine. This was her goal, and the goal of many other refugees. But not me, at least not yet. I wasn't thinking about emigration. I was too

My Aunt Riva and I.

preoccupied worrying about my parents and about Ilse and Klaus. But Aunt Riva talked ceaselessly about joining her in her quest.

"Come with me, Dago. Come to Palestine," she would say. But I would refuse, not wanting to give up hope that my parents survived.

When the subject of her own family came up, she seemed reluctant to say anything. It was obvious to me that something sad had happened. Seeing her reluctance to talk about it, I didn't push her. But eventually, with some gentle coaxing and many tears, she told me about her loss.

Riva had been forcibly confined with her husband, Meier Gutman, and her two children, Emanuel and Basia, in the Kovno ghetto. This was roughly one-quarter of the city that had been partitioned off to contain the Jewish population. Jews were not allowed to live in any other area. They were compelled to remain in the ghetto until moved by the Germans, to be relocated to labor camps in Poland, Estonia, and Latvia. These people were told that they would be well treated and would be employed as valuable workers in industries vital to the German war effort. That was the propaganda, intended to keep the Jews calm and to forestall resistance.

Eventually, the Gutman family's turn for relocation came. German military trucks drove into the ghetto and soldiers were assigned to help the crowds find seats on the trucks. As Riva's children were waiting their turn to climb into the trucks, a Lithuanian SS soldier took her little daughter, Basia, grabbed her legs, and swung her head against the truck. One look at the wound in her head left no doubt that she was dead. The SS man casually threw her body into a ditch in the side of the road. Riva saw it all.

The Lithuanian SS were said by some to be even more brutal than their German counterparts. They considered small children to be of no practical value to the Nazi war effort, and these children were often the first to be slaughtered.

Riva couldn't stop crying for a long time, recounting that particular event. Nor could I.

Following the murder of her daughter, Riva, her husband, and her son were sent first to a labor camp in Estonia and then to the Stutthof concentration camp, near Danzig, Poland. At Stutthof, Meier, Emanuel, and several others attempted to escape. They made it past the gates but had only an hour or two to enjoy their freedom. They were quickly recaptured and brought back to the camp, where the rest of the prisoners were assembled and forced to watch as they were executed.

Riva remained in Stutthof until the end of the war, used by the Germans for heavy labor. She suffered terribly, carrying out assignments that, under normal circumstances, would have been far beyond her capacity for physical labor. But it was succeed or die. When she flagged, she was beaten. Had she failed completely to carry out her assignments, she would have been executed.

When the Russian Red Army approached Stutthof, Riva and any other Jews who had survived to this point were forced by the SS to march toward Berlin. Again, she somehow managed to survive while others died.

By this time, a large part of the night had slipped away, and Riva had to return to Berlin the next day. She implored me to go back with her, urging me to accompany her to Palestine, but I refused. My desire to find my parents outweighed all other considerations. If I left Berlin, the chances that my parents would find me would be almost nil. The next morning, I accompanied Riva to the train station, where we said our good-byes. She planned to make at least one more trip to Berlin to earn additional passage money, and we would meet again when she returned.

About three weeks later, she came once more to the Kusitzkys. I felt something special with Riva. Although some things were hard for me to discuss, I held nothing back from her. There were no secrets that I could not reveal to her. I told her all about my experiences during my time as a U-boat, about Ilse and Klaus, the Gestapo prison, and all the rest. I told her everything. In return, she would talk about the Kovno ghetto and the camps. Somewhere along the line, we became very good friends, and when the day had passed, it seemed much too short. The time had come for her to return to Lodz.

At the station, she again tried to persuade me to return with her. Again, I refused. I still had hope. Riva left for Lodz, telling me that she would come back one last time. She hoped that, if by then I hadn't heard anything of my parents or Ilse, I would leave Berlin and come with her.

During those next few weeks, I continued to talk to people. I followed some leads, but they all ended up going nowhere. The Kusitzkys fed and housed me and gave me some of Heinz's old clothes. At long last I was able to shed the rags that I had worn since becoming a U-boat. The community center also helped, giving me a little money, which I used to take the train to and from Lübars.

Eventually, Riva returned to Berlin. We talked once more about emigrating to Palestine. It had been quite a while since I first started looking for my parents. Riva told me bluntly that there was little chance that I would find my parents if it hadn't happened by now. She forced me to make a decision I had been trying to avoid. By now, I had nearly given up hope. Although I felt as if I were being torn in two, I could not help but go along with her. My parents weren't coming back, and my future was not in Germany, the country that had taken everything from me that I had ever cared about. I agreed to go with her to Lodz.

I left Riva's Lodz address at the Jewish community center and prepared myself for a task I dreaded. Saying good-bye to the Kusitzkys was going to be difficult. They had given me food and shelter for quite a while, often at considerable risk to themselves. In some ways they had become the parents I no longer had, and I the son they had always wished for. Since everything of importance always took place in the kitchen, this is where I chose to make my good-byes.

"Stay here," Anni and Alex pleaded.

But I could not. Germany was part of my past, not of my future. I tried to explain that Berlin held too many bad memories for me to remain. I intended to make a new start in a new country. For me, that country would be Palestine.

Anni cried, "Stay with us until you establish yourself. We will help you. There is no need to go elsewhere. Things will be so much better from now on! You will see. Stay with us!"

Though it almost broke my heart, I had to say no.

She continued trying to persuade me. "How can you go to a country whose language you do not know? To a place you know nothing about? It will be too difficult."

I admitted the truth of what she said but told her that I still had to go.

They finally accepted my decision. Anni prepared a final packet of sandwiches for Riva and myself, and we departed the Kusitzky house. As we walked down the hill, I turned my head for a final look at the life I was leaving behind. Alex and Anni had been my shelter and comfort and I probably would not have survived without them. But I was twenty-two, the war was over, and the future beckoned. It was time to start a new life.

25

REFUGEE

WE TRAVELED FROM BERLIN TO LODZ, Poland, by train. Riva had purchased tickets for both of us at the Berlin station, since I was completely
without funds. She seemed confident that we would reach our destination
in Lodz; I was not so sure. I was traveling without identification papers of
any kind, and all traffic in and out of Berlin was now tightly controlled
by the Russian army.

Riva walked through several cars and eventually found one in which
several Jewish Red Army officers were sitting, some of whom were of
high rank. She recognized two of them as being from her hometown of
Kovno, Lithuania. Taking a seat next to them, Riva told them who we
were and about my lack of papers. The officers told her not to worry,
that they would take care of us.

As our train crossed into Poland, the Commandansky Patrolat—the
equivalent of the military police—walked through the train, checking
everyone's documents. When they came to us, I was petrified. But Riva
leaned over and whispered a few words to our new friends, and they
in turn summoned the patrol commander to a short conference. After
they finished talking, the commander saluted and continued down the
car with his troops.

An hour or so later, the Jewish officers left our train to board another
one headed to Kovno. Riva and I were now on our own. Before we had
traveled more than a few miles, another military patrol approached, again

asking for documents. This time, I had no one to intervene on my behalf. When we saw them coming, Riva told me to go into the bathroom and hide, but when I tried the door handle, it proved to be locked. There was nothing left to do but to take the door to the outside of the car. Sweating, I looked around, desperately seeking a place to hide. If I was found without papers, it would mean immediate arrest and incarceration.

Crouching, I stepped outside the car and stood on the platform, but there was nowhere to hide. They had almost finished checking our car and were heading my way. I cursed when I thought about the irony of surviving years of Nazi attempts to locate and arrest me only to be taken into custody now by Russian forces. There seemed no help for it. I was trapped.

I briefly considered trying to jump but quickly abandoned the idea, since I didn't think I would live through the fall. Then I noticed a ladder affixed to the end of the car, leading up to the roof. A last glance at the approaching patrol convinced me that I had no choice. Hoping that it would be as easy for me as for the heroes in the movies, I started climbing. The wind made the climb difficult, but fear gave me strength. I heaved myself onto the roof and lay down spread-eagle. The roof of the car was smooth, without grips of any kind. All I could do was lay down flat with my palms against the slick surface of the train's roof and hope that we wouldn't go around any sudden curves.

A few minutes later, the soldiers came out of the car and moved on to the next one. I waited a few minutes to be sure, came down the ladder, and went back inside, resuming my place next to Riva. She took one look at me, flushed and sweating, and asked, "What has happened? "

I told her about my retreat to the roof and how I had avoided the patrol. She warned me that I should not endanger myself again with these kinds of antics, even though I had explained to her that I had no other choice. Fortunately, we had no further complications along the way. A short while later, we arrived in Lodz. We made our way, as quickly as possible, to the apartment building where she lived.

Lodz was abuzz with activity, like a giant beehive, with people swarming everywhere. There were many Jewish survivors here, people of every type and description. The rumor mill had it that Lodz was the starting point for an established track to Palestine. Jews from all over

Europe gathered here in hopes of finding a way to get there. We had come to Lodz to connect with the guides that were supposedly available to escort refugees on an underground trip to Palestine. By car, train, ship, or foot, these guides were supposed to make the trip safe for those who could afford their price. Rumor said that they knew places where we would be able to pass without difficulty.

Merchandise of all kinds, especially different types of food, were being sold by vendors with pushcarts and on street corners. My experiences in Germany and an almost constant state of near-starvation had left me obsessed with food. I always felt hungry. Food and avoiding the lack of it was always on my mind. There was little enough food in Berlin, and it reassured me to see that Poland did not suffer the same problem.

Arriving at the apartment, we climbed the stairs to Riva's room. There were four flights, all filthy, covered with garbage that spread over the steps and landings. I had recovered enough so that the steps were not a problem for me. But the same wasn't true of Riva.

She was not in good physical condition, having suffered greatly in the camps. Aside from being in her fifties and quite rotund, the demands of physical labor and severe malnourishment had taken their toll on her. Riva had to stop on the landing of each set of stairs to catch her breath. On level ground she didn't have much of a problem, especially if she didn't have to go very fast. Stairs were another question.

Riva shared a two-room apartment with six other people. Although my new roommates made efforts to keep the apartment clean, it was difficult. The parts of the city I saw were incredibly filthy, with flies and garbage everywhere. In the apartment building, sanitation facilities were almost nonexistent. I had been given no forewarning about any of this and was horrified, but I resigned myself to living there. As with other situations I had encountered over the past few years, I had no choice but to endure. I just hoped our stay here would be a short one.

For some reason, Riva became melancholy. Perhaps the atmosphere made her think. She chose this time to talk about all the family members we had lost. Other than ourselves, we knew of no one in our family who had survived the war. Thirty-two beloved relatives murdered on my father's side alone. It seemed that Riva was all the family I had left.

Riva and I made eight people total, living in two small rooms. Two Lithuanian couples shared one room, and Riva and I shared another with a brother and sister, also Jews from Lithuania. All of these people were from Kovno and had known each other before the war. They had all been in different concentration camps and had somehow found each other after the war ended.

Europe was now in chaos, an anarchistic, burned-out shadow of its former self. Much of the governmental infrastructures had been destroyed by the war. With most of Europe in turmoil, border authorities had become corrupt, using their positions to extort bribes. To pass international borders, many of these authorities demanded a fee. Without money, it was impossible to pass. This situation repeated itself at every border, and sometimes even in the middle of a state or country, from one city to the next. Some areas were infested with armed bandits, preying on those trying to pass through.

There was little in the way of official information about emigration. This soon after the war, the embassies and consulates that still existed were not able to help. There were only rumors to guide us—and the rumors said that getting to Palestine was difficult, complex, and expensive. Without having the right connections, there was little chance of making it. There were also rumors that the British were prohibiting any more Jews from entering Palestine and that those attempting entry were being imprisoned.

We lingered in Lodz, waiting for the scouts who would take us to Palestine. Riva had enough money to get us there. But no scouts appeared, and eventually after four miserable weeks, our roommates gave up. Some of them heard that the route was no longer available. Others speculated that the scouts had been killed or arrested.

All of this discouraging news convinced my roommates that we had to make other plans. I wasn't able to participate in these discussions because I didn't speak Yiddish, and they wouldn't slow down enough for me to understand. Unable to distinguish fact from fiction, we decided to go to Germany. We had heard that Jewish organizations from the United States, with the assistance of the US Army, had set up camps for refugees there. It was said that Jews could stay in these camps while they were awaiting emigration to other countries. So we packed up our meager belongings, climbed down those filthy stairs one last time, and bid adieu to Lodz.

To forestall the difficulties that I had experienced on the way into Poland, it was decided that I should remain quiet. When the military patrols approached, my friends would put a blanket over my head, covering my face. The patrols were told that I was insane and that it was better not to disturb me, lest I become violent. Other times, the patrolmen were told that I had a contagious disease, which would inevitably send them scurrying to another part of the car.

When we arrived in Berlin, I led the others to the Jüdische Gemeinde. I was very anxious to find out if anything had been heard from my parents, but there was nothing. No word from my parents. No word from Ilse. Nothing had changed since I had been there four weeks ago.

I could not stop myself from giving up all hope. I was devastated. Riva tried to comfort me, but I was inconsolable. I could no longer delude myself that my parents were coming home. I let go of the last remaining shred of longing and steeled myself to face a future devoid of my parent's presence. Once again, I had no choice.

If I continued to hold on to the dream that they would return, I would never be able to break free from Berlin. In no way did I wish to forget my parents, but I now realized that if I was ever to make something of myself, I had to put the past behind me. My aunt and I would somehow take ourselves to Palestine, where we would start a new life, a new beginning.

Arriving at the community center, we were referred to the AJDC, the American Joint Distribution Committee office. After explaining our situation, they made arrangements for us to transfer to the Feldafing DP (Displaced Persons) camp in Bavaria. They provided funds for us to travel there, plus something extra for sustenance along the way. We had to leave almost immediately, so there was no time to visit the Kusitzkys or to do anything else.

Our travel route was from Berlin to Munich and then on to Feldafing. It had been explained to us that the camp was under the protection and authority of the US Army because it was located in the American occupation zone. The Feldafing camp administrators sent an American army truck to pick us up from the train station.

At first sight, Feldafing looked more like a vacation spot than a refugee camp, but closer inspection soon disabused us of that notion. Located near Starnberg, the home of the beautiful Lake Starnberg, were a series of houses that had been used as a training school for elite members of the Hitler Youth. The school was called NAPOLA, and the US Army had requisitioned it, its grounds, and another forty villas in the surrounding area. The entire sector was designated as a displaced persons camp for the use of the Jewish refugees, who were to remain there until they were able to emigrate to countries that would accept them.

It was rumored that General Eisenhower had ordered Germans removed from the villas to make the entire area available for use by Jewish refugees. Eisenhower had visited Dachau immediately after its liberation and had seen the results of Nazi handiwork for himself. He

General Eisenhower inspecting Camp Feldafing. *Photo by Marc Block, courtesy of USHMM Photo Archives.*

had publicly expressed his contempt for the Nazis on several occasions. One of these was his visit to the Feldafing DP camp on Yom Kippur in 1945. In what could only be termed an example of poetic justice, he ordered that these buildings be given over for our temporary use.

A small committee of refugees greeted us on arrival and directed us to our berthing area. We were assigned an apartment, a place called Villa Nordenholz. In spite of the name, our housing was anything but luxurious. There was one "large" room, approximately sixteen by twenty-four feet, one part of which contained one pair of bunk beds, two other single beds, a small table, and four chairs. That was all anyone could have possibly crammed into the available space. I slept there along with three others. There were two other sleeping spaces, really large closets. Riva slept in one and a young couple, the Schmidts (Smiths), shared the other. They were separated from the main bedroom only by thin curtains. Leible Schmidt was one of the Jewish police officers

DP Camp Feldafing in Southern Germany. The camp housed displaced persons (refugees). Shown is the camp council building, which acted as a center for the camp.

in the camp, and he wore an armband and a hat to that effect. Chana was a tiny young woman who attended the ORT school, learning how to be a seamstress.

Our living accommodations worked out to be about sixty square feet per person. A very small stove constituted our "kitchen" and another small space with a toilet was our bathroom. But in spite of the cramped quarters, it was warm, safe, and Nazi-free. And I was with family, my newly beloved aunt.

About 3,500,000 Jews lived in Poland before the war. The exact number of Jews who survived is not known, but the best estimates put the number at between 200,000 to 250,000.

Of those, several thousand returned to their hometowns in Poland, hoping that the end of the war and the defeat of Nazi Germany would

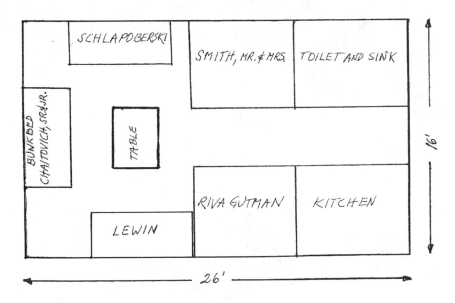

416 S.F. ÷ 7 = 60 S.F. PER PERSON
APPROXIMATE FLOORPLAN OF APARTMENT

Floor plan of room in DP Camp Feldafing, where I lived for four years.

also mean the end of the chronic anti-Semitism they had endured over the course of many years from the Polish population. But it was not to be.

After the war, there were anti-Semitic outbursts in some Polish cities resulting in beatings and murders of Jews. The worst of these took place in Kielce, a midsize town of about fifty thousand, 120 miles south of Warsaw. When Germany invaded Poland in 1939, approximately twenty-five thousand Jews lived in Kielce. After the war, two hundred people who had survived the concentration camps returned to Kielce to live there once again. On July 5, 1946, a rumor spread through Kielce that a Polish boy had been murdered by Jews. Poles in Kielce reacted to this lie by slaughtering forty-two Jewish men, women, and children.

The Polish government seemed unwilling or unable to suppress the anti-Jewish excesses. News of the pogrom in Kielce spread like wildfire, and large numbers of the Jews of Poland left, with most going to the US zone of occupation in Germany, where Feldafing and other camps were located. From there, they hoped and expected to emigrate to Palestine.

The populations of the camps swelled enormously with the Polish influx. When I got to Feldafing, the camp had nearly reached its maximum population of five thousand. The Polish Jews were distributed to DP camps all over West Germany, including Feldafing. I made friends with several of them. We talked about their experiences in Poland at great length, and they often expressed their disdain for the Poles. Many swore they would never return to Poland.

I wanted to forget about Germany and Germans. By the time I was ten years old I had been made aware of the reality of anti-Semitism. I soon became sick of living among people who despised me because of my religion.

My world was divided into two parts: those who lived outside the camp and those who lived inside. Outside the camp were enemies. It wasn't hard to find reminders of the hate campaign against the Jews. Some places still had paintings on their walls, with slogans like *JUDEN*

RAUS! ("JEWS OUT!"), JEWS ARE NOT WANTED HERE! But when the Allied armed forces took control of German territory, it wasn't long before all these signs disappeared. Suddenly, the Germans revealed that they had always liked Jews and had many Jewish friends. They were as surprised as anyone to learn that Jews had been mistreated or murdered. What a joke.

———————

Riva was highly respected by her peers. The younger people from Kovno would often gather around her, asking her advice on all types of things. I wasn't privy to their discussions, but I could see that she always gave freely of herself. I suppose that is what endeared her to many of the other Litvaks (Lithuanian Jews) from Kovno.

People who had survived the ordeals in the concentration camps were hardened, both physically and mentally. They had to be, or else they would have been dead. Those who were too sentimental weren't able to cope with the conditions in the camps. They died quickly.

As the days wore on, I did what I could to keep myself active and busy. But I wasn't really focused on life in Feldafing. My attention was on getting out; the camp was only a way station on the journey to Palestine. I wanted to leave this soil where so many of my people had perished.

We all felt that the only solution to the terrible tragedies of the Jewish people was a Jewish state in Palestine. Palestine was still under British rule, based on a League of Nations mandate. The hope and expectation of the Jews was that the State of Israel would eventually be established there.

Jewish Brigade soldiers, part of the British Army in Palestine, came to the DP camps to provide support and education. Their mission was to prepare the Jews to settle in Palestine, even though the British government was sharply limiting Jewish immigration. The soldiers organized all kinds of activities, both political (meaning Zionist) and cultural. All these heavily emphasized Jewish interests and aspirations.

I was amazed at the great number of people who were not only talented but also quite experienced in areas such as music, the arts, journalism, sports, theater, management, religion, education, and others. It was not long before two and then three theater groups (Amcho, Habima, and Partisans) began presenting plays and musical performances. Unfortunately for me, most of these plays were performed in Yiddish, a language I was still learning. But I liked listening to the music and watching the actors, even though my comprehension of the words was limited.

All of these activities were conducted by people from the camp population. Celebrities from the United States would sometimes come to the camp to help raise morale. The great composer and conductor Leonard Bernstein was one of these. He delivered an emotional address, lending encouragement to the Jews of the DP camp, then led the camp in singing the Zionist anthem, "Hatikvah" ("The Hope").

Three newspapers were published in the camp: *Das Freie Wort* (*The Free Word*), *Unterwegs* (*On the Road*), and *Agudath Israel*. All the newspapers were published in Yiddish. They wrote about anything and everything. The most intense discussions always revolved around the possibility of a Jewish homeland in Palestine and everything connected with it. They filled in the rest with current events, happenings at the camp, a little dose of gossip, who was getting married, who was born, and who had died.

From time to time, there would be some interchange of activities between Feldafing and other DP camps in the US zone of occupation. The orchestras and theater groups from Feldafing would travel to perform in the other camps and vice versa. The AJDC was a partner in nearly all our undertakings and supported them wholeheartedly. This also included the establishment of a library at Feldafing, with a selection of over one thousand books and over twenty newspapers in Yiddish, English, Russian, and German.

One of the absolute priorities was to provide schooling for the children in the camp. It was quite difficult to organize and equip schools, and a great deal had to be improvised to make it possible. Some of the problems were the lack of teachers, books, chairs, and desks. Some of the children knew only languages such as Polish, Russian, and Hungarian. Even though many knew Yiddish, it soon became clear that Hebrew had to be the common language in preparation for living in Palestine.

Some children had never had any schooling, or had not had any for the last several years. Some had never used a pen or pencil. It was a huge task to bring the schools into being. With the help of many in the camp and assistance from Jewish organizations in the United States, it was done. Children received basic education in a variety of subjects that would enable them to face the future with more confidence than they would have had otherwise.

There weren't many children in the camp, since there weren't many who had survived the war. Those that had were usually at least into their teenage years. Orphans lived in the children's block. They were taken care of mostly by educators. A few were extremely young. Some of the older camp residents would go to the children's block and play with them. They would try to give them the love they would have received from their parents, had they survived the Nazi terror.

There were a few *kibbutzim* near the camp to help prepare for emigration to Palestine. *Kibbutzim* were organizations in which people lived collectively. Everyone ate together and worked together. They grew fruits and vegetables, learning agriculture and farming. Most of those emigrating would eventually live on a *kibbutz* in Palestine.

As far as I could tell, I was the only German Jew in the Feldafing camp. Most of the people around me were Lithuanian Jews from Kovno. There were also Jews from other areas of Lithuania and Latvia. The majority of the survivors in Feldafing were originally from Poland and Hungary. A small number of German Jews returned to their hometowns, from which they decided whether or not to pursue their plans for emigration. I didn't do this because I wanted to be with my Aunt Riva and go to Palestine with her.

I made friends with a few Jewish men in the camp but not with any of the girls. There were fewer women than men in Feldafing. More men survived because the Nazis considered many of the women unfit for the heavy work in the concentration camps. More often than not, they were

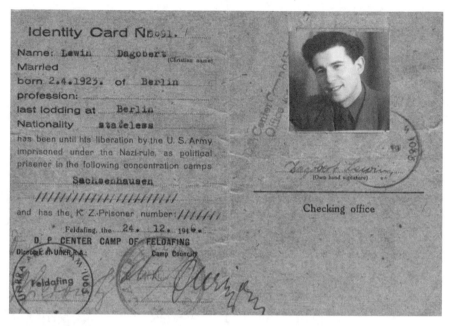

Identity card issued by DP Camp Feldafing administration.

looking for people who could lift heavy loads and could stand up under the demands of heavy physical labor.

Of the Jewish girls who had survived and were now living in the Feldafing camp, most were either already married or steadily dating. None of the rest caught my attention. Besides, I was still married to Ilse. If she was still alive.

Little by little, I made friends with other people. Many had lost their families in concentration camps, just as I had. We spent time playing soccer, running, practicing gymnastics, and swimming in the nearby lake. On one of our swimming days, a US Army truck pulled up to the lake with a number of American soldiers in the back. The soldiers jumped out and positioned themselves in a way that made no sense to us. They weren't facing us, so we weren't scared. One of the American soldiers produced a ball and another produced some wooden sticks.

We hadn't a clue what they were up to. We couldn't figure it out. One of them put something on his head that looked like a birdcage.

We still didn't know what they were doing.

Then one of them threw a ball at the man with a birdcage on his head. There was another man standing in front of the man with the birdcage, and he tried to hit the ball with one of the wooden sticks. But he didn't hit it. So the man who had thrown the ball the first time threw another ball at him. Eventually, the man hit the ball, way over the heads of the rest of them, and the ball disappeared.

We tried to ask the soldiers what they were doing, but these particular soldiers couldn't understand German, and we couldn't speak English. Later on, we were able to talk to some German-speaking soldiers, and they explained to us that what they were doing actually had a purpose and a name. It was called baseball. Though I didn't realize it at the time, this was my first step toward becoming an American.

Nearly everyone spoke Yiddish in the Feldafing camp. Very few spoke fluent German, and I rarely attempted to do so. In order to talk to anybody, I had to learn Yiddish. I had no formal instruction, so I just picked it up from Riva and the others in the room. I was fortunate that I had an aptitude for languages and didn't have a problem learning it.

Spiritually, much changed for me in those early days at Feldafing. Riva was quite religious, having been raised in an observant family in Kovno. Our roommate, Rabbi Schlapobersky, was strictly observant. Since I wasn't one to just sit around watching the world go by, I joined them. I learned to *daven* (pray).

There were several synagogues in Feldafing, but attendance was not overwhelming. It seemed to me that the level of religious pursuit didn't change much for people during the war. If they were Orthodox before the war, they were generally Orthodox after the war. Those who weren't before the war weren't observant in the camp.

As for me, I went through the motions of living an observant Jewish life, mostly because of my aunt and Rabbi Schlapobersky. They made some mild requests that I attend synagogue, but they gave nothing that could have been interpreted as a command.

Riva made Sabbath dinner. The traditional Jewish stew of beans and potatoes and sometimes beef, *cholent*, was her specialty. She cooked it on our little stove on Friday. Then she would put it under Rabbi Schlapo-bersky's mattress so that it would be warm for Sabbath lunch the next day. Everybody in our room would eat it as a special treat. Otherwise, we ate with everyone else in the mess hall cafeteria.

I did not feel totally comfortable in the DP camp. We were still in enemy territory, and the Germans would still take any opportunity to show displeasure and disdain for Jews. The German women who frat-ernized with the American soldiers frequently manipulated the soldiers into harrassing Jews when we were outside the DP camp.

My physical condition continued to improve. At Feldafing, the administration regularly distributed food packages of various kinds, some from the United States and some procured locally. The parcels from the United States nearly always came from the AJDC and UNRRA. They contained things such as chocolate bars, candy, canned goods, cookies, crackers, and, to the delight of many, cigarettes. I didn't smoke, so I traded the cigarettes for food.

The Chaitovitch father and son team who occupied the bunkbeds in our room were not religiously observant and fended for themselves, regardless of time and day. The young Chaitovitch had a girlfriend from Kovno who had survived the concentration camps just as he had. Young Chaitovitch was gone from our room most of the time, spending his hours with her instead of with us.

The older Chaitovitch was very considerate of Aunt Riva. He liked to do her little favors, to praise her, and to talk with her about the old days in Kovno. This older Chaitovitch was quite a go-getter, aggressive. He'd go and find food for her to cook. He obviously held her in high esteem.

Leible and Chana Schmidt always seemed to be fighting and arguing. It was almost expected that at certain intervals, Leible and Chana would fight. It was very difficult to have to listen to them all the time, since all that separated their fights and our ears was a thin curtain. First, Chana would raise her voice, then the fight would escalate, mostly with her yelling at him as he remained quiet. After their loud arguments, it would become very quiet, signifying that they had kissed and made up.

Rav. Schlapobersky was a big man, about six foot three and weighing two hundred pounds. He was very distinguished looking, yet young. He must have been a good worker, because he managed to survive in the concentration camps. He was the director of the Torah day school at Feldafing, a school that taught nearly 150 children.

Rav. Schlapobersky also had his eyes on my aunt Riva. Eventually, he asked her to marry him, but she turned him down; he was too slow. Then Chaitovitch asked her and she said no because he was too rough, too coarse.

Riva had spent her days visiting other people, most of whom she knew from Kovno or from the concentration camps. Otherwise, she read, wrote, and corresponded with her friends and relatives in Palestine. She attended courses to learn Hebrew to prepare herself for emigration to Palestine.

In the winter, the rooms were very cold, as the heating was completely inadequate. The villas around Feldafing were built to be summer houses, not to be inhabited during the winter. There were a few steam-heated radiators, which worked very poorly. We huddled in our blankets and sometimes we had to cover ourselves with coats and sleep in our clothes. But for us, it was still much better than where we had slept during the war.

The Jews of the camp mostly looked to the future, not the past. Few went around moaning about how they had lost their families. It is hard to say why. My opinion was that their minds were occupied with day-to-day living. No doubt many of them did not want to think about their losses, lest they become overwhelmed by their grief.

But in quiet moments, I did think about my parents.

When I thought of my father, I remembered how, when I was eight years old, I helped him in his first metal products shop. He had set it up in the basement of the 112 building on Koepenicker Strasse in Berlin. I remember pushing his wagon. When he expanded his business to a bigger place aboveground at the same address, his foreman, Herr Hoffman, who was a fair amateur artist, drew a picture of my father on a motorcycle. He titled it "Der Schnelle Leopold," "The Speedy Leopold."

Occasionally, pictures of the Gestapo dragging my parents away would pop up in my mind. Most of the time, I would instantly try to clamp down on these pictures, suppressing them. It did no good. I would still feel my grief rising to the surface, constricting my throat. Whenever I met someone from the concentration camps in the Lublin district of Poland, I would ask them if they knew anything about Trawniki, where my parents had been sent. But as always, no one did.

A few times, I saw camp residents have emotional breakdowns. One such instance happened while I was in the theater, watching a performance of a play written by another camp survivor. It depicted scenes from the concentration camps. In the middle of the performance, a man in the audience jumped up and started screaming at the top of his lungs, as tears flooded down his cheeks. He was yelling in Yiddish, "Dear God, what have I done to deserve this? My dearest wife, my little children, what did they do to deserve this? What have I done to deserve this? Where are you, God?"

He kept screaming this over and over again, crying. Others around him tried to calm him down, to no avail. He was eventually led out of the theater and taken back to his room. His frenzy was apparently contagious, as others in the audience began screaming and shouting. Everyone was upset, and the performance was stopped. But people understood and sympathized with the man's outbreak of emotion. I did too. I felt like weeping, though I didn't.

The curtain closed for ten minutes. Then the director appeared in front of the curtain. He said, "We all understand and sympathize with Moishele Cohen, and we feel the same way, but we must keep going. As the Americans say, 'The show must go on.' So we are now going to continue where we left off." The play proceeded. The next day, the camp newspapers had big articles and commentaries about the outbreak.

During another theatrical production, a woman got up, weeping uncontrollably. She began shouting derogatory remarks about the Germans in general and about the Lager Sylt concentration camp SS in particular. After she had expended her fury in denouncing the Germans she sat back down, and the people next to her helped to soothe her pain.

Though I had the same feelings as the others, I rarely broke down. The exception was when Riva would talk about the deaths of her children. She would cry and I would feel as though my heart was being torn out of me. This was not the deaths of strangers; this was more personal. It was the slaughter of Riva's children, my own family, and Riva's tears were the most bitter fruit yet borne by the seeds of hatred the Nazis had planted in me.

26

DIVORCE

FROM TIME TO TIME, the American Joint Distribution Committee sent a roster of survivors to the Feldafing camp listing those who had lived through the war. These lists were posted publicly and eagerly read by anyone who still had hope that their families might be alive. Though I no longer believed that my parents or Ilse had survived, I would still occasionally check the lists.

Late in the spring of 1946, I had just finished breakfast and decided to check the latest postings. I trekked through the mud to the administration building and waited for the old woman in front of me to finish. I was in no hurry, so I stood patiently. When I heard her sigh and walk away, head down and feet dragging, I knew what she had found. Nothing. The old woman trudged stolidly back toward the kitchen, in a kind of sad waltz that almost everyone in the camp had, by now, danced many times over.

Those who visited the bulletin board on a regular basis often became discouraged. The vast majority of missing friends and loved ones sought by camp residents were almost certainly dead, buried along with their identities in mass graves or burned to ashes in crematoria. But there was still a tiny flame of hope that never ceased to burn, the longing that today would be the day that the name would appear. For most, that day never came.

I approached the paper pinned to the wall and started scanning. No Leopold or Johanna. I traversed the *L*s. I saw "Lewin, Ilse Perl. Bergen-Belsen." And then, "Perl, Klaus. Bergen-Belsen."

I choked, sputtering, as I felt the blood drain from my face. Ilse! Ilse and Klaus were listed as survivors! I couldn't believe my eyes. I read both names over and over again. They had survived and were being housed at the Bergen-Belsen DP camp!

I turned around and, nearly plowing down a man who was standing behind me, ran through the mud to Villa Nordenholz. Riva was in the tiny kitchen, making lunch as I burst in, yelling that Ilse and Klaus were alive.

She gasped in surprise. "What? What did you say?"

"I said Ilse and Klaus are alive! They're on the list! I just saw it!"

"Oh my God! How wonderful!"

"A miracle from God," Rabbi Schlapobersky declared. Seeing my euphoria, the ever-practical rabbi asked, "So what are you going to do now?" His question caught me by surprise, quickly letting the wind out of my sails. Up until now, the prospect of Ilse having survived the war seemed dim, a fantasy that had little chance of coming true. But the rabbi's question forced me to think about the new realities of the situation.

Rabbi Schlapobersky could see the fizz going out of me. "You were married to her, right?" he asked me.

"Well, uh, yes," I said.

"So, do you want to continue being married to her?"

I stood there silently, hesitating. "I don't know," I said uneasily. "I just don't know. It is something I will have to think about." Did I want to resume my role as husband to a woman I had married only to protect? Did I want to be a father to a child who wasn't mine? I could see that these were questions that would take some intense soul-searching to figure out. At least they were alive.

Dazed by the sudden turn of events, I retreated onto my bed. A surrounding buzz, rising in volume, made me realize that the news was already spreading through the building. Soon I would be the target of a barrage of well-meaning questions. I turned around and unobtrusively left Villa Nordenholz, heading down to the lake.

I was elated that they were alive. Rabbi Schlapobersky was right; it was a miracle. But I had formed a strong bond with my aunt Riva that filled a place in me that had been left empty by my parents' disappearance. We had grown so close that I wasn't sure I wanted anyone else to interfere with that bond. I had married Ilse to save her life and the life of her child. Our hasty wedding had given her and Klaus the protection that only a marriage certificate could bring. And for a time, it had worked, protecting all of us.

But, as I examined my feelings, I had to admit that I didn't love her. During our time apart, I had almost forgotten that I was even married. Had the circumstances been different, I knew I would not have married her. I cared a great deal for both her and Klaus, but this affection was due to the bond formed by shared experiences and great danger, not love. We had been separated for almost two years. The question I now asked myself was, *What duty did I owe her?*

I stood there by the lake, with the cold wind whipping through my hair, and thought about the woman I had exchanged vows with. I had no idea what Ilse would expect of me or how she would feel about me when we met again. I tried to put it out of my mind, since there was nothing I could do about it until I saw her. I was left confused and uneasy by a future I knew I would have to face.

Over the next few days, there was a great deal of talk about all of this between Riva, Rabbi Schlapobersky, and myself. I was required to explain, at length, how we came to be together. They were very concerned that what brought Ilse and I together was anything but love.

"You aren't in love with her, Dago. You probably have never been in love with her," Riva said.

"It is not as though you had a real marriage," Rabbi Schlapobersky added. "You have had more than your share of misery. You are entitled to happiness, Dagobert! You deserve a new life!"

I was concerned that, whatever happened, I had to be fair to Ilse. Riva fumed. She thought that we were both better off with no marriage than a marriage without love, and she wasn't bashful about making her opinions known. She felt that if I returned to Ilse, any chance that I had for happiness would be lost to me. I could only shake my head in confusion.

Then the issue of Klaus came up. "He isn't yours!" Riva nearly screamed, "He's not flesh of your flesh!"

The fact that Klaus was another man's child bothered Riva immensely. If Klaus had been an orphaned family member, the child of a brother or cousin, then she would have considered it a righteous duty to raise him. But Klaus was no relation to us. He was the child of a stranger.

Riva continued, seething, "You know practically nothing about Klaus! You don't even know who his father was!"

It was true that I knew next to nothing about Klaus's father or the circumstances of his birth. Ilse never volunteered any information, and I never asked. It seemed to be something she had no wish to talk about. And if she had something to hide, I preferred to stay quiet about it rather than digging up something best left alone.

My relationship with Klaus was, at best, awkward. I was very fond of him, but the mystery surrounding his birth had always troubled me. The demands of survival placed upon me by the war had always pushed these types of questions into the background. I was only nineteen and very inexperienced when we got married. I never thought about the future or about what would become of our marriage after the war. I was too worried about surviving the moment. Until now, all of this had been something I had buried deep within my psyche, to be exhumed at a later date. That date had now arrived.

The entire discussion was hard for me. I knew that Riva and Rabbi Schlapobersky only wanted the best for me, but it was difficult to listen to them. As I sat there, trying to decide what to do, Riva and Rabbi Schlapobersky both watched me closely. I could see that they were concerned that I make the right decision. Schlapobersky could barely contain himself. He put his hand gently on my shoulder and turned me around to face him.

"Dago, you must give her a *get*, a Jewish divorce. It will be best for both of you. Then you can get on with your lives. If you don't do it now, you will end up doing it later. But by then, there may be children involved, not to mention the time you will have spent in a marriage you know is wrong."

After a few more days of this, I decided that I had no choice, I had to go to Bergen-Belsen. I had to see Ilse again. I had to be sure. And I had to see her in person. There were no telephones available in Bergen-Belsen and mail would have been too slow. If I was going to get a divorce, I wanted to get it over with as quickly as possible. I sent a telegram ahead, letting her know that I was alive and on my way to see her. Wasting no time, I bought a ticket to Belsen-Hone in the British occupation zone and left the next day.

Bergen-Belsen had been one of the largest Nazi concentration camps. After liberation, a DP camp was created in the area to house the survivors, much like Feldafing. Shortly before noon, palms sweating, I checked in at the guard house, asking to see Ilse Perl Lewin. The guard gave me directions to the little house where she now lived with Klaus. A few minutes later, I was knocking on her door.

And there she was. "Ilse!" I almost shouted. I really had not ever expected to see her again. And yet, there she was, my wife. I don't know what I expected. I didn't know if I would find her thin and skeletal or healthy-seeming on the outside but psychologically traumatized by her experiences. To all appearances, she looked to be in good shape.

"Oh my God! Oh my God! You're here!" she squealed, grabbing me around the shoulders, hugging me. "Come in, come in!" She yelled for Klaus, while leading me into a small, airy sitting room. After a few more minutes of exchanging hugs and smiles, we both sat at a small table near the door. The euphoria of our initial greeting died down as we got down to the business of catching up on events. Ilse said, "You go first, tell me what has happened to you."

So I started from the day we had been separated by the Gestapo. I told her about being sent to prison, my escape, and seeking refuge with the Lebrechts. Then about the Russians arriving in Berlin, my miraculous survival, and finally, about meeting Aunt Riva. She listened intently until I finished, then it was her turn.

Ilse reached across the table and clasped my hands. "We had a little baby boy, Dago," she said, looking away from me as if my presence there was too painful a reminder of what might have been. Tears slowly slid down her cheeks. "I named him Gad Lewin. He was born May 15, 1945, after Belsen was liberated, but he was very ill. We were all extremely hungry, malnourished. It goes without saying that the Nazis offered no medical care. I'm probably lucky that they didn't murder me, since I couldn't work.

"After the camp was liberated, Gad was born, but there was still very little available in the way of health care. Many thousands of prisoners were in desperate need of attention, but the few medical personnel here lacked the medicine and equipment they needed to help. He died when he was five months old, on October 4, 1945."

I sat there quietly, letting all of this sink in. I had been a father for five months and hadn't known it. I had a son who was born, lived his short life, and died, and I never so much as laid eyes on him. This was so far outside of my limited experience that I had no idea how to react. Another death in an ocean of deaths. But this was my firstborn son, a child who was part of me, and who I would now never know, who could never be replaced. Another reason to hate the Nazis, as if I needed any more.

"I wish I had been there," I said simply. "I wish I had been able to do something."

"It's over," she said curtly. "That part of our lives is done with, in the past. We grieve, but life must go on."

In the silence that followed, I heard a door close at the rear of the bungalow. I assumed that it was Klaus, finally obeying his mother's orders and making an appearance. But it wasn't Klaus. Someone else came into the room, a man dressed in the uniform of a British soldier. He was of medium build and was wearing a black eye patch.

"Oh! So sorry! I didn't mean to interrupt anything," he said, after he picked up on the tone of the conversation and saw that it was serious. As he walked over to Ilse, he looked perplexed, as if wondering what my business there was. I, in turn, wondered why he was here.

Ilse stood up and said, "Come in, Harold. Let me introduce you to Dagobert."

When he heard my name, the atmosphere grew awkward, thick with tension. It became clear to me that Harold was more than just a friend, and that this wasn't the first time he had heard my name. He had walked into her bungalow, unannounced and through a private back door. His posture, the way he looked at her, the unspoken undercurrent between them, all combined to announce a relationship as surely as if they had sent out engraved flyers proclaiming the fact.

I wondered if he lived with her. With my wife. As I realized what was happening here, I started getting angry. *Were they sleeping together?* I wondered. I had to work hard to suppress the possessive feelings that came flooding through me. After a moment, I got myself under control. This was ridiculous! I had not come here to reestablish a relationship with this woman. I had come here for a divorce.

Ilse, made uncomfortable by the unspoken tension between Harold and I, decided to attempt to lighten the atmosphere.

"Harold, Dago has come from Feldafing, in the American zone. He saw my name on the survivor list and came to visit me."

"How nice," Harold muttered unconvincingly, in true British fashion. After what seemed to be an eternity, he asked, "How's the weather in Feldafing these days?"

I blinked hard. Could I have heard him correctly? I fought to suppress a rising tide of irritation. I had just learned that my son lay dead in an unmarked grave and this man, who was sleeping with my wife, had the nerve to ask me about the weather? Somehow, I managed to keep silent. Apparently, the man was severely lacking in the social training the English were famous for. The fact that he was a British soldier just made it worse. I had no reason to love the British, who were actively blocking Jews from emigrating to Israel. Now one of them seemed to be forming a relationship with my wife.

At that instant, whatever doubts I may have had about my decision to seek a divorce vanished. It was as if I were seeing Ilse clearly for the first time. Riva was right. If we tried to continue as husband and wife, we would both be miserable. I couldn't put a name to what I felt for Ilse. Perhaps it was affection, or a sense of being needed, or maybe a type of comradeship, like soldiers develop in battle. Whatever it was, it wasn't love. Staying with Ilse would be the same as lying to her, and that would be a blueprint for disaster. Divorce was the only option.

As I realized this, any remaining inklings of fear and jealousy and doubt blew away like a puff of smoke in the wind. I was at peace with my decision.

Sometime later, Harold excused himself, leaving out of the back door. In absolute silence, Ilse and I both sat down at her table. The time had come.

"Ilse, I think we should talk about ending our legal relationship so that we can both go on with our lives. It seems that you have chosen a path with this soldier. I want to go to Palestine and build a new life. These two paths are not compatible."

She breathed deeply and stared down at the table, her hand brushing the same spot over and over as though cleaning it of dust. But she remained silent.

I continued. "My aunt Riva also survived the war and is in Feldafing with me. There is a rabbi, Rav. Schlapobersky, who lives in our room. They both feel the best way to go about this would be for you to come back with me to Feldafing, so we can meet before the rabbis there and get a divorce."

She pursed her lips, continuing to stare intently at a spot on the table. Finally she spoke. "So that is what you want, Dago?"

"Yes, Ilse," I said delicately. "It will be the best for both of us. We can both be free to get on with our lives and to leave the horror behind us."

She bit her bottom lip, still refusing to look at me. It was over and we both knew it. All that remained was to break the ties that still bound us as gently as possible.

"You are fond of this soldier, Harold?" I asked.

She continued to look down but nodded her head. "Yes. He is a good man," she replied.

"Do you want to marry him?" I asked.

She paused. "Yes, I do."

I nodded. "That is good. I hope he will treat you and Klaus well."

"He's a very good man," she said again.

There was another moment or two of tense silence. Then Ilse rose and announced, "Well, if we're to get divorced, we should do it immediately. Let me go and make arrangements so we can leave as soon as possible."

She excused herself and left the bungalow, presumably to make preparations for departure. I followed her outside and saw Klaus. I walked over to him, thinking that I would spend a little time with him. But he completely ignored me. He obviously didn't want to talk, which was a surprise to me. But I wasn't in the mood to play guessing games with an eight-year-old, so I shrugged my shoulders and kept walking.

Ilse was back after a half hour or so. She packed a bag and told me she was ready.

As we were walking away from her bungalow, heading for the train, I asked her if she would take me around the camp. We had a little while before we had to board, so she obliged me, showing me the various buildings where people now lived.

We came to a strange sight. There was a row of about twenty ovens, which Ilse told me were used to burn the bodies of the dead. A work detail of prisoners put the corpses on iron carriages. The carriages were pushed into the ovens, the doors were closed, and the bodies burned to ashes. Then the doors were opened, the carriages pulled out, and the next group of bodies loaded. The labor details worked around the clock, trying to keep up with the number of bodies to be burned.

"But this strategy," Ilse continued in a monotone, almost as if she were lecturing me, "was inefficient. A backlog of bodies piled up all around where we're standing. When the British liberated the camp, they found thousands of corpses strewn everywhere, rotting. The stench of the bodies was inescapable. The dead lay next to the living and the only way to tell them apart was to shake them. If they moved, they were considered to be alive and efforts were made to save them.

"The British soldiers were appalled by what they saw. To their everlasting credit, they tried hard to save the living. But they were totally unprepared to deal with the situation. About fourteen thousand prisoners died within five days of the Allies arrival. These people had been starved almost to death and were ravaged by disease. They were too debilitated to respond to food or medicine. For these thousands, the

British were too late. They were killed by the Nazis as surely as if the SS had machine-gunned them.

"The British were enraged by the slaughter. They ordered the entire population from the nearby town of Celle to come to the camp. Crying and wailing, the townspeople claimed that they had no idea that any of this was happening. The British ordered them to come back the next day, ready to work. No one was spared, not even the mayor. The townspeople were commanded to carry the bodies into a series of large trenches, which the British had prepared with huge earthmoving machines. Each one of these mass graves held hundreds of unidentified corpses. No one knew who they were, and no one will ever know. The townspeople covered the bodies with dirt, sealing them away forever."

By the time Ilse finished, it was time to leave. We boarded the train for Feldafing. It was not the most pleasant of trips. Ilse seemed depressed after telling me about the ovens. She seemed to have an urge to talk about the camp. When I asked her about the liberation, she stared out the window and started speaking as if to an invisible audience.

"A few weeks before we were liberated, there was a huge influx of new prisoners," she said. "The German armies were being pushed back. As the Russians freed Eastern Europe, prisoners from other camps were transferred here by forced marches. It is said that a quarter of a million people died or were murdered on these marches. The population of the camp doubled almost overnight. At that point, there were more than sixty thousand prisoners. The camp administrators made no attempt to provide more food or housing.

"These poor people were simply thrown into the camp, forced to seek whatever shelter they could find. There was no room for them in the regular barracks. Sanitary facilities were nonexistent. People relieved themselves wherever and whenever they could. The stench was horrific. Spotted fever, cholera, and tuberculosis were already a problem, then a raging typhus epidemic swept through the camp, killing 250 to 300 people every day. Bodies lay everywhere. People who were still alive slept next to corpses.

"On the day the British liberated the camp, April 15, 1945, I was in my third trimester of pregnancy. I was so weak that I could barely move. I didn't know it at the time, but Gad, our baby, would be born exactly a month later. I sent Klaus to get water from the only faucet still working in our area. He returned with the water, but he also had a chocolate bar. He told me that a soldier speaking a foreign language and wearing a beret had given it to him. Then I knew we were saved. I cried and cried with joy. I was too emaciated to do anything else. I had given up hope that we would survive."

After she finished, the rest of the journey was spent in awkward silence. There seemed no point in talking about our coming divorce. Ilse seemed shell-shocked, emotionless. There was no more romance, no talk of love, no pretense of future possibilities. It was an ordeal that she had to get through.

When we arrived at the camp, we went before the Bet Din—the tribunal of rabbis—and briefly told them our story. Rabbi Schlapobersky and Riva had already talked to them, so they knew what to expect. After the rabbis handed Ilse the written document, we thanked them and left. I took her back to the train station and we said our very awkward final good-byes, mumbling unconvincingly about staying in touch.

And then she was off. The last tie to my wartime life had been severed at last. It was time to start over.

27

END OF THE LINE

In 1946, my life began to return to some semblance of normalcy. I settled into something of a routine, attending lectures, cultural events, and meetings at the Feldafing DP Camp. My biggest problem was enduring the unending monotony of life in the camp. These activities helped to keep boredom at bay.

Riva's presence helped immensely in filling the hole in my life caused by my parents' absence. She was the one person I could confide in. During the war, Berlin had been filled with informers and *greifers*. These people were Nazi agents, including some Jewish ones, whose job it was to worm their way into a fugitive's confidence and then betray him to the Gestapo. I was already a naturally reticent person, reluctant to discuss personal matters. To survive as a fugitive, I had to learn how to keep my thoughts to myself and my mouth firmly closed. It was a lesson I had learned well, perhaps too well. With the constant need for secrecy and the danger inherent in trusting people in Nazi-controlled Berlin, it became second nature for me to avoid revealing my thoughts and feelings to others. This tendency toward secretiveness was now a habit that I found difficult to shed, even after the war ended.

Somehow, Riva put me at ease. I told her absolutely everything that happened and she reciprocated. Any major decision was made jointly after we had discussed it between us. If there was something she didn't know, I explained it to her. If she had to make a trip to Munich, I went with her. We were a team.

Our obsession, regardless of what else was going on, was the thought of moving to Palestine. All our decisions were made with this in mind. Like thousands of others, we dreamed of a new life in a country of our own, where religious beliefs would never be a justification for persecution and being Jewish would be a privilege instead of a curse.

Our dearest wish was to emigrate to Palestine together. We planned to move to Tel Aviv, where her brother lived. He had emigrated from Kovno before the war and now had an apartment in the city. They corresponded on a regular basis, so we had the advantage of knowing what conditions would be like before we arrived. There was also a possibility that Riva's brother would be able to help us get out of the DP camp.

Whenever Riva received a letter from him, we would drop what we were doing and open it immediately, hoping that it contained the news we prayed for. We couldn't wait to leave. At Feldafing, a normal life was impossible. We were worn out by the unending monotony. How people ate, how they slept, how they worked, and how they played, every aspect of life was abnormal and artificial. I was being ground down by the feeling of impermanence, of not being able to establish a home or life. We wanted out.

One day, Riva received another letter from her brother. It said that he had applied with the British governmental authorities in Palestine to allow Riva to immigrate under the quota system that they had established, which strictly limited the number of people allowed to move there. We were thrilled, at least until we read the rest of the letter. He told us that the British would not allow him to place an application for me. I was not a close relative and therefore not eligible to immigrate under their policies. He could not help me.

I was stunned. Separating from Riva, after all the years of being alone, seemed unthinkable. I could not imagine receiving worse news. After it all settled in, Riva and I had several long talks. She offered to forgo her opportunity to go to Palestine. "I'm not going without you, Dago," she said.

I exploded. "Absolutely not!" I screamed. "You have this opportunity. You must go! I will find my way there. I am not going to allow you to sit here in this camp if you can return to a normal society. I will find a way to follow you. You must go!"

Over the next few days, we had a number of stormy arguments, but eventually she agreed that I was right. Two long years after the war's conclusion, toward the end of 1947, Riva boarded a train for the first leg of her journey to Palestine.

At the time, I fully expected that I would follow shortly thereafter. Any sense of involvement I had with members of the camp community rapidly died out. I went through the motions of trying to appear sociable, but I lived through the letters I wrote to Riva and those I received back from her.

On May 14, 1948, the last British high commissioner left Palestine. Britain washed its hands of the entire affair, wanting nothing further to do with the constant fighting between Jews and Arabs. The same day, the new state of Israel was declared, with immediate recognition extended by the United States. In the early hours of May 15, units of the regular armies of Egypt, Jordan, Syria, and Iraq invaded with the supposed purpose of restoring order.

I was horrified by the prospect of war, but I also saw it as a possible opportunity to emigrate. Young Jewish males were being mobilized to go to Israel and fight. If I were selected, I would probably be able to gain entry into the country. To my vast disappointment, I was not chosen to go. Instead, I was told that it would be a long time, perhaps years, before I could hope to go to Israel.

———

Some months before Riva left, I learned that the ORT (Organization for Rehabilitation through Training) was going to open a vocational school in Feldafing. Notices were posted on bulletin boards that anybody who was experienced in the basic trades should apply for the position of instructor.

Excellent! I thought. I was thrilled by the idea. I took off across the camp to Villa Nordenholz to tell Riva. At first, she didn't understand that I wanted to apply for a position as an instructor. She presumed I would be a student. I had never told her much about my background in metalworking, so she was really not aware of my qualifications in that area. Gradually, it dawned on her that I might have the credentials to teach.

Riva smiled and hugged me. I was rotting at Feldafing, gradually losing my motivation as the days wore on. But teaching metalworking, this I knew I could do! I had a superb background in the field and superior training by first-class teachers. I was proud of my abilities in this area.

When I applied with ORT, I learned that all the teaching positions had already been filled except that of welding instructor. I was confident that I could teach this subject. My training as a *maschinenbauer* (machine builder) had included extensive experience in this field.

Welding is a complex activity, much more so than a casual onlooker might think. During my apprenticeship, I had spent more than a year

Camp Feldafing ORT School.

learning the ins and outs of gas and electric welding. I applied for the job and got it. Of course, it might have helped that no one else applied for it and that I was the only one in the camp who knew anything about welding.

The ORT school at the Feldafing DP Camp opened in February 1947 with 170 students and myself as its proud welding instructor. In the US zone of occupation, ORT had established sixty training schools in DP camps, instructing refugees who had survived the war. Of 250,000 survivors in Germany and Austria, about 30,000 received vocational training in ORT schools, selecting from among 350 courses in fifty different trades. Most of our students were young men, either a bit older or younger than myself. Some of the older ones had been professionals before the war but now wanted to learn trades. They were very serious about this because they realized that when they emigrated to another country, which all of them expected to do, a trade would place them in demand.

My daily routine began with a walk across the camp to the ORT school building. In the summer and fall, we frequently slogged through the mud. In the winter, the mud was replaced with ice and sludge. Cleaning shoes was a popular hobby at Feldafing. I now had two pairs of shoes, American army surplus, to replace the tattered pair I had worn all during my U-boat years. This bounty was courtesy of UNRRA, a United Nations organization that distributed various articles needed by those in the camps.

School usually started at 9:00 AM. We'd take an hour for lunch and then break for the day around 6:00 PM. I was given almost complete freedom to decide what to teach, when to teach it, and how to teach it. I had never been an instructor before, but it came easily to me. I cherished the interaction with my dozen or so students. Their interest in learning and the progress they made was extremely gratifying to me. For too long, I had been preoccupied with nothing but survival. It was tremendously stimulating to be in a learning environment again.

The job posed a real challenge. We were starting from scratch, with none of the materials or equipment we needed. Trips to Feldafing and Munich were required to buy steel and other metals, oxygen, and acetylene gas. We also needed various types of tools and machinery for the classroom. I drew a diagram of the space we would need and the layout of the machinery and material and was given authority to order the equipment.

I worked most closely with the instructors who taught courses in machine shop and sheet metal. They had more industrial experience than I, but I had more formal training. The machine shop instructor was from Lithuania, the sheet metal instructor from Poland. We worked very well together. Most of the students took classes from all three of us. When they graduated, they were experienced in all three disciplines.

During my tenure at the ORT school, I was informed that the king of Sweden, Gustav V, had made available a royal grant whose purpose was to afford an opportunity for selected ORT instructors in Europe to obtain advanced training in their specialties. The king had learned of the activities of ORT and was impressed enough with the good works they were doing to offer his help.

International Refugee Organization, Displaced Persons Professional Testing Board Certificate.

Twenty of us were chosen from among the more than eight hundred ORT instructors in Europe. Of course, I considered it to be a great honor to be included in this elite group. The Feldafing school director didn't have to twist my arm very hard to get me to participate.

The government of Sweden made all the arrangements for us to travel to Stockholm. We were lodged in the homes of local Swedes, two instructors per family. I was assigned, together with a machine shop instructor from the Feldafing school, to a nice family that didn't speak much German. We spoke no Swedish, but we still managed to get along well with them. Their house was near the streetcar line, so we were able to go anywhere we wanted with a minimum of inconvenience.

Stockholm was beautiful. We were there in the late summer and the weather was perfect for water sports. There were lots of lakes with hundreds of sailboats harbored at the shore. During the weekends, two or three of us would take off to explore the city. The girls there were beautiful and very friendly, the food was good and plentiful, and the people uniformly helpful. There were public saunas and baths, which we took frequent advantage of. The entire city seemed very clean and well-organized, much like Germany before the war, but with a population that seemed kinder and more open. All of this was a welcome change from the dreary mud and ice of Feldafing.

The training program was demanding, but the challenge was welcomed by everyone in our group. We spent many hours in classroom sessions, where expert instructors would acquaint us with the latest in metalworking technology and how best to pass this information on to our students. There were also a few classes, such as psychology, that weren't necessarily connected with metalworking but which were offered to increase our ability to deal with students from different cultures and backgrounds. There were practical sessions that gave us the opportunity to put into action what we were learning in the classroom.

Attending classes, for the first time since my apprenticeship, was tremendously fulfilling for me. It awakened in me a fierce craving to learn and gave my life the direction it had lacked for far too long.

ORT going-away party in Stockholm. Bert Lewyn in front row, fourth from left.

The Swedish ORT organization, forever trying to please us and take care of our needs, assigned to us two women and one man to act as our official guides. They took us to visit several factories in and near Stockholm and also included some factories where armaments and weapons were produced. One was an airplane factory, underground. We were told that the factory was actually carved out of rock and was virtually bombproof. One reason Hitler did not attack Sweden during WWII was because the Swedes were extremely well armed with an assortment of first-class weapons, including a substantial air force. It was generally taken for granted that had Hitler attacked Sweden, it would have cost the Germans dearly.

At the end of our stay, we had the expected going-away party, at which the school director issued diplomas to each of us. We never did get to meet the king, but we did spend some time with his personal representative. Pictures were taken and everybody got photographs. We told each other that we'd never lose touch, which, of course, we did almost immediately.

Finally, in mid-December 1948, my roommate and I left Stockholm. We traveled by train to a Swedish port, where the train was transferred onto a ferry. Once we reached Denmark, the train was shifted back onto solid ground and continued under its own power on toward Germany.

Not long after leaving Copenhagen, we realized that we were hungry, so we went into the dining car. There was a big sign over the door that said NO GERMANS ALLOWED. We looked at each other and shrugged, then stepped into the dining car. During WWII, German armies had occupied Denmark. Their treatment of the Danish population was brutal enough to create a reservoir of lingering resentment that did not vanish with the war's end. Germans were decidedly unpopular in Denmark and would probably remain that way for some time to come. Luckily, we had learned enough Swedish to order a meal. It might have not been the king's Swedish but it was enough to get by. So we ate silently, paid quickly, and departed as soon as possible.

In the last week of December 1948, I received a message from a Jewish chaplain in Munich. It had come by wire to the camp administrator and asked that I visit him as soon as possible. Upon receipt of the message, I arranged for a trip to Munich to visit the chaplain and left the next day.

When I arrived at the offices of the American Joint Distribution Committee, I was ushered in to see the chaplain. He wasted no time in explaining the purpose of his request.

"Rabbi Sam Geffen of Teaneck, New Jersey, has asked that I contact you to discuss the possibility of your communicating with his family by letter. It is possible that eventually you might be able to emigrate to the United States to be with them. Specifically, to Atlanta, Georgia."

This was a surprise to me. I knew nothing about Atlanta, Georgia. All I knew about the United States was that New York and my Uncle Benjamin were located there. I had vague memories of my parents writing letters to another relative in the United States, but who they were and where they lived I could not recall. It made no difference. I had no desire to go to America. All I wanted was to go to the newly declared State of Israel to join my aunt Riva.

"Do you know anything about the Geffen family?" the chaplain asked.

"No. Nothing," I said.

"Rabbi Sam Geffen's father is Rabbi Tobias Geffen. Rabbi Geffen's wife is your great aunt. She is the sister of your late grandmother."

My late grandmother. He was talking about my father's mother, I realized. I had never known her; she had died before I was born.

"Rabbi Geffen has been searching for your father. By chance, he stumbled across evidence of your existence instead."

I told the chaplain that I had never heard of the Geffens and knew nothing about Atlanta, but that I would be happy to write them. I also made it clear that I was resolved to emigrate to Israel to be with Aunt Riva. I had no idea that my father had written to Rabbi Geffen in 1936 asking for help, desperate for money, or that Geffen had responded with the assistance my father requested.

As I turned to leave, the chaplain let me know that he would be available to help me with any problems that came up. He said that he had tried to find me several times in the past with no success, but that he wanted to make sure that things went well for me from now on.

When I arrived back at Feldafing, I immediately went to my room and wrote to Riva. I told her about meeting the American chaplain and that Rabbi Geffen wanted to correspond with me. I told her I would send them a letter and enclose Riva's address, too, so they could write her. Finally, I would tell them that my plan was to emigrate to Israel.

Much to my surprise, I later learned that the Geffens had contacted Riva some time ago. They had already offered her sponsorship for emigration to Atlanta, but she had declined to accept their offer.

———————

Riva wrote me two successive letters. In each, she urged me to accept Rabbi Geffen's offer of sponsorship. She was of the opinion that I should not lightly dismiss the possibility of immigrating to America. She said that life was hard and uncertain in Israel and would be for some time to come. There were many problems with living in Israel, and many more were expected. While she missed me and would have liked for me to be there with her, her feeling was that I would be better off in America.

While I was shocked that Riva would urge me to go to America, it did have an impact on me. I began to rethink my goals. Everything I had heard, everyone I talked to, all said that America was truly the promised land, the golden country, with unlimited opportunities for those who wanted to work hard and build a new life for themselves. People lived well. Education was available to everybody. In short, no one had anything negative to say about America. Only positive things.

I was now twenty-five years old and ready to think seriously about my future. I was discouraged that, after so many years, I had accomplished so little. Even though I had fully intended to emigrate to Israel, it now appeared that my chances of actually doing so were becoming more remote as time went on. With every day that passed, life in the DP camp seemed to become a little emptier and a little harder to endure. I decided to think seriously about the Geffens' offer to correspond with them. But before I could even write to accept their invitation, I received letters from Rabbi Geffen saying that he would sponsor my coming to the United States.

This put things in a new light. There was now a real possibility that I could depart Germany soon, perhaps immediately. So when Riva encouraged me to accept the Geffens' offer to go to Atlanta, I folded. I had received an offer I couldn't refuse. If my departure could be arranged within the next few weeks, I would abandon my plan of going to Israel and move instead to the United States, to Atlanta, Georgia.

I got in touch with American officials in Munich. To my surprise, the entire affair moved with whirlwind speed. The American Consulate arranged background checks to make sure I was not a Communist. A medical exam, conducted by a US Army doctor, was administered to verify that I was in good health. Before I knew it, the day came to join several other people from Camp Feldafing to travel by train to Bremerhaven, Germany, where we were put through the final procedures and preparation for departure.

There was another medical check, detailed instructions on how to conduct ourselves on the ship, how to deal with the rigors of the journey, and what to expect once we arrived in the United States of America. We were given identification papers. I already had a DP index card, GO #166, Allied Expeditionary Forces. Everything I owned went

into a metal suitcase made of aircraft aluminum. I had purchased it in
Munich in a leather goods store that had no leather items for sale, but
they did have metal suitcases. Leather was now a very rare commodity,
but surplus aircraft-grade aluminum was readily available.

I was given a baggage check marked number 380, IRO, passen-
ger #183 on ship USAT *Mercey*. The actual sailing date was June 7,
1949. I had been in the DP camp for four years.

The ship carried four to five hundred passengers, mostly Jews. There
were a few non-Jewish passengers from Poland and Russia. But everyone
on the ship was a DP, a survivor of the Nazi Reich. Almost everyone
spoke Yiddish, which I was now fluent in, so I did not lack for company.

As I approached the ship, I felt a great sense of exhilaration. It was
hard to believe that I was finally leaving German soil, the land that had
caused me so much pain. When the ship actually broke loose of its
moorings, a tremendous shout went up from hundreds of throats. The
meaning of that shout was plain—it was a cry of great joy and great
relief. Everyone felt the same way: at last we were leaving the past behind.

The trip took twelve days, which I cannot say were the most pleasant of my life. There was a horrid stench throughout the entire sleeping
area, and some of the passengers themselves smelled pretty bad. The
heat was stifling and the ventilation poor, but we were glad to suffer the
heat and the stench for the reward of final liberation in a free country.

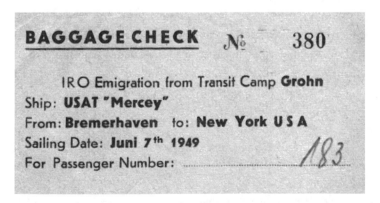

My baggage check for the journey from Bremerhaven to New
York on US Army
transport ship.

From what I could see, there were many more men than women on the ship, but all seemed to be in either good or fair physical condition. It was clear to me that those who had survived all of the various hardships during the war had made it because of their superior physical and mental condition. Those who were not in that category had less chance for survival. Of course, that is not to say that many men and women were not murdered in spite of their abilities. Many were. But the concept of "survival of the fittest" did seem to hold true.

Letter to Riva in Israel
Translated from Yiddish

June 20, 1949

Dear Riva,

Yesterday I arrived in New York. At the port, the wife of my uncle Alfred [my mother's brother who had immigrated to America just before the war] awaited me. They did not want me to travel to Uncle Geffen in Atlanta. They already had prepared a room for me. The AJDC wanted me to travel right away to Atlanta. But they (Alfred and Susi) insisted that I remain with them at an absolute minimum one week. They contacted Uncle Geffen by phone. He was not satisfied and disappointed that I did not come to him right away. But it was worked out so that I would come there one week later.

Now I am in New York the second day. The climate here is dangerously hot and moist. Such climate I am not accustomed to, and I feel bad accordingly. Uncle Geffen has here in NY three sons. Two are rabbis and one is a doctor. They have already telephoned here and they will come here soon to visit me.

We traveled by [the USS *Mercey* converted hospital] ship from Bermerhaven and it took twelve days for the journey. The weather was good the entire way, but the ship has rocked from side to side and front to back. Many people, especially women, were seasick. But I was not affected in any way and did not get sick. (It left me cold.) All of the twelve days we had to work. Some of us had to scratch off the old paint from the walls of the ship and paint them with new paint. The food was miserable and not enough of it.

The sleeping took place in a cabin with 90–100 men and there were no windows and the cabin was under the water line. In spite of several ventilators working (fans), it was a miracle that no one suffocated. My Uncle Alfred with his wife and son (thirteen years) have an apartment with four and a half rooms, kitchen and bath and all conveniences, on the fifth floor. No need to go up/down on steps as there is a lift. He works hard the whole day in a hotel as a waiter. She is in the apartment and does everything there in the household. The son goes to school and will be Bar Mitzvah in the next weeks.

I will remain here one week's time. Afterward I travel to Atlanta. For the time being I end this letter. Be healthy as I wish for you,

Your Dagobert.

As I wrote in my letter to Riva, two of Rabbi Geffen's sons, Joel and Sam Geffen, came to visit me in Uncle Alfred's apartment. They told me about Atlanta and their life there. They talked about the heat in the summer, but not to worry, people there knew how to dress so that the heat would not be too bothersome. They also told me about a cousin in New York, and that they would inform him of my arrival.

Not more than a few hours after their departure, I received a phone call from Stanley Lewin, the son of my Uncle Benjamin, who had visited us in Berlin when I was a young boy. Stanley insisted that I visit him and his family. Although I had made a commitment to stay with Uncle Alfred for at least one week, I asked him for permission to go with Stanley. At first Uncle Alfred was bitterly opposed to the idea, but he finally relented.

Stanley arrived within the hour, driving the largest automobile I had ever seen. As we drove through New York, I was amazed by the energy of the city, the big buildings, the hustle and bustle, and the traffic jams. Berlin was no backwater village, but somehow New York made an impression on me that made me feel like a country cousin.

When we arrived at Stanley's apartment, I was introduced to his wife, Margie, who took pains to make me feel at home. I remained with Stanley and his family several days before he took me to the train station for the trip to Atlanta. The train ride was long and uneventful, lasting almost twenty-two hours.

When the train pulled into the Union Station in Atlanta, there was only one person waiting on the platform. It was an elderly gentleman, somewhat hunched over, with a full gray beard, a hat and a black caftan-like coat, and walking stick. I had no doubt that this was Rabbi Tobias Geffen.

Somehow, he recognized me immediately. How, I don't know. He greeted me in Yiddish, which was a good thing, since I spoke no English. It occurred to me that I would be at a great disadvantage in this country until I learned the language and resolved to make this my top priority. With a porter carrying my aluminum suitcase, we ascended to street level and hailed a taxicab. It was only a short ride to the Geffen house at 593 Washington Street. As we walked into the house, Mrs. Geffen walked up to me and hugged and kissed me and screamed for some time about how happy she was to see me and to have me there. We talked until late into the night. After we had exhausted ourselves in conversation, Mrs. Geffen conducted me to a room that formerly belonged to one of their eight children, now all grown with families of their own. This room became my new home.

The next day, Louis Geffen, a son of Rabbi Geffen, came to visit me. We talked endlessly about everyone and everything in the Geffen family. They could not have made me feel more welcome. For the first time since my parents were arrested in 1942, I felt safe, at home. The peaceful life that was taken from me years ago, when the Gestapo first knocked on our door, had been restored to me.

At the Kusitzkys, I was always afraid. Even after the war, I was constantly on pins and needles, thinking about my parents all the time. Too much had happened in Germany for me ever to be at peace there. I knew that the day would come when, for the sake of my sanity, I would have to leave.

When I reached the Geffens, seven years of misery ended at last. On that day, June 27, 1949, I finally came home once again. Here, among family, I would eventually marry, establish my own machinery business, have five wonderful children and five grandchildren (so far).

But whatever the future holds, the nightmare of the Nazi holocaust will remain a memory, never to be forgotten.

DISPLACED PERSONS COMMISSION
WASHINGTON 25, D. C.

Dear Sir or Madam:

The Displaced Persons Commission welcomes you to the
United States of America.

The Congress of the United States of America has
established the Displaced Persons Commission to select for immigration to this country, persons displaced as a result of World
War II. Under the principles laid down by the Congress, you are
among those selected.

The Congress is interested in how displaced persons
fare after settling in the United States. So that the Congress
may be kept informed on this matter, it requires that each person who immigrated to the United States as the head of a family
or as a single person provide certain factual information.

The information is to be provided twice a year, for
two years. The reporting dates are July 1 and January 1. The
first report is required on the next reporting date after you
have been in the country 60 or more days. Each of the reports
must be in the mails to reach us by the date specified, but may
be mailed as much as fifteen days earlier.

The form for reporting is provided by the Displaced
Persons Commission. The form to be used will be available on
May 15 for the July 1 report and on November 15 for the January
1 report. It will be available at local offices of the U. S.
Immigration and Naturalization Service.

The Displaced Persons Commission wishes you every
success in your new life in the United States of America.

Sincerely,

Ugo Caruti, Chairman

Edward M. O'Connor

Harry N. Rosenfield

Letter from Displaced Persons Commission.

EPILOGUE

Bev Lewyn on the Conversations and Memories of Bert Lewyn

In every instance in writing this book, both Bert and I were completely committed to making this book as accurate as possible. Dragging out fifty-year-old memories is not an easy or simple process, but we searched for hard facts and for corroboration from the people in his story who were still alive. At every turn when we discovered something inaccurate or incomplete, we went back and corrected the text. The timeline of these memories and all the conversations in the book were written to the best of Bert's memory.

Bert was able to speak about his experiences quite easily, and he never once broke down even during my intense questioning of these excruciating and heartbreaking experiences. He was lucky to be able to distance himself from the emotions that he obviously felt during these moments. I do think this emotional distance helped him cope and go on to create a very successful life.

Since Bert's death, I have continued to research his story and have updated and included new information in this edition. Continuing research and additional materials from the Lewins' lives may be found on www.bertlewyn.com.

Dagobert Lewin

A few days after my arrival in Atlanta, I talked to Rabbi and Mrs. Geffen about the fact that I was now well rested and felt quite strong. It was time for me to find a job. They asked their son Louis to help me. Louis assisted me in getting a job working as a sewing-machine mechanic at the Berger Sewing Machine Company. The owner of the company, Bernie Berger, was a friend of Louis's. They were both Jewish war veterans and active in the Jewish War Veterans organization.

I started out earning the vast sum of forty-five cents an hour. There were other service men there who were paid more, but the presumption was that they were worth more because they could speak English and communicate with customers. I had no problem with this reasoning since my English was still very limited.

Shortly after starting my new job, I began attending night school on Washington Street. I had never graduated from any school, so the director of the night school thought I should start from the very beginning, the ninth grade. Within a few weeks, I was able to converse quite readily in English. Seven months later, I had earned my high school diploma.

For the next two years, I attended evening courses at the Georgia Institute of Technology. I took English, basic chemistry, algebra, geometry, etc. Meanwhile, I began working for W. P. Childs Machinery Company in Scottsdale, Georgia. The W. P. Childs company manufactured and sold woodworking and metalworking machinery. German equipment was considered to be among the best in the world, and I was able to help them introduce some German manufacturing techniques, which in turn allowed them to improve their machinery.

Life with the Geffens was good. It soon became clear to me that they were an extremely close-knit family. They had four sons and four daughters, each having their own families. All but one lived in cities other than Atlanta, but not a week went by without some or all of the children calling the Geffen parents, inquiring about their health or the latest news of the family.

There were frequent visitors at the Geffen house, and the general atmosphere was always one of warmth and genuine concern and interest. Uncle Tobias had been rabbi of the Shearith Israel synagogue in Atlanta since 1910. I accompanied him to Sabbath services on Friday and Saturday nearly every week. It was a new experience for me, because I had not regularly attended services for many years and those that I attended in my youth were Reform. The Shearith Israel was then an Orthodox synagogue.

An interesting bit of trivia was that Rabbi Geffen was one of the only people ever to see the secret formula for Coca-Cola. He was the rabbi who first certified the soft drink as being kosher for Passover, at the request of the Coca-Cola Company.

A few months after my arrival in Atlanta—as soon as I was able to converse in English—Aunt Hene Geffen decided it was time to find me a wife. She arranged dates for me with several of the young ladies in the Atlanta Jewish community. After a while, I had enough of this and asked her to please stop. She insisted on one more try and, as fate would have it, I met my future wife. Her name was Esther Sloan.

Wedding of Esther and Bert Lewyn, in the presence of the Geffen family, December 23, 1951, Atlanta, Georgia. *Left to right*, Mrs. Hene and Rabbi Tobias Geffen, Phyllis Simon, Lotti Simon, Bert and Esther Lewyn, Harold Simon, Louis Geffen, Anna Geffen, *kneeling*, David Geffen.

After making my case, emphasizing that I was not just a poor green-horn immigrant and that I would definitely make my mark, I convinced Esther to marry me. She did, on December 23, 1951. On our wedding invitation, Rabbi and Mrs. Geffen took the place of my parents, inviting guests to the wedding (along with Esther's mother, Eva Sloan).

Esther and I had five children: Andrea Jo (named after my mother Johanna), Lawrence David (named after my father Leopold and my grandfather Dovid), Marc Jonathan (who is married to Bev), Cynthia Jane, and Michael Evan. Andrea is married to Edward Krakovsky and they have two children, Jacob Aaron and Hannah Sloan. Bev and Marc have four daughters, Alexandra Eve, Rachel Madeline, Sarah Bena, and Rebecca Anna.

Very shortly after I arrived in the United States, I began to call myself "Bert" in social situations. No one had ever heard of "Dagobert." After Esther and I married, I became tired of my last name being mispronounced. When I applied for my naturalization papers, I Americanized my name to "Bert Lewyn" in hopes that both names could be pronounced correctly.

During my time at W. P. Childs I did quite well, selling their machinery in particular to the very large US Army–operated Redstone Arsenal in Huntsville, Alabama. The Redstone Arsenal used the machinery to make rockets, missiles, and other Allied military items. My knowledge of German came in handy because the arsenal was run by Werner von Braun and his department heads, nearly all of whom were from Germany. The US Army had hired von Braun and his team after WWII for their technical know-how.

These men had extensive knowledge in designing and building rockets, including the V-rockets that caused so much destruction in England. Even though my sentiments were such that I really didn't want to be around anything German, especially German people, this was business. I was able to suppress my negative feelings in order to do my job. We talked solely about technical things. I never told them about my background, and they never asked.

After six months at W. P. Childs, it became apparent to me that things weren't going to work out. My boss, Dick Childs, and I began to

Photo from grandson Jacob Krakovsky's bar mitzvah June 12, 2004. Back row from l to r: Marc Lewyn, Michael Lewyn, Lawrence Lewyn, Esther Lewyn, Bert Lewyn, Jacob Krakovsky, Andrea Lewyn Krakovsky, and Edward Krakovsky. Middle row granddaughters from l to r: Alexandra Lewyn, Rachel Lewyn, Sarah Lewyn, Sloan Krakovsky. Front row: Bev Saltzman Lewyn holding Rebecca Lewyn, and Cindy Lewyn.

have disagreements about what he owed me. I left the Childs company and followed two other former W. P. Childs salesmen, Jim Davis and Arnold Goldberg, who had started their own company after having similar experiences with Dick Childs. I left them after about three months, because DG Machinery & Gage Co. was a new company and there just wasn't enough money to support all three of our families.

In 1952, from the basement of my mother-in-law's house, I formed my own company. It was initially called the Bert Lewyn Co., but eventually I changed the name to Lewyn Machinery Co., Inc. My company sold woodworking machinery to manufacturers of wood products. With the support of my wife, Esther, I threw myself into the work with an enthusiasm usually reserved for the very young or the insane. Virtually every waking moment was spent in that dirt-floor basement, pounding on my typewriter and organizing my new business. Esther's mother began to suspect that I might not be entirely rational and harangued

Esther about her new husband every chance she got. Undeterred by the criticism, I went on to make a net profit of thirty-four dollars my first year in business.

In the second year my net profit soared to $725 and my third year in business I reached $3,000. I spent most of my time traveling the South in my car, calling on customers old and new. I did well enough to hire my first employee in 1961. In 1963, battling anxiety all the way, I bought a plot of land on Jackson Parkway and built the first ten thousand square foot building to house my business.

For many years, I sold machinery manufactured in the United States, mostly from a company located in Wisconsin. Unfortunately, their equipment became somewhat old-fashioned and it soon was clear that they were reluctant to make the changes needed to remain competitive with the Europeans. In 1975, an Israeli friend, who was an engineering consultant to the woodworking industry, recommended that I contact a German manufacturer, Koch Maschinen. My friend told me that he had extensive dealings with this German company and that they had become friends, both inside and outside the office.

Up to that point, I had steered clear of any involvement with German manufacturers. Then, in 1974, the International Machinery Exposition took place in Hanover, as it does every two years. I attended this exposition along with my friend. He insisted on introducing me to the people at Koch Maschinen, to which I reluctantly agreed.

The long and short of it is that, in 1976, I began a business relationship with Koch Maschinen of Bielefeld, Germany. I introduced their machines to the United States market, sold them, and serviced them for ten years, until finally I was bought out by the Koch family. I remained with the company until 1991. To this day, I still count the Koch family among my friends, something I thought would never happen in view of the fact that I had once turned my back on Germans and Germany for what I thought was forever.

In all that time, I never told them about my background or about my experiences during the Hitler years. I never wanted to talk about what had happened to me and my family. I didn't want to discuss it with anyone, not support groups, not with friends, not with coworkers.

In the years since I arrived in the United States, I had tried to forget the details of my life in Germany. I told Esther a little about it when we got married and mentioned a few very sketchy details to my children, but that was all. I didn't avoid the subject, but I volunteered no information and spoke in the most general terms possible. When my children asked me about it, I would inevitably respond with, "I'll tell you more when you get older."

Other than myself and my aunt Riva, the only survivor in my family was my first cousin, Dov Levin. Dov is the son of Hirsch, my father's brother. He was in the Kovno ghetto with Riva and the rest of my relatives. He escaped from the ghetto into the forests, where he became a partisan, fighting the Germans by blowing up their rail lines and committing other acts of sabotage. After the war, Dov walked from Lithuania to Italy. From there, he went by ship to Palestine, the entire journey taking about ten months. Soon after his arrival, he joined the Haganah and fought in the 1948 War of Independence. He became a professor of contemporary Jewish history at Hebrew University in Jerusalem and has authored fourteen books and over four hundred articles. He is the world's foremost expert on the history of the Jews in Lithuania, Latvia, and Estonia during the Nazi period.

In 1980, Dov and his wife, Bilah, came with me to Destin, Florida, for a vacation. He insisted that I make some sort of record of my experiences in Berlin during the Hitler years. I tried to discourage him, but he refused to be deterred. We purchased a tape recorder and tapes from the neighborhood drugstore and sat for hours, with him interviewing me, relentlessly dragging out my story. Once the tapes were complete, I made no further effort, for many years, to record any aspect of my history.

I retired from the machinery business in 1991 and soon began to toy with the idea of writing this book. I wanted my children and grandchildren to know my history, as much as I could remember about myself, my parents, and their families. I realized the best way to accomplish this would be to write, but even though I knew that time was rushing by, I never got around to doing much, other than jotting down a few notes.

In 1992, my son Marc and my daughter-in-law Bev returned once again to Destin. On the way down they listened to the tapes of Dov's interviews from over a decade before. Bev was fascinated with my story and suggested that it should be recorded in book form, for our family and for posterity.

By the fall of 1993, I still had done little to make the book a reality. Bev suggested that we take her upcoming maternity leave from CNN and use this time to write the book. Six years later, after numerous revelations and adventures in self-discovery, here we are, complete at last.

Bev Lewyn

After the book was published, Bert enjoyed speaking about his story to school and community groups around the country.

He had two more granddaughters, Sarah Lewyn (named for Sara Hene Geffen, his aunt who brought him to Atlanta) and Rebecca Lewyn, bringing Esther and Bert's total number of grandchildren to six. Bert continued to be active in his family's real estate business until he became ill.

Bert died at home on January 3, 2016, surrounded by his family. Even toward the end of his life when his short-term memory failed him, he did not appear to suffer from the terrible memories of his younger years as some in his family feared might happen. Though his ability to communicate waned, when he did communicate he maintained his charming wit and sense of humor.

His wife, Esther, says that he spent his time during the early decades of their marriage "trying very hard to forget" what had happened. He threw himself into work. He didn't join survivors' organizations. He virtually never talked about years in Berlin, not even with his wife. He only told his children about his past when they were in their teens.

In June 2016 my husband, Marc, and I took our four daughters to Berlin to visit key sites in their grandfather's life in Berlin and to walk in his footsteps. Some of the newer photos in this edition are from that trip.

On June 15, 2018, Bert's family returned to 70 Koepenicker Strasse in Berlin to witness the laying of the brass *Stolpersteines* or "stumbling stone" plaques to commemorate that Dagobert, Leopold, and Johanna had lived there and had been victims of the Holocaust.

Ilse Perl Lewin and Klaus Perl

After Ilse came with me back to Feldafing to receive our *get*—our religious divorce—Ilse returned to Bergen-Belsen, and we lost contact with each other. She eventually married Harold Nestor Murray, the British soldier she met after the liberation of Bergen Belsen. She had no more children.

Strange as it may sound, in 1993 when we began the writing of this book, I had no recollection of Ilse whatsoever. I did not remember her when Dov was interviewing me in Florida, nor when Bev began a more detailed interrogation.

After a few months of working with Bev, she jokingly commented to me that my story was amazing, like something straight out of Hollywood, but that it lacked a love interest. We got quite a chuckle out of that, but her comment must have jarred something in my mind, because memories of Ilse seemed to appear out of nowhere.

The next time we met, I told Bev about Ilse. By this time, I could recall the incident of meeting her at her aunt's house, of her seducing me, of meeting Klaus, and then of us *posing* as husband and wife while we lived at Herr Braun's apartment.

After that, I remembered nothing except the events that occurred after I visited her at Bergen-Belsen. I incorrectly remembered us seeking a religious divorce because Riva and Rabbi Schlapobersky told us to proceed with it "just in case anyone should have thought we were really married."

It was only after we started rereading letters that Anni Kusitzky had sent me after the war that questions and contradictions arose. One of Anni's letters mentioned that Ilse and Klaus had recently come to Berlin to visit her.

This was a startling revelation, since I had no memories of Ilse ever meeting the Kusitzkys. How in the world had Ilse known them? And though I could stretch my imagination to having Ilse meet them once or twice, I couldn't believe that she would have known them well enough to visit after the war.

Much of the research done to establish my history was performed through archives in Berlin. I had requested several of these archives to send me any documentation they had concerning my parents or myself. Imagine my shock when, included in the documents about my parents, were papers regarding my "wife"—Ilse Perl Lewin—a woman I had no recollection of marrying.

My last memories of Ilse were of us living together in Herr Braun's apartment in Berlin, pretending to be married. Yet Ilse's deportation papers, which I now held in my hand, were dated January 5, 1945. This was almost the same day that I recall being arrested by the Gestapo. Coincidence? Before today, I had imagined that Ilse was arrested shortly after our time together at Herr Braun's, since I had no further memory of her after this period. But these papers clearly established that Ilse was still around after our time together at Braun's apartment. I was also puzzled that the papers gave Ilse's last name as Lewin.

There were too many unanswered questions here. I decided to try to contact Ilse. I had no idea whether she was still even alive, but my curiosity would not allow me to rest without at least making the effort to find her.

Anni's letter had mentioned that Ilse was married to an orthopedist from London, so I put search notices in the journal of the British

Orthopedic Association. I called the Wiener Library and the Association of Jewish Refugees, both in London, and ran notices in their publications. I also ran a notice in a journal published by the mayor of Berlin, distributed to Jewish ex-Berliners.

In a book written by Dr. Inge Lammel of Berlin, it was mentioned that Ilse and Klaus were deported to Bergen-Belsen in January 1945. I contacted Dr. Lammel and explained that I was trying to contact Ilse. She did not know where Ilse was, but she gave me the name and phone number of a friend of Ilse's, a Mrs. Alice Fink of Chicago.

I tried to call Mrs. Fink, but she refused to talk to me. Not wishing to give up on my most promising lead, I wrote to Mrs. Fink, enclosing an unsealed letter to Ilse and asking her to please forward it. The letter explained the situation and asked for her help in answering some questions.

More than six months went by with no word from Ilse. We gave up. We decided to finish the book as best we could, even with the questions and contradictions that remained.

Then, in June 1996, Ilse called. She said that she had heard that I was searching for her but had hesitated to contact me, fearing to reopen a chapter of her life that was best left in the past.

Klaus and his children told her that she owed me nothing and did not need to contact me. Later I learned that she did feel that some type of debt existed between us. Eventually, she said that her curiosity got the best of her and decided to risk a call.

In talking to me and in reading the questions I had prepared, it became apparent to her that I had forgotten much of what we had experienced together.

I was caught entirely off-guard when she told me that we had not been just posing as husband and wife but that we had been legally married. We had gone to the equivalent of city hall and been officially married, with appropriate documentation. This was a complete and total surprise to me. From a copy of a civil divorce decree, Ilse read aloud the date of our wedding, December 12, 1942. That was over two months before the Fabrikaktion of February 27, 1943. I didn't remember knowing Ilse before then.

She also told me that the Gestapo had arrested us together at the Kusitzkys, when I only remembered myself being there. She mentioned

Paul Richter's house in the country and how she had been there with me, even though I had no recollection of her being present. But she remembered many details that I remembered, plus a few that escaped me.

She told me that she would respond in writing to my questions. "Do you want to know the bad as well as the good?" she asked me.

"Yes," I said, without hesitation. Whatever the reason for my faulty memory, I wanted to know the truth.

When my daughter-in-law Bev learned of this "bad as well as good" comment, she asked, "Dad, are you prepared to learn that there was a pregnancy? Even a baby?" Here, I drew a blank. I had no memory whatsoever, one way or the other.

Sure enough, the next day Ilse informed me that we had parented a baby boy. He was born on May 13, 1945, in the Belsen DP camp, one month after Belsen was liberated. Ilse had named him Gad Lewin. The conditions in the camp were abominable, and Gad did not survive for long, dying on October 4, 1945. Ilse even enclosed a picture of Gad's grave.

All of this was very difficult to grasp. Nothing seemed to stimulate my missing memories. It was as though those events—the marriage, the pregnancy, the baby's death—never occurred. It was very hard to make them seem real.

I wanted to meet with Ilse again, face-to-face. But Ilse did not want to tell me where she lived or to give me her address. I offered to come to England, but again, she refused. Her husband was very ill and she did not want to leave his side. Any letters I might have for her had to be sent via Klaus.

There are still questions that remain, but after the death of Ilse's husband a few months later, she seemed to lose interest in the project. Nonetheless, I am grateful for a source of information I otherwise would not have had.

Bev Lewyn

During the writing of this book, after learning that he had forgotten that Ilse and he had been legally wed and had a child together, Bert pushed the information aside and kept going. According to Esther, he never spoke of his late son again.

Gad Lewin, May 13, 1945–October 4, 1945.

When I recently asked Esther why she thought he could have forgotten the existence of a child, she said that since he lost so many family members, this child would have "just been yet another one lost." In that context, perhaps it is a little easier to understand.

During the book-writing process, I had the opportunity to consult with Eli Stein, a trauma-specialized therapist in Minnesota. When I

Ilse in center, Esther Lewyn to Ilse's right, and Ilse's friend Alice Fink on the left.

asked Stein about Bert's memory suppression, he explained that exceedinngly painful memories can be likened to a house. To move forward, instead of burning down the whole house, trauma survivors may just throw away the key. Dr. Stein speculated that for Bert, Ilse was the key. And so he "threw her away" by forgetting her presence.

Marc and I visited Ilse at her home in England in the spring of 1999. Ilse was very gracious and told us that while it was a marriage of unusual circumstances, she had loved Dagobert. She said the tension was so high while they were living illegally that her son, Klaus (sometimes spelled Claus), did not want her to talk to Bert; he was concerned she would become upset.

Eventually, Ilse, Bert, and Esther met and had an enjoyable time together. There is a photo of Bert on a couch with Esther on one side and Ilse on this other: "his two wives," the women exclaimed.

Ilse died on September 22, 2010. The notice of her death says that her son, Klaus (Claus) died before her.

Günther Gerson

In spite of vigorous efforts and unlike other people I met during the war years, I have been unable to contact Günther Gerson. I have, however, talked to at least one individual who was with Günther in prison.

Apparently, Günther was arrested while impersonating an SS officer. I was told that he was stopped in a department store wearing an SS uniform minus the uniform hat. A patrol checking for deserters demanded his identity papers, which he was unable to produce. He was taken into custody and transported to the same prison, located in the Jewish Hospital pathology building, where I had been incarcerated.

Günther's whereabouts after the war ended are unknown. There was a rumor that he was living in Argentina. Wherever he is, I would certainly love to talk to him.

Bev Lewyn

When we first wrote the book, Bert vividly remembered Günther Gerson, his escapades with him, and Günther's girlfriend and her father. We tried repeatedly to find Günther while we were writing the original book but were repeatedly unsuccessful. In the years since this book was first published, I occasionally tried to search for Günther online but always came up dry.

Until the summer of 2018.

My first breakthrough came a few years prior from Barbara Schieb, a researcher at the Silent Heroes Memorial Center in Berlin. Barbara reported that Günther's girlfriend was actually named Eleonore/Ellen Stindt—*not* Ella Berg, as Bert had recalled (the names have been corrected in this edition). Eleonore's father, Bruno Stindt, was a cameraman in Berlin for Paramount News/Pictures. It seems Bert's memory about Bruno Stindt having fantastic Nazi connections was indeed correct. In the spring 1977 international film magazine *Sight & Sound*, director and screenwriter Jonathan Lewis says in the article "Before Hindsight" that

Bruno Stindt was "Hitler's favorite cameraman" and that Stindt supplied not only Paramount with footage but also Movietone and other companies who couldn't gain access to it on their own.

Bruno Stindt was not Jewish, but according to Barbara Schieb, his wife (Eleonore's mother) Tilla Stindt, was. Eleonore and her brother, Gerhard Stindt, would thus have been potential targets of the Third Reich. Bruno Stindt was able to use his Paramount contacts to ask Franklin Delano Roosevelt's private secretary to help get his son Gerhard out of Germany, and Gerhard did go to the United States. At some point Gerhard starting using the name Gary and became a prominent reporter for NBC News.

In July 2018, Barbara shared with me the names of Günther's parents: Else and Hermann Gerson. Contrary to Bert's memory that Günther's mother died first and that his father remarried, she said Günther's father, Hermann, died in 1931 and his mother, Else, committed suicide in 1937, so neither of his parents were alive while Dagobert and Günther were U-Boats. Barbara also said that Günther had a sister, Senta, who became the foster child of Tilla Stindt after Else Gerson committed suicide. Barbara's records indicate that Günther's guardian was his uncle.

Newly armed with Günther's parents' names, I searched online for them and soon had a breakthrough. I found Günther's parents listed on a family heritage website and reached out to the man in charge. I told him I had been looking for Günther Gerson for years to no avail and asked if perhaps I had found the correct family. As luck would have it, he said I had. He explained that Günther had changed his name to Gerald Garson after immigrating to Chicago after the war. That is why we never found him. He also gave me the contact information of Günther's daughter, Dr. Sharon Garson Glass.

Dr. Glass and I spoke on the phone, and she told me that she only discovered her father had changed his name after he died of a heart attack in Chicago in 2005. She found a letter and some documents that told her more about his life before coming to America.

In 1969, Gerald wrote a letter to a judge in Illinois describing his life. In the letter he wrote that his father, Hermann Gerson, had been partners in a ladies' garments manufacturing business, not the jewelry business Bert had recalled. While Hermann was alive, Günther's family was very well off. After Hermann's death, financial difficulties forced Günther's mother, Else, to get a job, and they had to move out of their large apartment in Berlin-Templehof into a smaller apartment. Else had difficulty adjusting to the new lifestyle and she was constantly harassed for having married a Jew and having half-Jewish children. Günther's mother's German Protestant family cooled their relations with them, and his father's family began to leave Germany for England, South Africa, and South America. When the situation became even more difficult, his letter says that Else put Günther in the "12th jewish orphanage in the suburb of Pankow."

This comment that Günther was in the Pankow orphanage was a big surprise to me, as Bert never mentioned Günther being in the orphanage and Bert's childhood friend at the Waisenhaus, Dr. Leslie Baruch Brent, also doesn't recall the name. I asked the people presently maintaining the orphanage records and they found no trace of a Günther Gerson. They asked another orphanage in the area about him as well, and they too had no records of a Günther Gerson being in their orphanage.

Günther's letter recalls a life in the orphanage very similar to Dagobert's. Günther wrote that he attended school, had his bar mitzvah there, and visited his mother and sister every weekend. The letter to the judge states Günther ultimately stayed in the orphanage for six years.

Once the war began and his sister, Senta, disappeared off the streets, presumably picked up by the Gestapo, Günther, like Dagobert, says he decided to go underground and live illegally. Gunther says he slept during days in bombed-out buildings, fields, or basements, and during the night stole food, breaking into stores to obtain the necessary items to stay alive. Günther's letter does not mention the Stindts and living with them or working for Bruno Stindt.

His letter then says "soon I found myself in the company of other 'illegals' who formed underground sabotage teams, conducting extremely dangerous demolition and sabotage activities against the German military." Gunther says the group was "well armed," which was fascinating to read, given that Dagobert was captured at the Kusitzkys with a crate of weapons—and he could not recall why or how he had all those weapons.

Günther was arrested on December 13, 1944, very near the time that Dagobert would have been arrested. Eugen Herman-Friede, a teenager in the same Gestapo prison where Dagobert was held, says Günther was arrested because he was caught wearing a Gestapo uniform without the appropriate hat. Barbara Schieb corroborates that Günther was kept for a time in the Gestapo prison at the Jewish Hospital. Later he was moved to the prison in the basement of the Gestapo headquarters on Prinz Albrecht-Strasse.

Günther's letter says "in order to make me tell them what they wanted to know, [the Gestapo] subjected me to extremely painful torture and starvation." The torture included thumb screws, Russian roulette, severe beatings, treatments with a red hot needle, and being hung by his heels and revived with cold water when he passed out. He says that the torture was responsible for him losing 70 percent of his hearing, which diverges from Bert's memory that Günther was hard of hearing even during the time they were U-boats. Günther's daughter and Barbara Schieb concur that the hearing loss was a result of the torture, so I have removed from this edition Bert's descriptions of Günther being hard of hearing while a U-boat. Barbara thinks it is quite likely that Günther and Dagobert would have seen each other in Berlin in the days after the war. Perhaps Bert recalling that Günther was hard of hearing stemmed from postwar memories and not from the time they were U-boats. Photos and documents also indicate Bert's memory of Günther being blond with blue eyes was also incorrect. I have removed those descriptions in this edition as well.

Gerald's letter says he escaped from the Prinz Albrecht Strasse prison in February 1945 and became "one of only two survivors of it"—he says he later learned the rest of the prisoners were taken outside and shot in the neck and thrown in the rubble. When the war was over, Günther was granted one of the first immigration visas to the United States and arrived in New York on June 18, 1946.

Günther Simon Gerson at some point became Gerald Symon Garson. He married Evelyn Jorczak in 1952 in Chicago and they had two

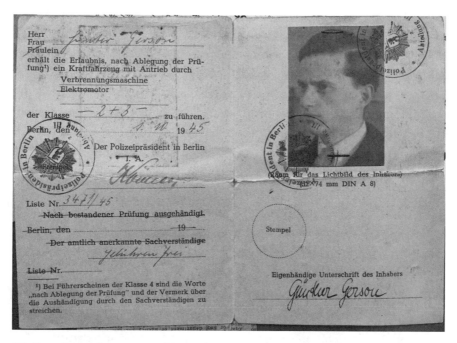

Günther Gerson's postwar driver's license.

daughters: Sharon, born August 29, 1959, and Marcella (Marcy), born December 19, 1961. Gerald died of a heart attack in Chicago in 2005.

Barbara Schieb says Günther's girlfriend Eleonore Stindt gave birth to Günther's son, Michael Franklin Stindt, on April 25, 1945, in Berlin-Templehof. Gunther visited Michael in Germany when Michael was ten years old, and he wanted to take Michael back to the United States, but Eleonore said no and so Michael stayed in Munich with her. Günther apparently had little to do with his son. His compensation file does not even mention the boy, nor does his October 2, 1946, application for US citizenship. When I spoke with her, Günther's daughter Sharon was unaware that her father had fathered a son before he emigrated to the United States. She wants to talk to him, and as of this writing Barbara plans to put them in touch with each another.

Alex and Anni Kusitzky

I kept in touch with Alex and Anni after the war. I went back to visit them in the 1970s with my wife, Esther, and son Michael, but by then Alex had died and Anni had sold the house and moved to an apartment.

In almost all of our contacts via letters and in person, Anni begged me to come back to Germany and never could understand why I did not wish to live there. "I'll take care of you," she would say. She wrote me long letters, filled with much emotion. Here are excerpts from a few letters, translated from the German:

> I don't understand this world and don't believe in it. I can well understand that [your] Auntie [Riva] Gutman feels lonesome. She will very often think about her dear ones who have perished so terribly. I hope that the scoundrels who have committed these crimes will have received just punishment. All guilt will be weighed on this Earth. We don't want to think about the terrible deeds committed, when we do, we must shame ourselves to be German. Now, dear Dagobert, you don't stand alone in this wide great world and that you have a dear good woman who understands you and loves you. That I wish for you.

> Tell me dear Dagobert, don't you long for your home where you lived your childhood and youth? . . . How did you ever have the thought of going to America, such a strange and foreign land, so far away. I cannot understand this. Here, with us, are so many possibilities to advance and improve. You are not a blockhead and could obtain a highly respected position and make a lot of money. But then again, you were very young and maybe you were intrigued by the lust for adventure . . .

> Dear Dagobert, I don't understand you at all. Why have you landed in such a faraway strange and black part of the Earth. After all, you are a German and will remain a German and your mother tongue is German. For all the things in the world, I would not have gone to live [in America.]
> Yes, with what then happened one must be ashamed to be a German. But dear Dagobert, the loving God has saved you from this terrible fate, the annihilation. Do not forget to thank him for having

saved you, that you live and can enjoy the beauty of the world and that you have healthy limbs and body. The almighty will judge and deal with those who are guilty and have brought on all the misery.

You really have no business living in the South of the United States because you are not accustomed to the hot weather and you don't really understand these people. You'll never be satisfied and you shouldn't be there. I want to urge you to come back to Berlin. I will help you to build a good life and things are much better here now than they used to be under the Nazis. Besides all of that, you are a German. You are not an American. Don't dawdle just pack your bags and come back here.

Anni later wrote that she had hidden me because it was the right thing to do. She said she was not interested in gaining glory for what she had done. "God alone knows what I have done and he will handle it."

Anni felt it was her mission to help the sick and incapacitated. She sponsored families from Siberia and Russia and helped them emigrate to Germany. She also spent much of her time with the needy or people who had been disabled by medical conditions, keeping them company, shopping for them, doing their laundry, etc.

She also spent a few years helping her son, Heinz, who was injured in a fall from a horse when the Germans were retreating from the advancing Russian army. After the accident, Heinz suffered from epileptic seizures, which troubled him for many years. It was very hard on Anni to care for him and to see him go through such a horrible period.

Anni died in 1979. I was contacted in 1995 or 1996 by an author in Lübars who asked me to send information about Anni and Alex and how they protected me during the war. The book, *Lübars Bilder Buch* (Lübars Picture Book) by Diesbach and Hensel (published 1997 by Haude and Spener) has pictures of Anni and her house and mentions her as being a hero for what she did for me. The author requested my photograph in 1997, which he incorporated in his book with these comments, translated from the German:

Bert Lewyn moved away in 1949 after miraculous rescue from the murderous land of Poets, Thinkers and Cowards, who paid no heed to the warnings of what was happening. Afterwards, they never knew anything about it.

Bev Lewyn

In June 2016 my husband, Marc, and I took our daughters to Berlin to visit the sites where their grandfather lived, worked, or hid. We went to Lübars, now a lovely suburb in the horse country outside Berlin. It was very difficult to find the original Kusitsky house on Benekendorfstrasse as the land has been subdivided and the house is no longer visible from the road. Eventually, a neighbor helped us find it and we walked up the same hill Dagobert had walked, past the gate, and up the stairs. Halfway up the hill, next to the walkway, was a beautiful pond. The man who lives in the Kusitsky house now explained that a crater made in the ground from a bomb during the war had been turned in into a pond. And so something lovely came out of that terrifying day.

Crater from the bomb in the Kusitskys' yard is now a lovely pond.

Heinz, Horst, Jenny, and Leo Lebrecht

After the war ended in May 1945, I moved with the Lebrechts from Lorenzstrasse (the tiny apartment in the bottom of the Nazi headquarters building) to a larger place at 95 Ringstrasse. Shortly thereafter, I left them to go live with the Kusitzkys.

I had no subsequent contact with them until 1997. After we began working on this book, I started trying to locate them. After several failed attempts, I spoke with Barbara Schieb, an author who has written about wartime Berlin. She suggested I send a letter to Heinz in care of the Central Kartei (Central Records) office in Berlin.

I asked them to please forward the letter to Heinz. They did this and in 1997 I received a call from Heinz, now Henry. I met with him at his home outside Los Angeles the same year. He is married and has a daughter and grandchildren. Henry is retired from his emblem manufacturing business and is also writing a book on his experiences during the war.

The Lebrecht boys came over to the United States in the 1950s with their parents, and they all lived in California. Their parents died there.

Horst Dobriner

Horst Dobriner, my friend from the orphan's home whose mother and stepfather hid me while I was a Uboat, was transported to Auschwitz in 1943 and was murdered there by the SS. He was twenty years old.

Riva Levin Gutman and Dov Levin

When she first immigrated to Palestine in 1947, Riva lived with her brother and sister-in-law in Tel Aviv. After learning Hebrew in an *ulpan* (an intensive course), she then became a social worker in Nes Ziona, a town about an hour from Tel Aviv. She worked with children, either orphans or children who were somehow disturbed. Eventually, she became the director of the institution.

After her arrival in Palestine, Riva found my first cousin (and her nephew) Dov Levin. Riva became for Dov what she had been to me, a surrogate mother. Dov and his wife, Bilha, had three children: daughters Nitzana and Basmat and a son, Zvika. All three children grew to consider Riva as their grandmother. Riva remarried very briefly but the marriage only lasted a few months.

Riva and I remained very close after I went to the United States and married. I visited her in Israel when I could. She still used the furniture I had bought and shipped to her when I was in the DP camp.

Riva died in 1979. After her death, Dov discovered that Riva had saved the letters I had written to her, including those I had written from Feldafing. After Dov forwarded the letters to me, I translated them from Yiddish into English. Some of these translations are included in this book.

My granddaughter Rachel (daughter of my son Marc and daughter-in-law Bev) is named for her.

Boris Levin

Original name Ozerac-Beras Davidovich Levinas, Uncle Boris's name, occupation, and reputation saved my life when the Russians burst into the Lebrechts' apartment.

His daughter, her husband, and their grown children now live in Scranton, Pennsylvania, and are members of a synagogue where my cousin, David Geffen, is the rabbi. David met this woman, recognized her name, and made the connection to me. We've been in touch since I began writing this book, and she has sent me many translated documents about her father and his career.

It was through these documents that I learned my uncle Boris had fought and been wounded in the battle at the village Kosino. He and his Red Army comrades fought the Germans as they tried to advance toward Moscow.

After finishing his education in France, Boris moved to Moscow in 1930 and worked as the senior engineer at the Central Administration of Power Economy. In 1937 he was the head of testing of electrical equipment for large-scale industry. He authored several books for use in electrical engineering courses in educational institutions. After WWII, he was instrumental in the engineering reconstruction of power plants and related industries in the USSR.

My Parents: Leopold Lewin and Johanna Wolff Lewin

For nearly sixty years, I had no confirmation of what had happened to my parents. I had the postcard that had told me that in 1942 they were in Trawniki, Poland. But I had nothing else. In all that time, I had never met anyone who had been in Trawniki.

Then, in January 1994, my daughter-in-law Bev went to Jerusalem to the research library of the Holocaust memorial, Yad Vashem. There she was shown a copy of the Gedenkbuch (Remembrance Book), a large compilation that details the fates of Berlin Jews deported to the East. She looked up my parents and brought back Xerox copies of the pages that concerned them. Below is a translation of the relevant section from the Gedenkbuch as well as a reproduction from the German.

> Lewin, Leopold
> born September 7, 1891 in Kovno, Lithuania.
> address before deportation: Berlin S.O.16, Koepenickerstr, 70.
> Deported 3-28-42, [transport] No. 11.
> Place of Death: Trawniki, Poland.
> Fate: declared dead
>
> Lewin, Johanna (nee Wolff)
> born July 29, 1897 in Natkischken, District Tilsit, East Prussia, Germany.
> address before deportation: Berlin S.O.16, Koepenickerstr, 70.
> Deported 3-28-42, [transport] No. 11.
> Place of Death: Trawniki, Poland.
> Fate: declared dead

It was the first and only official word I ever had on them. This was the only documentation that existed that revealed that my parents had been murdered.

But why was there so little known about Trawniki? I had inquired of different people over the years but could find no one who knew anything about it. Why were there no survivors telling their tales of that concentration camp? On August 24, 1997, I finally found out why.

I was reading *Letzte Spuren* (*Last Traces*), edition Hentrich, a book in German published by a German publisher, from whom I had ordered several Holocaust-related books. Part of the book is a reprint of the diary of Rudolf Neumann, the manager of the factory of the Schultz company. Here is what I learned:

Trawniki was a forced labor concentration camp directly next to a training camp for Ukranian SS troops. These Ukranian SS were the ones who guarded the Jews.

Trawniki became, in essence, a commercial enterprise not unlike Schindler's factory from *Schindler's List*. Unfortunately, there was no Schindler to save the Jews from being executed. The German company Schultz—formerly located in Warsaw where it had used the Jews in the Warsaw ghetto as laborers—relocated to Trawniki after the Warsaw ghetto was burned down following the famous Warsaw ghetto uprising.

Some of the Warsaw ghetto Jews were relocated to Trawniki with the Schultz company. Others were shipped in from other locations, including Berlin. The Schultz company also moved their equipment and machinery from the Warsaw ghetto area to Trawniki.

The Jewish slaves were forced to work in Schultz's production of clothing, including making fur coats, fur hats, shoes, and other things, all destined to be supplied to the Wehrmacht of the German Reich in their ongoing war against Russia and the cold, cruel weather.

I believe that my parents were sent to Trawniki because of my father's experience with machines. I suspect he was forced to maintain the Schultz machines.

The manager of the company, a man by the name of Rudolf Neumann, was quite humane and friendly toward the Jews working there, and the Jews there held him in high esteem. Neumann wrote in his diary about Trawniki and its last days. From reading excerpts of his diary, I have been able to piece together a picture of the last days of the Trawniki camp.

The number of Jews working varied slightly but hovered around six thousand, about half men and the other half women and children. On November 3, 1943, between 5:00 AM and 6:00 AM, an unfamiliar contingent of SS guards appeared, blocking entrances and exits to the camp.

They chased the Jews out of the barracks and into an adjacent area. There, the SS forced the Jews to take off their clothes and to throw them onto piles, then to run to previously excavated ditches. The new victims were forced to lie down on the already executed victims in the ditches. Several of the SS commandos—each consisting of four to five soldiers, positioned along the ditches—shot the victims with their machine guns.

The excavated ditches were not quite enough to hold all the victims. The SS took the several hundred remaining Jews to a sand excavation site next to the ditches and shot them there. All the while, several trucks equipped with loud speakers were blaring music so as to drown out the screams of the victims and the constant shootings.

By 4:00 PM that day, six thousand men, women, and children had been murdered. My parents may have been among them.

The SS contingent left the camp later that same day. The dead corpses were burned. It took three weeks to accomplish this and was done by Jewish prisoners brought there from another concentration camp in the area. Ukrainer SS troops supervised and watched the Jewish prisoners while they were burning the corpses. Once the grisly deed was done, the Jews themselves were shot and then burned by the Ukrainer SS troops.

It appeared from reading Neuman's diary that the Schultz company had not known this was going to happen.

And this is why I had never found any Jewish survivors who knew anything about Trawniki. They were all murdered. There was no one was left to tell the story.

Bev Lewyn

In 1993 when we began writing this book, I went to the research library at Yad Vashem in Jerusalem and found the first proof of what had happened to Bert's parents. That Gedenkbuch (or memory book) contained the records that the Nazis had kept on every victim, and it listed Leopold and Johanna Lewin's destination as the Trawniki concentration camp and said they were declared dead.

Years later, once the USSR fell, historians got access to more information that had previously been unavailable. That new information led to the publishing of an updated version of the Gedenkbuch.

We now know that that Johanna and Leopold Lewin were deported on March 28, 1942, and were made to leave the train at the Trawniki station. From there they were made to walk twelve kilometers to a ghetto near Lublin called Piaski. They had to live in the Piaski ghetto under

Lewin, Karl-Heinz	Berlin	05.12.28	verschollen	Riga
Lewin, Karoline, geb. Bruehl	Berlin	26.05.94	verschollen	Auschwitz
Lewin, Karoline, geb. Lewin	Berlin	05.12.76	verschollen	Minsk
Lewin, Klara	Berlin	21.02.67	09.03.43	Theresienstadt
Lewin, Klara	Berlin	19.09.93	verschollen	Auschwitz
Lewin, Klara, geb. Lewin	Gelsenkirchen	09.02.93	verschollen	Riga
Lewin, Klara, geb. Lewinski	Berlin	25.12.66	31.01.43	Theresienstadt
Lewin, Klara, geb. Wolf	Frankfurt am Main	11.06.90	für tot erklärt	unbekannt
Lewin, Kurt	Berlin	18.01.01	verschollen	Auschwitz
Lewin, Kurt	Berlin	16.07.01	11.10.42	Sachsenhausen
Lewin, Kurt	Berlin	07.08.02	verschollen	Auschwitz
Lewin, Kurt	Berlin	04.04.85	verschollen	Auschwitz
Lewin, Laura, geb. Loewy	München	11.05.90	verschollen	Riga
Lewin, Laura, geb. Rosenthal	Berlin	29.11.61	26.01.43	Theresienstadt
Lewin, Lazar	Berlin	22.10.83	07.08.41	Freitod
Lewin, Lea	Mannheim	29.11.09	für tot erklärt	Gurs
Lewin, Lea Pia	Berlin	22.07.34	verschollen	Auschwitz
Lewin, Lena, geb. Aberstein	Bendorf	22.11.74	31.05.42	Bendorf-Sayn
Lewin, Lena, geb. Hirsch	Berlin	14.07.85	verschollen	Riga
Lewin, Leo	Berlin	31.05.04	verschollen	Osten
Lewin, Leo	Berlin	29.03.59	verschollen	Minsk
Lewin, Leo	Berlin	06.11.61	00.02.44	Theresienstadt
Lewin, Leo	Berlin	28.10.83	08.03.43	Freitod
Lewin, Leonhard	Bork (1)	23.09.68	verschollen	Minsk
Lewin, Leopold	Berlin (2)	21.12.60	16.09.42	Freitod
Lewin, Leopold	Berlin	07.09.91	für tot erklärt	Trawniki
Lewin, Leopold	Berlin	20.05.95	verschollen	Auschwitz
Lewin, Lewin-I.	Berlin	11.12.74	00.04.44	Theresienstadt
Lewin, Liesbeth	Berlin	23.11.79	verschollen	Trawniki
Lewin, Lieselotte, geb. Wolff	Berlin	19.06.20	verschollen	Auschwitz
Lewin, Lilli	Berlin (2)	16.11.24	verschollen	Litzmannstadt/Lodz
Lewin, Lina	Berlin	26.08.95	verschollen	Riga
Lewin, Lina, geb. Fehlowicz	Fürth	15.02.90	für tot erklärt	Auschwitz
Lewin, Lina, geb. Lewin	Essen	04.09.75	verschollen	Izbica
Lewin, Lippmann	Frankfurt am Main	21.07.99	21.01.43	Auschwitz
Lewin, Lisbeth	Bendorf	29.06.18	15.08.41	Bendorf-Sayn
Lewin, Lisbeth, geb. Schwarz	Berlin	19.11.84	verschollen	Majdanek/Lublin
Lewin, Lothar	Hagen	21.07.25	verschollen	Buchenwald
Lewin, Lothar	Berlin	15.11.31	verschollen	Trawniki
Lewin, Lotte	Berlin	08.03.15	verschollen	Riga
Lewin, Lotte, geb. Steinweg	Düsseldorf	12.04.22	verschollen	Minsk
Lewin, Lotte, geb. Zade	Berlin	22.12.95	verschollen	Auschwitz
Lewin, Louis	Berlin	19.07.66	verschollen	Minsk
Lewin, Louis	Berlin	28.09.68	verschollen	Minsk
Lewin, Lucian	Berlin	02.01.31	verschollen	Riga
Lewin, Lucie	Berlin	14.02.03	verschollen	Auschwitz
Lewin, Lucie, geb. Markus	Berlin	06.03.20	verschollen	Auschwitz
Lewin, Ludwig	Berlin	19.04.07	verschollen	Auschwitz
Lewin, Ludwig	Berlin	29.10.09	verschollen	Mittelbau-Dora
Lewin, Ludwig	Berlin	10.01.64	18.01.43	Theresienstadt
Lewin, Ludwig	Fürth	10.07.85	für tot erklärt	Auschwitz
Lewin, Ludwig	Berlin	29.02.96	verschollen	Auschwitz
Lewin, Lutz	Berlin	19.01.25	verschollen	Auschwitz
Lewin, Magdalene, geb. Brieger	Berlin	14.02.84	verschollen	Auschwitz
Lewin, Manfred	Berlin	08.09.22	verschollen	Auschwitz
Lewin, Manfred	Nürnberg	29.01.25	für tot erklärt	Riga
Lewin, Manfred	Berlin	02.08.33	verschollen	Osten
Lewin, Mannheim	Berlin	21.07.82	verschollen	Auschwitz
Lewin, Margarete, geb. Cohn	Berlin	25.06.99	verschollen	Auschwitz
Lewin, Margarete, geb. Fraenkel	Berlin	26.10.80	verschollen	Auschwitz
Lewin, Margarete, geb. Goldmann	Berlin	18.12.85	verschollen	Riga
Lewin, Margarete, geb. Hartmann	Berlin	23.08.09	verschollen	Auschwitz
Lewin, Margarete, geb. Jacoby	Berlin	10.04.92	verschollen	Auschwitz
Lewin, Margarete, geb. Levy	Berlin	30.05.90	verschollen	Auschwitz
Lewin, Margarete, geb. Markuse	Berlin	09.10.88	verschollen	Riga
Lewin, Margot	Berlin	02.10.16	verschollen	Auschwitz
Lewin, Margot	Berlin	16.06.21	verschollen	Litzmannstadt/Lodz
Lewin, Margot	Berlin	30.07.27	verschollen	Litzmannstadt/Lodz
Lewin, Margot, geb. Margoliner	Berlin	10.12.10	00.03.43	Auschwitz
Lewin, Margot, geb. Schaul	Berlin	12.07.10	verschollen	Auschwitz

Remembrance book (Edition Hentrich), page no. 871 out of a total of 1,400 pages, listing fifty-five thousand names of deported Berlin Jews. My father, Leopold Lewin, is indicated by the horizontal lines.

Lewin, Hilde	Berlin	30.11.29	verschollen	Riga
Lewin, Hilde	Berlin	18.03.95	09.03.42	Litzmannstadt/Lodz
Lewin, Hilde, geb. Eisner	Berlin	18.07.71	09.10.42	Theresienstadt
Lewin, Hilde, geb. Gerson	Düsseldorf	20.01.95	22.03.45	Bergen-Belsen
Lewin, Hildegard	Berlin	26.03.20	verschollen	Auschwitz
Lewin, Horst	Berlin	01.01.27	23.01.45	Dachau
Lewin, Horst	Berlin	24.01.27	verschollen	Trawniki
Lewin, Hubert	Berlin	14.04.91	verschollen	Auschwitz
Lewin, Hugo	Berlin (1)	05.05.25	verschollen	Auschwitz
Lewin, Hugo	Berlin (1)	24.04.70	00.04.43	Theresienstadt
Lewin, Hugo	Berlin	24.06.79	verschollen	Riga
Lewin, Hugo	Berlin	18.05.87	verschollen	Litzmannstadt/Lodz
Lewin, Hugo	Berlin	05.01.95	verschollen	Riga
Lewin, Ida	Berlin	22.03.84	verschollen	Litzmannstadt/Lodz
Lewin, Ida	Berlin	26.11.97	03.11.42	Litzmannstadt/Lodz
Lewin, Ida, geb. Czollack	Berlin	19.09.92	verschollen	Auschwitz
Lewin, Ida, geb. Hamlet	Bremen	04.07.78	28.07.42	Minsk
Lewin, Ilse	Nordrach	25.07.09	verschollen	Auschwitz
Lewin, Ilse	München	12.12.26	verschollen	Riga
Lewin, Ilse	Kassel (1)	16.08.99	für tot erklärt	Sobibor
Lewin, Ilse, geb. Loeffler	Berlin	01.06.08	verschollen	Auschwitz
Lewin, Ilse, geb. Neumann	Berlin	08.07.14	verschollen	Trawniki
Lewin, Ilse Erna	Berlin	16.07.21	verschollen	Auschwitz
Lewin, Inge	Berlin	26.09.36	verschollen	Auschwitz
Lewin, Ingolf	Berlin	11.07.33	verschollen	Riga
Lewin, Irma	Berlin	19.03.04	verschollen	Auschwitz
Lewin, Irma, geb. Lang	Berlin	05.10.97	verschollen	Auschwitz
Lewin, Irma, geb. Sondheim	Kleinlangheim	30.05.90	verschollen	Auschwitz
Lewin, Isidor	Berlin	10.10.91	03.05.42	Litzmannstadt/Lodz
Lewin, Israel F.	Frankfurt am Main	23.12.73	21.09.42	Theresienstadt
Lewin, Jakob	Berlin	06.02.00	21.07.41	Buchenwald
Lewin, Jakob	Berlin	19.10.04	verschollen	Auschwitz
Lewin, Jakob	Mönchengladbach	25.05.22	verschollen	Auschwitz
Lewin, Jakob	Duisburg	28.10.60	verschollen	Minsk
Lewin, Jakob	Berlin	24.02.68	verschollen	Theresienstadt
Lewin, Jakob	Berlin	12.09.82	verschollen	Auschwitz
Lewin, Jakob	Berlin	06.12.82	verschollen	Osten
Lewin, Jeanette	Berlin	17.12.69	verschollen	Minsk
Lewin, Jennette, geb. Dann	Frankfurt am Main	31.10.57	10.11.42	Theresienstadt
Lewin, Jenni	Berlin	21.01.71	12.01.43	Theresienstadt
Lewin, Jenni, geb. Schein	Berlin	23.07.77	verschollen	Riga
Lewin, Jenny	Berlin	19.06.72	verschollen	Minsk
Lewin, Jenny, geb. Gramse	Berlin	13.11.78	verschollen	Riga
Lewin, Jenny, geb. Kaspari	Berlin	24.01.09	verschollen	Auschwitz
Lewin, Jenny, geb. Koeln	Berlin	30.12.90	verschollen	Auschwitz
Lewin, Jette, geb. Lesser	Berlin	08.02.56	verschollen	Minsk
Lewin, Jette J.	Berlin	27.02.70	verschollen	Minsk
Lewin, Joachim	Berlin	11.10.35	verschollen	Auschwitz
Lewin, Joachim	Berlin	22.12.37	00.03.43	Auschwitz
Lewin, Joachim	Berlin (1)	28.01.99	28.11.44	Bergen-Belsen
Lewin, Johanna, geb. Bender	Berlin	04.01.72	15.09.42	Theresienstadt
Lewin, Johanna, geb. Hirschel	Berlin	16.07.80	22.10.42	Freitod
Lewin, Johanna, geb. Muenzer	Berlin	30.10.90	verschollen	Litzmannstadt/Lodz
Lewin, Johanna, geb. Rogasinski	Berlin	26.06.78	00.04.43	Auschwitz
Lewin, Johanna, geb. Rubert	Berlin	10.07.76	verschollen	Auschwitz
Lewin, Johanna, geb. Wolff	Berlin	29.07.97	für tot erklärt	Trawniki
Lewin, Johanna, geb. Wolfsfeld	Berlin	28.07.82	verschollen	Auschwitz
Lewin, Joseph	Bielefeld	23.03.76	06.06.44	Theresienstadt
Lewin, Joseph	Berlin	06.01.99	verschollen	Auschwitz
Lewin, Judis	Berlin	17.10.41	verschollen	Auschwitz
Lewin, Judith	Hagen	14.12.21	verschollen	Auschwitz
Lewin, Juergen	Berlin	04.04.34	verschollen	Litzmannstadt/Lodz
Lewin, Julius	Düsseldorf	26.06.12	verschollen	Minsk
Lewin, Julius	Berlin	25.07.77	10.12.41	Litzmannstadt/Lodz
Lewin, Julius	Berlin	26.12.77	verschollen	Minsk
Lewin, Julius	Frankfurt am Main	15.05.90	verschollen	Minsk
Lewin, Julius	Berlin	11.01.94	verschollen	Litzmannstadt/Lodz
Lewin, Julius	Berlin	27.05.94	verschollen	Auschwitz
Lewin, Julius	Berlin	13.08.96	verschollen	Auschwitz
Lewin, Jutta	Wuppertal	19.12.18	verschollen	Izbica
Lewin, Jutta	Berlin	14.02.35	verschollen	Riga
Lewin, Kaete, geb. Gruenspan	Berlin	21.09.10	verschollen	Warschau

Remembrance book (Edition Hentrich), page no. 870 out of a total of 1,400 pages, listing fifty-five thousand names of deported Jews. My mother, Johanna Lewin Geb. Wolff, is indicated by the horizontal lines.

horrible living conditions with no proper rooms, scarce food, no sanitary facilities, and hard work. Since they were both deaf, it would have been difficult for them to hear and therefore to comply with shouted instructions from the Nazi guards.

There was a transport of two thousand Jews from Piaski to the Belzec death camp on April 11, 1942. The next transport from Piaski was sent to the Sobibor death camp on July 22, 1942. In November 1942 about one thousand Jews were shot to death at the local Piaski Jewish cemetery. We do not know whether Johanna and Leopold died in Piaski, Belzec, or Sobibor.

Levin Family

Not shown in this picture are my parents, Leopold and Johanna Lewin, who were living in Berlin, Germany, and my uncle Boris Levin, living in Moscow, Russia. *Front row:* Basva, Chana, Sarah, Mordecai, Dov-Berl. *Middle row:* Chave, Hirsh, Minne, Emanuel, Dovid, Benjamin,

My family in Kovno, Lithuania. Only four of them survived the Holocaust.

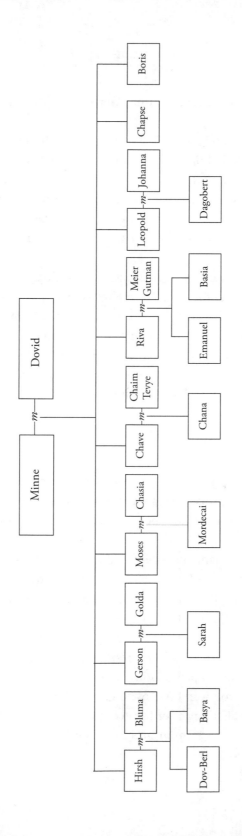

Riva. *Back row:* Chaim Tevye, Bluma, Gerson, Golda, Chapse, Chasia, Moses, Meier Gutman.

This photograph, along with others, was originally sent by my grandfather Dovid Levin to Rabbi Tobias Geffen in Atlanta. When Rabbi Geffen passed away, the Geffen family transferred Rabbi Geffen's archives to the American-Jewish Historical Society in Waltham, Massachusetts. My son Marc Lewyn requested and obtained various papers from these archives including several photographs that are now in my possession and are included in this book.

The only survivors of the Holocaust of those listed are:

Benjamin, who had emigrated from Kovno to America before Hitler's rise to power. Riva, who survived the concentration camps. Dov-Berl, who had escaped from the Kovno ghetto, joined the military partisans and their operations against the Germans, survived the war, and undertook a ten-month journey, mostly by foot, to Palestine (now Israel). Chapse, who emigrated to Palestine before Israel became a state and before Hitler's rule in Europe.

Wolff Family

My grandmother on my mother's side was Henriette Wolff, who lived in Heydekrug (when it was German and Silute when it was Lithuanian).

My mother had three brothers—Herbert, Salli, and Alfred—as well as one sister, Irma.

Herbert, Salli, and Irma were deported to the ghetto in Kovno, where they were murdered by the Lithuanian SS. Alfred managed to escape and made his way to America with his wife, Susie, and son, Peter.

Other than Alfred, no one in my mother's family survived. They all perished in killing camps or in the Kovno ghetto. I have documentation of the murder of my uncle Salli, my mother's brother. Lithuanian uniformed SS robbed him, raped a woman with him, and murdered them both in Uncle Salli's room in the Kovno ghetto. The Jewish ghetto police made a horrific, detailed report of the events. The original report, written in German as well as the translation into English, are in my possession.

Leslie Baruch Brent (born Lothar Baruch)

Bev Lewyn

After the original publication of the book, the new owners of the building that housed the Judische Waisenhaus restored the building and organized reunions of the surviving residents who had lived at the home. Bert and Esther attended a few of them, and this allowed Bert to become reacquainted with some of his old friends from those days. Chief among them was his friend Leslie Baruch Brent (born Lothar Baruch), who tells me they were best friends there and ran up to the orphanage attic together to hide when the Hitler Youth attacked. Leslie Brent went on one of the first kinder transports to England. He grew up to become a British immunologist and zoologist and is the codiscoverer with Peter Medawar and Rupert Billingham of "acquired immunological tolerance," which became fundamental to the practice of tissue and organ transplants. Medawar shared the 1960 Nobel Prize in Physiology or Medicine for the discovery. In June 2016 Marc and I took our daughters to Berlin and attended a meeting at the Waisenhaus and met with Dr. Brent. He had vivid memories of that day the Hitler Youth attacked the orphanage, and I have added his detail of running into the attic to this edition.

Oskar Klimt

Bev Lewyn

While this cigar-chomping, tool-stuffed, odd-English-phrase-speaking man did exist and Bert vividly remembered him and his experiences working for him, Bert drew a complete blank in regards to his name. We used the name "Oskar Klimt" as an ode to Oskar Schindler and Gustav Klimt.

APPENDIX I
APPRENTICESHIP

DURING 1936, Nazi persecution of the Jews decreased markedly. Visitors from all over the world would soon be arriving in Berlin to attend the Olympic games and Hitler knew it was in his best interests for Germany to show a friendly face to all and sundry. The ubiquitous signs declaring JUDEN UNERWÜNSCHT (JEWS NOT WELCOME) mysteriously disappeared from public places and Nazi abuses of the Jewish population suddenly dwindled away as the country went on its best behavior. This artificial calm was not to last, but it was enough to sway many German Jews into thinking that the leopard had changed its spots, that henceforth things would be better.

My father was one of those who hoped that the downswing in Nazi harassment would be permanent. Partly because of this, he was hesitant to consider emigrating from Germany, even though my uncle Benjamin tried repeatedly to convince him to leave, or at least to send me to live with him in America.

My parents were disinclined to take such a drastic step. The thought of sending their only son away, not knowing whether they would ever see him again, was more than they could bear. But it must have caused them to devote more attention to the future, because shortly after this my father enrolled me in an apprenticeship program sponsored by the Jewish Community.

Living anything like a normal life was becoming an impossibility for anyone of Jewish descent. German society was being hypnotized by the speeches of Hitler and by his promises of a better tomorrow, once Germany was made Judenrein (free of Jews). The leader of the nation was telling so many lies so often that the German people became convinced that the Jews were the cause of all their problems and that, conversely, their expulsion would mean the return of good times for all.

Emigration was on the minds of many Jewish families. When Jews made inquiries at the consulates of countries that welcomed immigrants, they learned that professionals such as doctors, lawyers, and bankers had low priorities in being considered for immigration visas. There were few job openings for German-speaking white-collar workers.

Preferred applicants were those who could help alleviate the chronic shortages in certain trades. Near the top of the list were the trades of machinist, metalworkers, and machine builders. Naturally, proof of training or experience was required with the visa application.

The program my father enrolled me in was designed to train suitable candidates in machine building and metalworking. I was fortunate to have been selected for participation. And once I began attending, I was able to live with my parents again, commuting every day to and from their apartment. This was quite welcome as, during my years in the Orphan's Home, I only rarely saw them. Using the local S-Bahn, the commute was an easy one, to and from Wernerwerke (Siemensstadt).

Classes were conducted in a building owned by a company known as Fleck und Söhne. They were manufacturers of precision machine tools such as lathes and milling machines. Their factory occupied the first and second floors. On the second floor, about eight thousand square feet were given over for use by the apprenticeship program.

The class was made up of about thirty apprentices and four instructors. These instructors were all experts, with years of experience in their particular specialties. They did a wonderful job of passing on their expertise and know-how to the apprentices. At the same time, they insisted on strict discipline and impeccable performance from everyone.

Herr Schmidt taught welding in all its aspects, both gas and electric. This man duplicated or created conditions that were comparable to actual industry situations. This included gas and electric welding overhead and vertically, such as might be encountered in ship or bridge building. After undergoing Herr Schmidt's training, we felt that we were equipped to handle any welding application that might come along.

The lead instructor and general manager was Herr Kaminski. He was most involved with teaching the use of so-called chip-making machines, such as lathes, mills, grinders, drills, etc., as required in the precision machining of parts and components.

A third instructor was Herr Tichauer. His forte was metal forming, such as forging, blacksmithing, bending, punching, and coping. He was particularly skilled with anything that had to do with blacksmithing. For example, he instructed us in such basic skills as the forging and machining of various types of tools, such as chisels, screwdrivers, hammers, tongues, ornamental iron structures, and many others.

Lastly, there was Herr Lederman. Up until two years earlier, he had been the chief engineer and chief designer of the Loewe company in Berlin, a large, well-known, and well-respected builder of machine tools. Their machines were used not only in Germany but throughout Europe. Because he was Jewish, Lederman was dismissed from the company. This was the Loewe company's loss and our gain. His experience, ability, and effectiveness at passing on knowledge to the apprentices was outstanding. His dismissal was made even more ironic by the fact that, like some other highly successful machinery companies in Berlin, the Loewe company was originally founded and operated by Jews.

Lederman was a genius when it came to machine design. We could well understand why he was the chief designer and chief engineer of the Loewe company for so many years. He was responsible for the design of many of their high-grade machine tools, which were in use throughout Europe.

After being discharged from the company, Lederman volunteered to teach several subjects in our program. These included machine drawings, parts manufacturing, and metallurgy and several others. I took all of these classes from him. Lederman taught us in a few months what would usually have taken years to learn.

The instructors continuously inspected our work to make sure that it met the high standards they demanded. If something failed to meet their criteria, they required repeat performances. For example, one of the basic essential requirements in machine building and metalworking is the mastery of hand filing. As a training exercise, filing was used to produce surfaces, angles, and sizes of steel blocks from a rough blank to a finished product.

We were given a steel cube measuring roughly three inches on all sides. When finished, all four sides had to be in perfect rectangular relationships. In addition, each side had to be perfectly flat with tolerances of plus or minus one-tenth of a millimeter, roughly the thickness of a human hair.

On the average, a student would spend about a month filing his block, which would be intermittently inspected by the instructors. The instructors were insistent on near-perfection. When we thought that we had it right, we presented the block to the instructor. He inspected it by means of a precision square, and if he found it to be less than nearly perfect, he handed it back to the apprentice with appropriate comments, explaining what was wrong and instructing them to continue filing.

All day long, day after day, we would stand at the workbench, the block of steel clamped in the vice, filing away. The instructors would walk up and down the rows of workbenches, checking our work. We each had three files: a coarse, a medium, and a fine. The files had to be laid on the workbench in such a manner as to be perfectly straight.

It was not unusual to finish with a block one and a half inches to two inches per side. This is amazing considering the original size of the three-inch cube. Some people may not appreciate the amount of metal thus removed by hand filing, but I want to emphasize that there was a phenomenal amount of persistence and patience necessary for this endeavor. We were not allowed to move on to the next section of the course until our blocks met the specifications required by the instructors.

It may seem that the instructors were overdoing it, but one has to remember that it was a great privilege for us to be allowed to attend the course at all. We were expendable. For every student attending the course, there were many others who would have very much liked to take his place. We were learning not just how to file but also perseverance and self-discipline. The famous German reputation for quality craftsmanship was being taught to a new generation.

All of the instructors insisted on strict discipline, not only as it concerned behavior but perhaps even more importantly as it concerned our performance in each subject. They wanted only serious students. They were extremely pleased with all the students who were attending, for their seriousness, their ability and willingness to learn.

By the time I finished the course, I had made up my mind never to use another file, but it was not to be. Never say never, because never is a long time. The mastery of filing I obtained from this course very possibly saved my life, as is recounted earlier.

Toward the conclusion of the three-and-a-half-year course, every apprentice was required to design and manufacture one or two typical objects. I chose a bench-mounted punching and shearing machine, manually operated, as well as a lock and two keys, utilizing the wing key design. Both of these items had to be designed using all proper standards in effect at the time. This design had to be approved by two of the instructors, one of which was Lederman and the other Kaminski.

I was successful in completing both objects (the punching and shearing machine, as well as the lock and keys). Both were inspected by all instructors, and I received the highest possible grade, which was very satisfying. There were also oral and written examinations. After passing both, I got a diploma with a statement to that effect.

I made quite a few good friends during the apprenticeship. How many of them survived the Holocaust, I don't know, but one who did was Harold Baum. I succeeded in tracking him down in 1999. Harold had participated in the same apprenticeship program as I, albeit a shorter version. He was fortunate enough to have been able to leave Berlin in 1941, to immigrate to America. He now lives in Florida.

Recently, Harold informed me that Herr Lederman had not survived the war. He was about to be arrested by the Gestapo when he threw himself in front of a moving S-Bahn train. Like so many others, Lederman committed suicide rather than face whatever agonies the concentration camp would bring him. In this manner, one more unique, talented, irreplaceable soul was lost to Hitler's madness.

APPENDIX II
KRISTALLNACHT

EARLY IN THE MORNING OF NOVEMBER 10, 1938, I was walking to the S-Bahn station Jannowitzbrücke. The train would take me to the Berlin-Siemensstadt station, from where I could walk to the apprenticeship program I attended. I was fifteen years old.

As I took my seat, I looked out over the city. The train tracks were high up above street level, affording views over great distances above the city. As the train pulled out of the station, I noticed several columns of smoke rising from the city.

I didn't think much about it, but when I arrived at the FLECK building, I noticed that none of my classmates had changed into their work uniforms. Instead, a heated discussion was taking place about reports from the newspapers and radios that a seventeen-year-old Jew named Herschel Grynszpan had shot and killed Ernst vom Rath, the legation secretary at the German embassy in Paris.

The motive for the assassination was the recent expulsion of thousands of Jews of Polish extraction, Grynszpan's family among them, by the Nazi government. Many of these people had lived in Germany for years. The Jews were taken by rail to the Polish border, where Gestapo guards attempted to force them to enter Poland. However, Polish border guards refused to allow them entry, trapping the Jews in a no-man's-land between the two competing forces. They had no choice but to live there as best they could. When Herschel Grynszpan received a postcard from his sister detailing the family's plight, he decided to take revenge by assassinating the highest-ranking German official he could find.

German newspapers and radio covered the story for days. Even though this was the single, isolated act of a grief-stricken teenager, the media was broadcasting the theme of "collective responsibility" for the killing. In other words, this was a murder for which all Jews were somehow equally responsible and should be equally punished.

My classmates were also debating the reasons behind the beating of Jews on the streets and the destruction of Jewish businesses and synagogues. They were talking about how Jews were being attacked, mostly elderly men and men with beards. Many of my classmates had seen it happen, witnessing the fires and the destruction. It suddenly became clear to me what the columns of smoke meant. Buildings were burning.

Suddenly, the lead instructor, Kaminski, came out of his office, waving his arms and shouting, "Everybody quiet! I have just spoken with the head of the Jüdische Gemeinde and have been informed that the demonstrations against Jews and destruction of their property are continuing today. For our own protection, we should all go home till further notice."

Within a few minutes, all of the students had scattered in different directions. I headed for the city, alternating between the S-Bahn, the U-Bahn, and walking. Something very unusual was taking place and I wanted to see it with my own eyes.

I could not imagine that everything I heard was true, especially the burning of Berlin's synagogues. My first stop was one of the larger synagogues in Berlin, the Fasanenstrasse synagogue. When I got there, the fires were still burning and the air was thick with smoke. A great portion of the building was already in ruins. Spectators filled the sidewalk on the far side of the street, watching the building burn. There were a few firemen who stood around with the rest, watching the fire burn, making no attempt to extinguish it.

As I mixed with the crowd, I overheard people say that the firemen were there to protect the building next to the synagogue, not the synagogue itself. The people watching seemed to enjoy seeing the fire and the destruction as if it were some kind of Roman circus put on for their amusement.

Mingling with the crowd were a number of brownshirted SA men, storm troopers. They were agitating the throng, urging action against the Jews, calling the burning of the synagogue "just the beginning." I remember them making comments such as, "We must get rid of the Jews, they are our misfortune," and similar nuggets.

When I had seen enough, I departed as unobtrusively as possible and made my way to the Prinzregentenstrasse synagogue, where the situation was similar but the crowd more hostile and unruly. I learned that a member of the synagogue and his family had died in the fire. There too, SA thugs incited the mobs that cheered the burnings. In all cases, it was taken for granted that members of the SA had set the fires.

In 1938, there were twelve major synagogues plus several other smaller ones in Berlin and hundreds of others throughout Germany. In Berlin, only three survived.

After getting my fill of watching the synagogues burn, I started to make my way home. On my way there, I was witness to further destruction of another kind. Large mobs of people were swarming around Jewish-owned department stores, smashing display windows, and looting the stores of all types of merchandise. I saw them carrying away furs, jewelry, silver, clothes, furniture, you name it. In the larger stores, the mobs would make their way up to the higher floors and toss the goods out the window, down to their waiting accomplices, who would collect them and carry them away.

In some of the stores, the SA and Hitler Youth led the way in smashing anything and everything in a ferocious orgy of vandalism. I saw a piano and other large items thrown out of an upstairs window just for the sheer love of destruction.

These events would become known as Kristallnacht, or Night of Broken Glass. But these calamities were not enough to satisfy the Nazi mania for Jew bashing. Two days later, on November 12, 1938, they also decreed a fine of one billion marks (about $400 million) to be paid by all German Jews collectively, as punishment for the death of vom Rath. In addition, repair and restoration of the buildings and businesses destroyed during the riots was commanded by the Nazis. These repairs were to be performed at the expense of the Jewish owners. If they had insurance and received compensation, the German government confiscated that money.

After Kristallnacht, it became obvious that emigration was absolutely and immediately necessary. My father and I stood in line at the Bolivian and then at the Chilean embassies, trying desperately to apply for a visa. The lines went around the block a few times as hundreds of people waited and hoped for a chance to leave the country. After waiting sometimes for days and nights, we discovered no more applications were being taken.

After Germany attacked Poland on September 1, 1939, England and France declared war on Germany two days later. The Nazi government eventually blocked all emigration. No more Jews were allowed to leave.

The Nazis alleged that Kristallnacht was simply a spontaneous reaction of the Aryan people to Grynszpan's crime. I did not know it at the time, but confidential Nazi documents recovered after the war showed that Reinhard Heydrich, the deputy chief of the Gestapo, had ordered that there be no interference with the burning of synagogues unless the fires endangered German property. This document proved that the entire uprising was a preplanned, organized event instituted by the Nazi government, not an impulsive act of the "Volk" (the people) as Hitler wished the rest of the world to believe.

Marc and Bev Lewyn at the
Oranienburger Strasse synagogue.

Rebuilt Oranienburger Strasse
synagogue, 1997.

Author in front of the building that formerly
housed the Gustav Genschow Waffenfabrik (weapons factory).

ACKNOWLEDGMENTS

For this edition Bev Lewyn would like to thank Barbara Schieb of the Silent Heroes Memorial Center in Berlin, Dr. Sharon Garson Glass, and Rachel Lewyn.

For additional materials uncovered during Bert and Bev Lewyn's research through each edition of the text, please visit www.bertlewyn. com. Here you will find letters, photos, and other information from Bev Lewyn.